FAMILIAR INSECTS
OF AMERICA

FAMILIAR INSECTS

Illustrations by CARL BURGER
Schematic drawings by NANCY LLOYD

HARPER & ROW, PUBLISHERS *New York and Evanston*

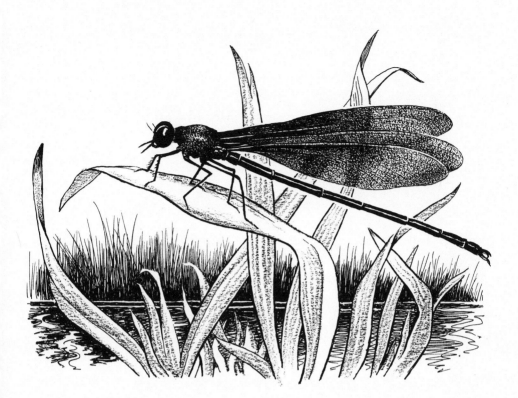

OF AMERICA

by WILL BARKER

foreword by HILARY J. DEASON

In Memory of Glenn Williams

FAMILIAR INSECTS OF AMERICA

CONTENTS

FOREWORD

by HILARY J. DEASON
American Association for the Advancement of Science

The fascinating world of insects has attracted the attention of people throughout history. The plague of locusts that invaded Egypt in the time of Moses is an early account of a disastrous insect depredation, and other great phenomena have been reported in later history. It is written that John the Baptist subsisted on a diet of dried locusts and wild honey. Pliny's natural history of Rome is filled with unlikely stories of insects based on fantasy and lore rather than on factual observation. Take, for example, his account of the oriental locusts which grew to such great size that their legs were dried and used for saws.

My introduction to the insect world was equally unenlightened, although by that time many observations had been factually recorded and the science of entomology was well developed. From the jumbled memories of my elementary school days I recall the observation of our second-grade teacher: "Insects are the most abundant form of life. Some day they will become so abundant that they will be able to kill all other kinds of animal life. Then they will take over the world!" Her assertion was not founded on scientific knowledge; she was merely stating a layman's popular misconception of that day. This notion probably arose from the experience of that small town with invasions of house flies, ants, mosquitoes, grasshoppers, and gnats, each in season. Also, all children became quite familiar with other commonplace insects such as lice and fleas which were supported in numbers by dogs, chickens, and even a few of our schoolmates.

My poor understanding of the insect world improved somewhat as I became a little older. I recall spending many hours on summer days in our back yard where a multitude of winged distractions kept attention from the book I was trying to read. From that close range, what was going on about me was wonderful: ants carrying sticks, spiders spinning their webs or feeding on a luckless fly the web had captured, bees sipping at the blossoms and flying back and forth from their hive, butterflies emerging from their cocoons, a praying mantis motionless and barely discernible on her twig, a ladybug sunning itself on a tall blade of grass. I wanted to know more about these insects which had become so interesting. No informing book could be found, at home, at my grandmother's, at my friends' homes; and there was no public library in that town.

Although many of the individual ways of the omnipresent small creatures remain an enigma to the present day, man has learned how to control many of the harmful ones and to utilize efficiently those that are beneficial and productive. Books about insects written for the professional worker and for the laymen are numerous, yet the average man is not too well-informed concerning the insect life that surrounds him. Will Barker's book, *Familiar Insects of America*, is therefore a welcome and significant addition to published literature in the field. The book demonstrates the author's ability to describe lucidly, accurately, and in an absorbing manner the story of various insect groups. It will help the academically talented young person and the nonspecialist adult alike to understand the principles of classification, the basic details of natural history, the economic relationships, and other interesting facts about the common insects of North America. He who reads the book will find that he has gained good general knowledge of America's insect life, and has enjoyed the process. The serious reader eager for further study will find included a recommended reading list.

I do not believe that the writer of Proverbs 6:6, "Go to the ant, thou sluggard; consider her ways and be wise," was advocating a serious study of entomology. Nevertheless he certainly did indicate that a thorough study of the lives and habits of ants (and by implication of all insects) would reveal conduct, industry, and fortitude mankind could beneficially emulate. Mr. Barker's book should be available everywhere young people are busy preparing themselves for and adjusting their lives to the world in which they live.

I am confident this book will become as well-known and well-used as Will Barker's *Familiar Animals of America*.

viii

INTRODUCTION

. . . , *each crawling insect, holds a rank*
Important in the plan of Him who fram'd
This scale of beings.
STILLINGFLEET

Insects constitute 70 to 80 per cent of all known animals. These
six-legged creatures have been one of the most numerous forms of
animal life ever since the Carboniferous period. This time in the
history of our planet began some 200,000,000 years ago, and was
one in which great ferns were the predominant plant form. The
insects dominated this period—when coal and oil were beginning
to form and when dragonflies sped through the air on wings with
a spread of two feet.

Specimens of this first dragonfly type have been found in rock
formations in France; in the Elmo limestone of eastern Kansas; and
in a limestone formation of northeastern Oklahoma. Throughout
the world the story of our earliest insects is told in nearly one
hundred and fifty rock formations that typify various geological
periods. One of the earliest fossil fragments is that of a small insect
that might be a springtail. This fragment was found in Scotland
imbedded in a dark flintlike rock formed in Devonian times—
approximately 350 million years ago.

Many fossilized insects date from the Permian and Carboniferous
periods, and many are somewhat like today's mayflies and cockroaches. If you wish to trace the story of insects in North America,
there are areas other than eastern Kansas and northeastern Okla-

homa to explore. The coal beds of Pennsylvania and the shales of Florissant, Colorado, are good places to look as well as localities at White River, Colorado; Green River, Wyoming; and Quesnal in British Columbia.

Though there were more insects on this continent in times gone by than there are today, these animals are still so numerous and fly through the air in such multitudes that in 1951 a swarm of grasshoppers in the West was estimated to be one hundred miles long and three miles wide. At other times insects in caterpillar form have been known to crawl across railroad tracks in such numbers that they have brought trains to a halt. They also honeycomb the earth with tunnels and runways of varying sizes.

Water is not free of them either, for they skim over its surface, swim through it, and crawl across the bottom of pond, lake, or stream. And though marine insects are not so numerous as those of land or fresh-water environments, you will find some in coast-wise waters or at sea, where one species of water strider rides the waves hundreds of miles offshore.

On a world-wide basis the insects of these various habitats number nearly one million identified species. They belong to a large group, or phylum, of animals known as *Arthropoda*—a name derived from the Greek, *arthron*, jointed, and *podos*, of a foot. Insects are not the only animals with jointed appendages classed as arthropods, for such near relatives as the centipede, the lobster, the spider, and the scorpion belong in this grouping, too.

In order that one lot of arthropods may be distinguished from another, those with like characteristics are separated into various classes. As a class the insects are the *Hexapoda*, the zoological way of saying that these are the true or six-legged insects, but more commonly the class to which these six-legged animals belong is referred to as *Insecta*. The animal groups most frequently referred to in *Familiar Insects of America* are: Order, Family, Genus, and Species.

The classification of animals and plants—taxonomy—is a science in itself. The order of precedence in this classification is as rigidly adhered to as the seating arrangements for a formal dinner at the White House, and follows a descending scale like this:

Kingdom
Phylum
Class
Subclass
Order
Suborder
Superfamily
Family
Subfamily
Tribe
Genus
Subgenus
Species
Subspecies

Various characteristics differentiate insects from all other animals. In its adult form an insect is an animal that has a hard outside skeleton, known as the exoskeleton, and a body distinguished by three main divisions: head, thorax, and abdomen.

An insect is further distinguished by one pair of antennae, or feelers on the head, and three pairs of legs attached to the thorax.

Though most winged insects have two pairs of wings, there are some such as the fly that have only one pair. These, like the legs, are attached to the thorax.

The minute holes along each side of an insect's body are known as spiracles. An insect breathes through these openings, and the air so inhaled passes into tiny tubes, the "tracheae," that act as air-conveying ducts. These tubes are so numerous that they reach nearly every nerve in the body. Getting air in this way means that the blood of an insect carries no oxygen. And without oxygen there is no hemoglobin—the respiratory pigment in the red corpuscles of animals with backbones, the vertebrates. Because it lacks hemoglobin, the blood of an insect is not red.

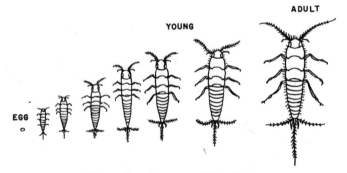

Direct Development (Silverfish)

The mouth parts of our various insects are of two major types: biting and chewing, and sucking; the second type of mouth may be for sucking only, for piercing and sucking, or for lapping. The biters, chewers, and all other types of feeders reach adulthood either by a simple form of development or one that is known as metamorphosis—changes in form and structure and usually a change in food and habits, too. Some insects undergo a metamorphosis that is not radical, but for others the changes are marked and abrupt.

The first type of development is the least spectacular. The bristletails and the springtails (the *Thysanura* and the *Collembola*), reach maturity without any metamorphosis whatsoever. At hatching one of these insects is a miniature of the parents, and merely increases in size, as man does, until it reaches adulthood.

xii

A less simple type of growth is the form of development known as incomplete, or direct, metamorphosis. At the time of hatching an insect that reaches adulthood in this way is a tiny, wingless replica of the parents. Such an insect becomes an adult by a series of molts, or form-sheddings. After each molt it emerges from the old form a slightly larger individual. If one of these insects is to be winged, a little swelling is noticeable on each side of the thorax after the first or second molt. These swollen spots are the wings-to-be. And with each molt they increase in size and become more truly winglike. The last molt produces an insect that is fully winged.

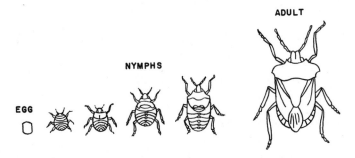

Incomplete or Direct Metamorphosis (True Bug)

Insects that undergo an incomplete metamorphosis are unique in that the wings develop externally. Another feature of their development is that at no time during the process of growing up are they inactive. And the stages in their lives are only three: egg, nymph, and imago—the adult or perfect form.

Yet another group of insects reaches adulthood by means of a complete, or indirect metamorphosis. Insects such as the bee, the beetle, and the butterfly undergo several radical changes in form before they achieve the adult state. An insect that develops in this manner passes through four life stages: egg, active larval stage (maggot or caterpillar), inactive pupal stage, and active adult. (One exception to the general rule of inactive pupal stage among these insects is the so-called rain-barrel mosquito that does not become quiescent at this time.)

To sum up an indirect or complete metamorphosis, it can be said that the young insect bears no resemblance whatsoever to the adult and will undergo radical changes before it becomes an adult. Furthermore, the wing development of such an insect is internal, and the wings themselves appear only *after* the last molt.

Any of these insects, from aphids (the *Homoptera*) to those in the order *Zoraptera* (little-known insects resembling small termites), are an integral part of their particular plant and animal communities. We cannot get along with some of them and we

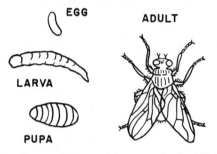

Complete or indirect Metamorphosis (Fly)

cannot get along without some of the others. Many classed as injurious because they threaten our economy are preyed upon by other animals. The most numerous of these predators are other insects. Next are the birds that carry on a daily warfare against insects, intensified at the time the young are in the nest.

A *Farmer's Bulletin,* issued by the United States Department of Agriculture, lists a number of insects classified as agricultural pests, and also gives the numbers of birds that feed on them. Here are some of the insects and the species of birds from this list:

Insect	*Number of Birds*
Alfalfa weevil	50
Billbug	110
Cotton-boll weevil	66
Cutworm	98
Japanese beetle	175
White grub	95
Wireworm	205

One of the most spectacular controls of insects by birds took place in 1848. The Mormon colony in Utah was less than a year old, and the prospect seemed good for an excellent harvest—greatly needed not only for the infant colony itself but also for additional members who were expected at any moment.

Shortly before harvest time, the sun darkened as if a sudden eclipse had taken place. The darkening was caused by swarming grasshoppers (later to be known as Mormon crickets). These ancient enemies of man settled on the crops and began to feed voraciously. As the 'hoppers fed, the colonists knew that possible starvation was on the way with every insect bite. Then the despairing people heard a great mewling—raucous cries that heralded the approach of hungry gulls. The birds dropped down out of the sky onto the 'hopper-laden grain and devoured the swarm. For deliverence from starvation, the Mormons eventually erected a monument to the gulls.

This monument in Salt Lake City is probably the first concrete tribute in America to Economic Ornithology. The first American publication having to do with entomology was published in 1806. Fred Val. Melsheimer, Minister of the Gospel, compiled a list of 1,363 insects accompanied by a short textual preface. This little pamphlet—now valued at no less than $150 and perhaps more—was titled *A Catalogue of Insects of Pennsylvania*, and the Reverend Mr. Melsheimer began his preface by saying:

I hereby offer to the Friends of Natural History a Catalogue of Insects, in the Collection of which I have spent my Hours of Recreation for some years past. To the best of my knowledge, I have but few predecessors in the United States in this Undertaking. For this Reason I may calculate on the Indulgence of the experienced Naturalist; in case some slight errors should be found in it, . . . Should the present Undertaking meet the Approbation of the Friends of Natural History in the United States, then this Catalogue will be continued from Time to Time. . . .

Thomas Say, author of *American Entomology*, issued in three volumes between 1824 and 1828, is said to have called Melsheimer "the parent of American entomology." Now Say is considered the father of that branch of natural science having to do with insects. Say was troubled by the lack of scientific interest in America and, in commenting on it, he contrasted Europe with America regarding the subject in the Preface of his *American Entomology*. This is what he wrote:

But little, I might almost say nothing, has yet been done in the United States in relation to the very interesting and important science upon which this work is intended to treat. While, in other departments of natural history, we have publications honourable to the republic, there is not, as far as I know, in the archives of American science, the record of an indigenous work on this subject.

Titian Ramsay Peale illustrated *American Entomology*, more interesting today for its asides than for the information contained therein. With reference to the leafhopper and the walkingstick, Say wrote:

Dead leaves shed by the parent tree are said to change gradually into animals of singular shape, and to have changed their place of abode under the eye of the historians who related the wonderful tale. Dead sticks also are said to sprout legs to move from place to place, and perform all the functions of a living body.

Since publication in 1806 of Melsheimer's list of 1,363 American insects, the number of known insects for North America is more than 82,000, and they constitute a diversified population. Of this host a few representative species and a few that are unusual or exotic (that is, imported) have been selected as subjects for *Familiar Insects of America*. The sequence in which the orders appear, chapter by chapter, is not the usual accepted scientific one. For we have written about the most common or the most "important" groups first. Thus, Chapter 1 is about well-known, common insects—grasshoppers, crickets, katydids, and their allies, the *Orthoptera*. This group is the Eighth Order under *Insecta* as listed in the *Bulletin of the Entomological Society of America*. In Chapter 11, "Other Orders"—the last one in the book—the sequence of the orders written about is the accepted scientific one, discounting groups already covered or omitted because they are little known or presumed to have less appeal than some others.

The names of insects are frequently subject to change as, after due consideration and deliberation, entomologists select the most definitive for each and every species. Though we have tried to use the most recent, generally accepted common and scientific names, we may have erred in some instances. Consequently among the scientific names in particular, you may find one that is not current.

Furthermore if the selections for this book still seem arbitrary, it is because a single volume could do little more than list all the species known to occur north of the Rio Grande. The choice is also based on a selection of beneficial and harmful insects, those with differing ways of life, and species that you and I are likely to see in a country with Arctic and subtropical regions, mountainous terrain both east and west, and arid lowlands, fertile plains, and well-watered valleys.

You will find insects in the plant and animal communities of all these regions. In the high valleys of our western mountains where shadows come early in the afternoon, you can see the butterflies known as Parnassians. These low-flying creatures drift back and forth above grassy alpine meadows or flit in and out of rock-rimmed cul-de-sacs. To see Parnassians you have to be in their vicinity during the brightest hours of their day, for as soon as the mountain peaks cut off the sunlight, these butterflies seemingly vanish from their mountain haunts. Now they have settled themselves for the night among the grasses.

If you visit one of the five great American deserts you may see long lines of harvester ants on their way to gather seeds. The harvest gathered by these colonial insects is brought back to the cone-shaped anthills and turned over to the workers—other members of the colony that crack the shells, then store some of the kernels underground while feeding others to the young. Then in your particular neighborhood, you may hear the lazy drone of the bumble bee, see the intermittent flash of the firefly, or discover to your dismay that a cutworm has sheared off recently set-out tomato plants.

Though these and other insects are somewhat familiar, we may not know as much about them as we think we do. *Familiar Insects of America* attempts to give as much information as possible within space limitations about our more common insect allies and those that are called foes. If any of the information so generously furnished me by the individuals and institutions listed below is misinterpreted the fault is entirely mine.

I want to thank each of these for help given at various points in the preparation of this book:

M. L. Du Mars, Foreign Agricultural Service; Ashley B. Gurney and Philip Luginbill, Jr., Agricultural Research Service; Alfred Stefferud, Editor, *The Yearbook of Agriculture;* Division of Information and Education, Forest Service, United States Department of Agriculture. Ralph E. Crabill and all other members of the Division of Entomology, United States National Museum. Educational Materials Laboratory, Office of Education, and Public Health Service, United States Department of Health, Education, and Welfare. Office of Climatology, Weather Bureau, United States Department of Commerce. Fish and Wildlife Service, United States Department of the Interior. Entomological Society of America. Frank W. Lara, National Wildlife Federation. Kenneth B. Pomeroy, American Forestry Association. A. U. Spear, Information Officer, Florida Livestock Board. American Forest Products Industries, Inc. Sport Fishing Institute. World Health Organization. Staff, Mt. Pleasant Library, District of Columbia. John Pallister, Department of Insects and Spiders, American Museum of Natural History.

Dr. Alexander B. Klots and his wife, Elsie B. Klots, are due a special acknowledgment for reading this book in proof. To them I wish to express my appreciation for taking the time to read it and to thank them for their interest and suggestions regarding it.

And again I should like to mention particularly one person with whom I have worked previously on the putting together of books. This is Carl Burger, whose accurate, artistic illustrations are so much a part of *Familiar Animals of America* and *Winter-Sleeping Wildlife*. Now my especial thanks to him for the painstaking care with which he executed the illustrations for *Familiar Insects of America*.

W. B.

Washington, D. C.
January, 1960

Only if we know and face the truth about the world, whether the world of physics and chemistry, or of geology and biology, or of mind and behavior, shall we be able to see what is our own true place in the world.

—Sir Julian Huxley

1 GRASSHOPPERS, CRICKETS, KATYDIDS, and ALLIES

Happy are the grasshoppers' lives
Because they all have noiseless wives.
ANON.

If this couplet is true, then the cricket and the katydid should also be happy, for their wives are as noiseless as those of the grasshopper. All three insects belong to families in which the males have the ability to make that form of music known as stridulation. This shrill, creaking serenade comes late in summer when male grasshoppers, crickets, and katydids are trying to attract mates, and thus ensure another generation of music-makers for the summer to come.

The ability to make music by scraping one wing across another is not the only unusual characteristic that distinguishes these three families of insects. The short-horned grasshopper, the familiar brown or blackish brown field cricket, and the green-eyed katydid with its threadlike antennae are undoubtedly three of the best broad-jumpers among animals. If some entrepreneur were to stage an animal Olympics these insects would place first in most jumping events. And the reason is that they have greatly enlarged thighs on each hind leg.

This enlargement makes it possible for the grasshopper and its jumping relatives to cover amazing distances in relation to individual weights. One of the short-horned grasshoppers can be said to outjump the kangaroo if you equate the distance jumped by each animal to the weight of each. If an adult kangaroo could make a leap comparable to that of an adult grasshopper, the kangaroo's leap would measure 1,200 feet—about one-fourth of a mile.

The three other families in the order *Orthoptera* are composed of insects that creep, crawl, or run. They are the native and imported mantids; the hard-to-find walkingsticks; and the odorous, hitch-hiking cockroaches. The scientific name for all six families derives from two Greek words: *orthos*, straight; and *pteron*, a wing.

Yet not all insects in this order are winged. Species such as the cave and camel crickets are wingless, while others only have remnants. The species that are winged have two pairs in which the structure differs. The forewings are leathery and heavily veined, and bring to mind a piece of parchment on which a design has been stenciled. They act as wing covers for the less sturdy hind wings that fold fanlike when the insect rests.

The *Orthoptera* can be further distinguished by biting mouth parts; antennae, or feelers, that vary in length from moderate to extremely long. Each has several eyes, some of which are simple and others that are compound. They undergo an incomplete metamorphosis, also known as a direct metamorphosis. This is a series of molts that starts in infancy and continues until the final, or adult, form is achieved. A molt occurs when the growing insect becomes too large for its old skin, which then splits to release a larger version of the baby insect—at hatching time so much like its parents that except for wings it is well-nigh a perfect miniature.

The grasshopper and its close relatives have been with us since Triassic times—an era that began 190,000,000 years ago toward the close of the age of reptiles. The cockroach dates from the Upper Carboniferous Age—the age of invertebrates and primitive vertebrates that began some 250,000,000 years ago.

A world-wide census of *Orthoptera* at the end of 1948 showed that there were about 22,500 species in the order. Of these in North America above the Rio Grande, the noisy and noiseless species combined to give us slightly more than 1,000 species, many of which are troublemakers. In commenting on this order, the late Professor of Entomology at Cornell University, John Henry Comstock, wrote:

Although the song of the katydid and the chirp of the cricket are most often associated with recollections of pleasant evenings spent in the country, we cannot forget that to members of this order are due some of the most terrible insect scourges man has ever known.

Grasshoppers, Crickets, and Katydids

During the hot dry summer of 1865 General Alfred Sully had a lot of trouble with insects in the vicinity of Sioux City, Iowa, where the General and his troops were bivouacked. They were on their way to Indian Territory and the short sojourn in Iowa coincided with the arrival of swarms of grasshoppers passing through the same area. The insects so harassed the military that the General reported the action to the St. Paul *Press*.

The only thing spoken of about here is the grasshoppers. They are awful; they have actually eaten holes in my wagon covers and in the 'paulins that cover my stores. A soldier on his way here lay down to sleep in the middle of the day on the prairie. The troops had been marching all night. His comrades noticed him covered with grasshoppers, and woke him. His throat and wrists were bleeding from the bites of these insects. This is no fiction.

As a rule grasshoppers do not prey on men, but they have long been one of our worst insect enemies. Man has suffered from their depredations seemingly since the world began, and General Sully is not the only complainant on record with regard to the behavior of these insects. The Egyptians, the Hebrews, and the Greeks all had words about the grasshopper and the damage this flying insect causes. You can find one such reference in a book of the Old Testament. The third verse in the second chapter of Joel states: "The land is as the garden of Eden before them, and behind them a desolate wilderness; yea, and nothing shall escape them."

The commentators of eras long since gone referred to the grasshopper as a "locust," for which the equivalent Latin word is "a burned place." The first settlers in North America learned of these "burned places" soon after their arrival. Grasshoppers attacked the scanty crops of the Massachusetts colony in 1740. The colonists bound brush together, and with these primitive controls swept millions of insects into the ocean.

Seventy-odd years later swarming grasshoppers destroyed the crops of settlers in Minnesota. Then in 1877 as the covered wagons lurched their way West, the canvas-topped vehicles were temporarily halted by swarms of grasshoppers. The foraging insects left many a home-seeker without grass for his animals and with no food for himself and his family.

The greatest grasshopper damage occurs in the West. It takes place in areas where the average annual rainfall is 10 to 30 inches. From 1925 to 1949 the value of the crops lost as a result of grasshopper outbreaks in twenty-three western states was more than $779,500,000.

The species that cause the greatest loss are the 'hoppers usually known as "general feeders." These insects devour entire crops of small grains, corn, soybeans, cotton, alfalfa, clover, and various grasses. At times they are so numerous and so voracious that they eat corn stalks right down to the ground, then start on trees. And as the General learned they will even chew on man.

The man-eating species might have been one of six hundred identified for the United States and Canada. The areas in the United States where 'hoppers cause the greatest damage are apt to harbor more than one hundred different species. But at least 90 per cent of crop damage is caused by such grasshoppers as the clear-winged; the differential; the two-striped; the red-legged; and the migratory. A sixth, the American Grasshopper (*Schistocera americana*), occasionally ruins field crops in Alabama, Florida, Georgia, Louisiana, and Mississippi. The migratory, two-striped, and the red-legged grasshoppers have nation-wide distribution. And though the red-legged is the most common, the migratory is probably the most destructive.

The list of debits is far longer than the one of credits when it comes to record-keeping for the grasshopper. But there are a few favorable entries to be made for this insect. The grasshopper makes good live bait, and trout fishermen use the insect as such. 'Hoppers are in the diets of various game birds including the wild turkey, and are fed upon by unpenned domestic fowls among which is the turkey.

Some native Americans formerly ate these insects, but today they are not much favored in spite of being sold roasted, in cans, as cocktail food. Nevertheless if you are interested in knowing how to prepare grasshoppers for the table, thirty-three recipes are available. Grasshopper cooking is discussed in a pamphlet published by the Republic of the Philippines.

Migratory Grasshopper
Melanoplus bilituratus

The Migratory Grasshopper is a one-inch, reddish brown insect with an irregular black patch on the neck or collar. It is one of the short-horned grasshoppers, so called because the antennae or feelers are about as long as, or perhaps slightly longer than, the thorax—that body part between the head and the abdomen.

This grasshopper occurs in cropped fields or idle lands in which the soil is well drained or light. It thrives where the average annual rainfall is 10 to 30 inches, and where the climate is subhumid or semiarid. In such areas the migratory grasshopper and the four other highly destructive species gather in swarms in outbreak years. The species named for its migratory impulse often travels hundreds of miles. And wherever these sharp-toothed insects pause, crop and range plants are destroyed, soil erosion follows because ground cover has been devoured, and there is other damage that may be directly or indirectly attributed to an infestation. An example of indirect damage is the forced sale of cattle because all forage is gone.

In 1938 migratory grasshoppers gathered by the millions in North and South Dakota. These states served as points of departure for the insects that first invaded Minnesota, Montana, and Nebraska, and then eventually crossed the border into the provinces of Manitoba and Saskatchewan. Winds from the southeast helped some swarms in their long-range movements. By 1940 the swarming Dakota grasshoppers had produced a third generation. And by 1940 the crop damage for which the insects were responsible and the money spent on their control amounted to more than $62,000,000.

The worst grasshopper plague in twenty years was predicted early in the summer of 1958. In western Kansas and eastern Colorado and in Nebraska, the Texas Panhandle, and New Mexico, the

Migratory Grasshopper, *Melanoplus bilituratus*, laying eggs

wheat farmers and the cattlemen were anticipating a good season. Then came an announcement from an entomologist that the 'hoppers were coming—coming out of the ground in numbers estimated at 600 to one square yard. This many to a square yard is ten times the number considered a bad infestation—about 60 to the square yard.

The 'hoppers that crawled out of the ground early in the summer of 1958 hatched from eggs laid the previous spring and fall. The eggs of a grasshopper result from a single mating between mature insects; one mating is sufficient to fertilize several lots of eggs. The eggs are deposited by the female in pods in well-defined breeding places.

Once the female is ready to lay her eggs, she searches for the right spot in which to deposit them. She probes the soil or the sod, first at one spot, then at another. When she finally locates a spot to her liking, she starts a bore, or tunnel, with the ovipositor. This is a specialized egg-laying organ at the end of the abdomen; it consists of three pairs of jointed styles—hard, sharp prongs that can bore into the ground.

The pincerlike ovipositor moves around until it gets a good "bite" on the ground. Then the insect exerts pressure from above so that the organ digs in. This action pulls the abdomen after the ovipositor and at the same time elongates the abdomen. As the valves of the ovipositor expand and contract, the soil is pushed sideways. This forms a firm-walled tunnel in which to store the eggs.

Now the female is ready to commence egg-laying. The valves of the ovipositor open to release some eggs. They are immediately enveloped by a discharge of a thin, sticky substance. As the eggs are expelled, the abdomen shortens. After the last egg is deposited in the tunnel, all are then covered by a final coat of the gluey substance. As soon as this coat hardens the eggs are protected against either too little or too much rain.

The number of egg pods laid by a female varies with the species, available food, and the weather. (One breeding ground of the clear-winged grasshopper had an average of 25,000 eggs to the square yard.) The migratory grasshopper, a medium-sized species, sometimes lays as many as 21 pods, with 15 to 20 eggs to each pod. An egg is about the size of a grain of rice and has about the same shape. This 'hopper and other crop-eating species are *not* able to survive the winter except in the egg state.

Each year in northern states there is only a single generation of the migratory grasshopper. But in the South there is apt to be more than one generation a season. Kansas, for instance, frequently has two generations, and Arizona often has three.

Growth of a young 'hopper within the egg is governed by hereditary forces and by moisture and temperature. During April, May, or June, the embryo within the egg swells and swells until it finally cracks open the shell. Even after it emerges from the shell, the embryo is not a free-moving individual. It is encased in a sheath that has the appearance of cellophane. The sheath holds the legs and feelers close to the still-soft body.

As it wriggles and squirms it way toward the surface, the flying grasshopper-to-be is protected by the sheath. Ordinarily it does not have to force upward more than an inch. But drifting soil may cause a journey of several inches. The first 'hopper out of the shell is a trail blazer; those that hatch subsequently follow the number-one insect like so many horses following the lead mount.

Once the 'hopper is above ground, it sheds the enveloping sheath. Now with legs, feelers, and biting mouth parts free, the newly hatched 'hopper is set to walk, jump, and eat. For a short time after it emerges, the tiny insect is white. But after a few hours in the sunlight, it takes on the characteristic coloring of its particular species.

Except for size and the lack of wings, the just-out-of-the-ground 'hopper resembles its parents. In this respect it is unlike many other insects. A fly, for instance, has a larval stage before it becomes mature; and a butterfly has a resting period known as "pupation" before it reaches the adult stage.

The young grasshopper of any species becomes an adult by a series of molts—a way of growing up that is called an incomplete metamorphosis. It grows a new body covering every so often, then sheds the old one. To reach the adult stage requires 40 to 60 days. During this interval there are periodic body splits down the insect's back. And after each split a slightly larger and more fully developed 'hopper emerges.

The time finally arrives when the last molt is to take place—the one from which the grasshopper emerges with wings. But before actually molting the insect has to get in position to do so. It hangs upside down, and with all six feet grips twig, plant stalk, or any other perch on which it has crawled. Then, all wrong-side-to and motionless, it hangs until the old and final skin splits down the back.

With gravity as an aid, the emerging adult slowly pulls its antennae and legs from the confines of the last skin to be shucked. Once free it rights itself. The reversed position lets the wings hang straight down as they unfold. Slow, pulsating movements of the body force blood and air into the wings. When they are finally inflated, they dry, stiffen, and acquire color. And lastly the under-wings are folded and fall into position beneath the upper wings—narrower, but a protection because they are harder. Such wings are typical of the insects in this order, the straight-winged insects.

If you were to make a detailed study of the features of the grass-hopper—the morphology—you would want to note in particular the arrangement of the five eyes. There are two large compound eyes made up of many facets, or sight units, and three small simple ones known as the "ocelli." The large eyes are paired and on either side of the head. Two of the small eyes are above the antennae, while the third is equidistant from the others but slightly below them.

Opinions differ about the functions of these simple eyes; one theory is that they are for seeing nearby objects, while another is that they are to measure light intensity. And they may also act as some sort of regulator for the nerves and muscles of the large, many-faceted eyes that permit an unusually wide range of vision.

A molt is an interval of quiet for the grasshopper; the process may last from one to three hours. To prepare for this casting off and renewing, the insect goes without food and rests for about twenty-four hours. Immediately after each molt another quiet interval occurs during which the external body parts harden.

The swarming or mass flights of grasshoppers occur when the insects are unusually abundant. There are times, however, when it seems that mass flights are induced by shortages of foods. Swarming frequently originates where plants and grasses are short and where the prevailing midday temperature of the air is more than 75° F. Generally the insects start to fly when the temperature of the air is between 75° and 89° F., and when that on the ground is 100° F.

or a few degrees warmer. And there has to be a gentle breeze—the kind that ripples a field of wheat in a series of green waves.

Migratory grasshoppers take off against the wind, then bank to fly with it. They are helped in the upward flight by warm air rising from the hot ground. In an amazingly short time the insects are high in the sky, glittering like so many bits of metal shavings in the harsh light from the sun. Though there are no altitude records for the migratory grasshopper, the insect has often been reported by airplane pilots at several thousand feet. And during the 1958 grasshopper plague in Colorado, the *Rocky Mountain News* stated that pilots were climbing 10,500 feet to get above the clouds of grasshoppers in the eastern part of the state.

As the migratory grasshopper flies with the winds, it sometimes travels 25 to 50 miles a day; a season's flight may be hundreds of miles. The swarming 'hoppers of 1938 flew 500 miles in three weeks —from central South Dakota to central Montana.

Not all the insects of a mass movement survive until the end of the road is reached. Grasshoppers are preyed upon or controlled by various animals including other insects. Among insect enemies are the flesh, tangle-veined, and bee flies and the ground and blister beetles. These insects use grasshoppers and eggs as hosts for their young. The maggots of the bee fly and the two beetles are often such effective controls that they have been known to destroy 40 to 60 per cent of the grasshopper eggs in a given area.

Spiders, good-sized game fishes, and birds (except doves and pigeons) eat grasshoppers. Among rodent predators is the grasshopper mouse—a stockily built little mammal one-fifth of whose diet consists of grasshoppers and other insects. Though these and other natural controls destroy numberless grasshoppers, their combined efforts are not enough.

Man-made measures such as seeding, proper tillage, and the use of insecticides and pesticides are also necessary. This goes without saying when it is a matter of record that the 1938 grain damage by grasshoppers in Saskatchewan, Canada, was estimated at more than $35,000,000. During the summer and fall of 1956 surveys were made in the United States to determine grasshopper damage on cropland and rangeland. The survey revealed that cropland in more than fifteen states and rangeland in some 20,000,000 acres in more than sixteen states were threatened by the grosshopper—a truly formidable enemy but one that Vachel Lindsay must have liked when he wrote this in *The Sante Fé Trail:*

> I want live things in their pride to remain.
> I will not kill one grasshopper in vain
> Though he eats a hole in my shirt like a door.
> I let him out, give him one chance more.
> Perhaps, while he gnaws my hat in his whim,
> Grasshopper lyrics occur to him.

Mormon Cricket
Anabrus simplex

If there are twenty Mormon crickets in each square yard of an acre, then the amount of forage lost each day will amount to twenty pounds—the daily requirement of one cow. Though these large wingless grasshoppers are considered less destructive than many others, their voracious appetites make them a constant crop threat in intermountain and far western states.

The damage to range plants by Mormon crickets is general throughout the Rocky Mountain region. But the area in which this almost black insect does the greatest harm is the shrubby desert range of northern Nevada. No wonder the insect is feared, for it feeds on more than 250 kinds of range plants!

Cultivated crops are not immune; the insects eat small grains, alfalfa, and truck crops.

The Mormon cricket has been feared by the rancher and the farmer ever since the western United States was first settled. Then, as now, the crickets swarmed down from the mountains. These insect hordes threatened complete destruction of the crops and ultimately the starvation of the early settlers. Such migrations into some of Utah's first Mormon settlements prompted the common name of this insect.

Areas of certain mountain ranges are the permanent breeding grounds of the Mormon cricket. There are breeding grounds in the Big Horn Mountains of Wyoming, the Pryor Mountains of

Montana, and the Independence Mountains of Nevada. Here and in certain other areas the female lays its eggs in sandy, loamlike soil. This has to be light and well-drained, and is usually on a slope with a southern, eastern, or western exposure. In the really sandy regions of Washington and Idaho, the eggs are deposited in the crowns of bunchgrass, whose tufts make a nest any hen should envy.

The eggs of the Mormon cricket are about ¼ inch long, rounded at either end, and dark brown when thrust into the ground by the ovipositor. The eggs are in the ground only a short time when they undergo a change in color and in form. The dark brown becomes a dull gray and one of the rounded ends becomes larger than the other.

Midsummer is the season when the female lays her eggs. The preferred time of day seems to be the afternoon. Throughout the egg-laying period there are intervals of rest. Also throughout the egg-laying period, the smaller male "sings." The singing usually occurs in the forenoon. Though a female may lay as many as 250 eggs, the average is 150. And the eggs are laid one at a time.

A young Mormon cricket develops within the egg during the warm weather, so that by the time the ground freezes it is fully formed. If the weather is abnormally warm, it may hatch late in February. But the more normal hatching time starts about the beginning of April.

The young cricket, or nymph, is about ¼ inch in length. Except for the white on the edges of the shield right behind the head, the nymph is predominantly black. The differences in size and color are the only characteristics that distinguish the young insect from its parents.

There are seven sharply defined periods of growth before the Mormon cricket becomes an adult. Each period is separated by a molt, the quiet interval when the outer skin is shed. By the time a nymph is a third grown, it may be any one of three colors: tan, black, or light green. Sixty days or so after it emerges from the ground, the insect is ready for its final molt. Once this has taken place, a full-grown cricket crawls out of the last skin to be shed. The adult has three color stages: first, reddish brown; then, dark olive green; and finally, near black.

The best-known peculiarity of the Mormon cricket is undoubtedly the mass migration. One is apt to start on a day when the air temperature is 65° to 75° F. and when that of the soil surface is 75° to 125° F. The velocity of the wind must be no greater than 25 miles an hour. The day, however, may be either clear or partly cloudy.

A band of Mormon crickets acts as a single unit. Each insect in the same band marches in the same direction. If marching Mormon crickets have to split to get around an obstacle that they cannot get over, they reassemble afterward.

These migrating insects travel half a mile or even a mile in one day. They may cover 25 to 30 miles in a single season—provided that there are fifty favorable days in the season. Though it is possible for an outbreak of the crickets to reach its peak in one year, it usually takes two or three years for a real infestation to develop.

Mormon crickets are generally controlled by poisoned baits. These may be either wet or dry. The use of baits to save crops is safe—always provided you spread them in the amounts recommended. As a rule with proper precaution, there is no danger of poisoning either domestic or wild animals.

The insects are also checked by the use of oil on water in irrigation ditches or that in streams. The oily film kills migrating crickets, for they march right into whatever water they come to, then kick themselves into the current and float along. Sometimes a cricket armada goes only a short distance; at other times it is water-borne for mile after mile. But sooner or later the individuals come ashore to start new infestations.

Fence barriers also protect crops, and baited metal strips are used, too. The strips halt the insects, which then feed on the poisoned bait and subsequently die.

The years in which Mormon crickets reached the largest recorded outbreak proportions were the 1930's. An estimate of the losses attributed to the insect in 1938 was about 15 per cent of the forage on 13 million acres of range land. The estimated crop damage of varying intensity occurred on 35,000 acres.

By 1949, however, the effect of widespread campaigns to control the Mormon cricket was apparent. The crop damage was confined to 230 acres, while the damage to range plants was classified as slight on about 200,000 acres.

Field Cricket
Acheta assimilis

About one hundred years after General Alfred Sully had his trouble with grasshoppers, another professional man in an entirely different field was momentarily defeated by a single insect in this

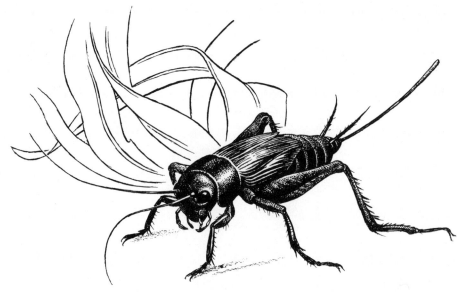

FIELD CRICKET (female), *Acheta assimilis*

same order. The man was Isaac Stern, the noted violinist, and the troublemaker was a lone cricket, secreted in a palm.

No one knows whether the cricket was trying to attract a mate, distract Mr. Stern, or merely fiddling for fun. But its high-pitched *treet-treet-treet* was such that Mr. Stern had to stop playing a Brahms concerto. Bow in hand, the violinist announced that he could not compete with a cricket.

After a five-minute search ushers located the source of the disturbance in a potted palm. They rushed pot, palm, and the cricket outside. Then with competition eliminated, Mr. Stern and the orchestra resumed their Miami Beach concert—interrupted by a single cricket on the night of June 17, 1957.

The well-known field cricket is one of more than two thousand species. It is a black insect about ⅝ inch in length; has antennae, or feelers; chewing mouth parts; and two pairs of wings. The wings fold over the back. Rarely used for flying, they are equipped with special sound organs that are frequently used for "fiddling." On one front wing is a ridged membrane; on the opposing front wing there are also ridges. But these are different; they are serrated along the edge, notched somewhat in the manner of the cutting edge of a saw. To make its music, the cricket draws one wing across the other. This fiddling creates a variety of sound combinations.

In addition to the *treet-treet-treet*, a stopper for Mr. Stern, the field cricket has two other combinations in its repertoire. Sometimes it fiddles a *cree-cree-cree*, and then again it makes its "strings" hum with a *gru-gru-gru*. Any of this male music is picked up by the female whose "ears" are located just below the front knee joints.

You can have cricket music throughout a great part of North America. The insect is found in most sections of the United States as well as in southern Canada and in northern Mexico. On this vast range the females lay their eggs in the ground each fall. The young overwinter in the egg stage, then emerge the following spring as nymphs. They have an incomplete metamorphosis, undergoing a series of molts before they become full-grown.

Crickets make good pets, and during the summer of 1959 when I was on the staff of the Junior Naturalists Training Program, Accokeek, Maryland, some of the youngsters taking the course made cricket cages for the species they caught on field trips. The Chinese and Japanese have kept these insects for centuries, and house them in elaborate cages. Owners in both countries stage cricket fights, with males commanding good prices. One comparable to our field cricket is worth $50 to $100, and one fighter named "Genghis Khan," so the story runs, did so well in a single bout that it won for its owner $90,000.

Field crickets often chew the twine on bundles of grain. The damage caused by this species is not so great as that of some of the others. The mole cricket, a large nocturnal species, feeds on the roots of lawn grasses. The burrowing of the insect, known scientifically as *Gryllotalpa hexadactyla*, as it feeds also uproots seedlings and hastens the drying out of the soil. In one night a single mole cricket can damage several yards of recently seeded lawn.

In this country the cricket is not the problem insect that the grasshopper is. But in New Zealand there was a plague of crickets in June 1957. Pastures were destroyed on the Huaraki Plains in the northern part of the country. And in some places the insects actually moved right into farmhouses, where they stripped paper from the walls, chewed the upholstery on furniture, and ate the clothes in the closets.

Ordinarily the cricket is a vegetarian, but when food is scarce or the insect is numerous, it becomes omnivorous. The diet includes other crickets, shoe linings, and, as one southern family learned, the crickets on their hearth developed a great fondness for striped T-shirts.

In the cricket family, the *Gryllidae*, there is a delicate pale-green insect that measures nearly three-fourths of an inch in length. This is the tree cricket, and in most instances it is apt to be a species in the genus *Oecanthus*. It trills all through the night from a perch in a tree, in a treelike shrub, and even in high-growing grass. One of these crickets is only a little less noisy than the katydid, presumably the loudest music-maker of all these insects. A trilling tree cricket synchronizes its music with all the other crickets of the same species in the neighborhood. The insects thus become a cricket chorale whose music is as monotonous as someone practicing the same scale for hours on end.

A tree cricket has a varied diet that includes weaker members of its family; the leaves and blossoms of a number of plants; and occasionally ripening fruits. The female punctures the stems of raspberry plants and similar fruit-bearing plants at the time she is ready to lay her eggs. These punctures make "nests" into which she drops her eggs. The tiny holes provide safe overwintering cul-de-sacs for tree crickets in the egg stage, but they damage the canes of the plants. Tree crickets can be controlled by burning raspberry and other canes, and by poisoned baits when the nymphs emerge in the spring.

Angular-winged Katydid
Microcentrum retinerve

The angular-winged katydid is one of the "long-horned" grass-hoppers. It can be identified by its long, threadlike antennae, or feelers. The insect is about 2 inches in length, has chewing mouth parts like other *Orthoptera*, and four good-sized wings that fold

ANGULAR-WINGED KATYDID, *Microcentrum retinerve;* eggs on edges of leaves

over the back. It is more easily heard than seen, for its foliage-green color blends so well with its surroundings.

The male is the noisy member of the family. He is the one that sounds off with "Katy did! Katy didn't!" The frequency of the call on a summer evening is often as much as once a second. The persistent, repetitious call is the result of rubbing the ridges of one outer wing, the wing cover, back and forth across the rasps of the

GRASSHOPPERS, CRICKETS, KATYDIDS, AND ALLIES   17

opposing wing cover. This sound is received by the female who catches it with "ears" that are on the front legs.

Early in the fall the female lays her eggs. She uses an exceptionally long ovipositor to deposit them on leaves and twigs. The oval-shaped eggs are placed in a pattern that reminds you of overlapping shingles. This arrangement gives the eggs the appearance of some kind of tree scale.

Once the winter is over the young katydid emerges from its protective casing. It resembles the parents, but is, of course, much smaller. It is also much lighter in color and there are no wings. Before it acquires wings the katydid has to pass through the type of growing-up peculiar to the insects that undergo an incomplete metamorphosis—by changing a little at a time.

The northern katydid has one brood a year, but those in the South usually have two. And the northern katydid, like the woodchuck and the woolly bear caterpillar, has a reputation as a weather prophet. The first katydid call of the season in the North is supposed to mean that in six weeks there will be frost. But as a weather forecaster the katydid is no more reliable than the woodchuck and the woolly bear. And it is much less destructive than these other two animals. Though the katydid feeds mostly on the leaves of trees, it does no great damage.

MANTIDS
Family Mantidae

H. G. Wells said that considering the size of the female praying mantis, it is one of the most awe-inspiring of created beings when aroused. The scientist and writer once had an encounter with what must have been an enraged mantid. For Wells said this particular insect reared herself menacingly, then brought her claws forward, and rattled her wings to produce a "quite horrid sound." He commented that he could no more have touched the menacing little beast than he could have walked up to a snarling tiger.

Of the world's more than 1,500 species of mantids, we have some twenty native or introduced species in the United States. One, the praying mantid, or mantis, has been described as a "pious fraud." Undoubtedly this is because the insect assumes a seemingly worshipful position as it waits for prey. Perched on a leaf or twig, the mantid holds itself immobile, with the long spiked forelegs in front of the shiny triangular head.

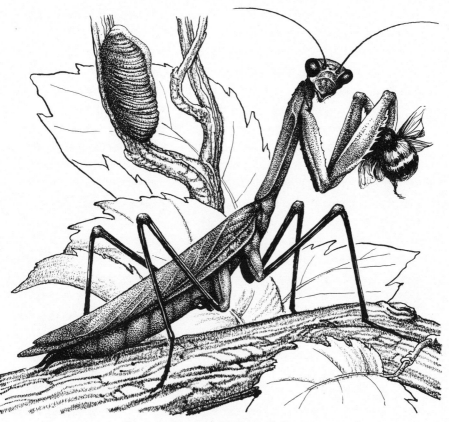

PRAYING MANTIS, *Mantis religiosa*

This immobility is a great aid in hunting, but camouflage also helps. The upper part of the body is long, thin, and a greenish brown, while the lower part is flattened and more green than brown. A color combination such as this makes the praying mantid well-nigh invisible to the other insects on which it feeds. Some of these are flies, crickets, grasshoppers, and roaches—all ancient enemies of man. The insect eats honey bees and some mantids seem to prefer the bee above all else.

When prey comes within reach of a waiting mantid, it is snatched and held in the toothed claws of the powerful forelegs. The prey is held fast by the lower leg that closes knifelike against the upper leg. Spines on the upper leg holds the prey in place like meat skewered on the tines of a fork. The mouth has strong cutting jaws that enable the insect to bite through the hard outside skeleton, the exoskeleton, of insect prey.

A praying mantid often makes a leisurely meal. When it has devoured its prey, it cleans out any food particles left in the spines, and finally washes its face in the manner of a cat. The amount of food eaten in a day often equals the insect's own weight.

The end of summer and the early fall is mating season for the various mantids. Some species mate more than once, but usually a single mating is sufficient to fertilize the eggs. Though it is generally supposed that the female bites off the male's head once a mating is consummated, this is not always so. Such behavior depends upon the species, and is also apt to take place among caged insects.

The female lays several hundred eggs before frost. Laid in clusters of varying numbers, the eggs are attached to the branches of shrubs and trees or to the stems of grasses. They are deposited in layers and protected by a foamy secretion that hardens a few minutes after it is exposed to the air. This forms a light brown, brown, or grayish brown case in which the eggs can overwinter in safety unless the season is unusually severe. On the southernmost parts of its range in this counrty and in tropical and subtropical regions, also, the mantid enters a quiet interval known as the "diapause." This inactive period occurs during extremely dry weather or at the time of the rainy season.

The wingless young hatch in the spring and leave the nest or egg case in what looks like a living chain of tiny mantids. They start feeding on plant lice or other small insects almost at once, and continue eating pest insects during a life that is only one season long. They are fully grown by late summer and, depending upon the species, measure 2½ to 4 inches in length. By this time, too, they have acquired their nearly transparent wings. The males are apt to be the stronger fliers. As a rule these insects do not make flights of any great distance, and at the time a female is ready to lay her eggs she flies but little.

Of the native or introduced species, probably one of the commonest in the East is the Carolina mantis (*Stagmomantis carolina*). The range of this native mantid is from Pennsylvania across the Middle West to Colorado and south into Mexico. Edwin Way Teale has reported it in the neighborhood of Baldwin on Long Island. A number of species closely related to the Carolina mantis have more restricted ranges than our commonest eastern form. One close relative is in Florida and three are members of various plant and animal communities throughout the Southwest.

The most widespread mantid of the West has a range that covers much of the Great Plains area and extends north into British Columbia and south from central Texas into Mexico. This is the minor mantis (*Litaneutria minor*)—a light buff to dark brown species that seems to prefer the ground for its habitat. Perhaps it lives where it does because it is less conspicuous than if it were constantly above ground in the various grasses of its range.

Though these mantids and such others as the unicorn mantid of Arizona only and the grizzled mantis of the Southeast are native mantids, they are not always the species that come to mind when we think of these unique tropical and subtropical insects.

The mantid so frequently pictured is the European mantis—the species classified as *Mantis religiosa* by Carolus Linnaeus, who might well be called the father of binomial nomenclature. In *Praying Mantids Of The United States: Native and Introduced*,* Ashley B. Gurney has this to say about *M. religiosa*:

This is a widespread species of northern Africa, southern Europe, and temperate Asia. It appeared at Rochester, N. Y., in 1899, probably the result of eggs being introduced on nursery stock. . . . Adults are about 2 to 2½ inches long and the wings cover the abdomen when folded. Egg masses are rather more bulky than those of the Carolina mantis, but less so than those of the Chinese mantis and differently shaped.

---

* Smithsonian Publication 4037, published separately from the Institution's *Annual Report of 1950*.

The Chinese mantis (*Tenodera aridifolia sinensis*) mentioned by Dr. Gurney is another introduced species. It was first noticed near Philadelphia in 1896, but now has spread until its range is from New Haven, Connecticut, coastwise as far south as Virginia. There are localized populations of these mantids elsewhere, and egg masses have been distributed in Illinois. This distribution took place in 1949, and the mantids that hatched from the two hundred distributed cases have increased appreciably the mantid population in Warren County. Colonies have been started in California and probably in Ohio where a dealer in biological supplies has been distributing egg cases.

A species closely related to the Chinese mantis was first discovered in 1926 near Aberdeen, Maryland. This is the narrow-winged mantis (*Tenodera angustipennis*)—a species that can be differentiated from the Chinese form because its hind wings are not darkened nearly so much and because it is smaller and much less robust. This mantid is now found on a range that extends from Connecticut to Virginia.

Though mantids in the vicinity of an apiary can make short work of the bees therein, the insects are regarded as beneficial—the only ones of the order in this category. In fact these insects are of such value to the farmer and gardener that there is a market for the egg cases, the *oöthecae*. One dealer in these cases is located on Long Island, and a farmer in the neighborhood gets fringe benefits.

From the day the praying-mantis dealer went into business, the delighted but puzzled farmer has not been troubled by red spiders or other bean pests. Surplus mantids freed by the dealer or those that escape rid the bean patches of pests.

Walkingstick
Diapheromera femorata

The walking stick is one of the most perfect examples of passive mimicry. The length of this wingless insect is three or four inches, but the breadth is barely an eighth of an inch, or nearly the size of a terminal twig. This twiglike resemblance is further enhanced by a series of body rings that are similar in appearance to the growth rings on a twig.

In addition to looking like the twig of an oak, cherry, locust, or walnut tree, the position a walkingstick assumes on its chosen perch adds greatly to the illusion that it is a tree growth. The creature holds its two front legs ahead of it so that they parallel the stick or twig on which it rests. Its grayish brown color also helps to make it indistinguishable from its preferred habitat on a range that includes the better part of the United States.

The walkingstick feeds on the leaves of its favored trees and many others and those of various shrubs and bushes. Only in one area does this feeding do enough damage to warrant control. The excepted area is Michigan where the name for the walkingstick in some parts of the state is "jack-pine horse." Under this pseudonym the insect becomes a pest every so often and in a way that is peculiarly its own as the people in parts of Crawford, Dickinson, and Ogemaw counties well know.

Every other year in even-numbered years the walkingstick becomes one of the delinquent members of its plant and animal community. In these years it damages enough trees to be considered a pest. An explanation for this tree injury in even-numbered alternate years in parts of Michigan and the general lack of damage elsewhere may be due to the egg-laying habits of the female. The prolonged period of incubation for the eggs is also a possible explanation for this cyclic damage.

The female lays about one hundred eggs. She is the only known insect that makes absolutely no provision for their protection. A female releases her eggs from wherever she happens to be, and they drop willy-nilly to the ground without so much as even "a glance in their direction" from her. Some eggs hatch the following spring, but for many others a full year may have to elapse from the time they were dropped until the embryo within develops sufficiently and has enough strength to break out of the shell.

Although spring arrives officially March 21, it is usually at a later date that the first young walkingsticks emerge. A recently hatched walkingstick is a springtime green—a color that is in keeping with the young foliage and one that protects the equally young insects from would-be predators. During the summer the insect undergoes five or six molts and by fall the green of spring and early summer has been replaced by the adult grayish brown. Now the walkingstick or jack-pine horse is such a good example of passive mimicry that it is almost impossible to locate. It is at the top of its mimetic form, designed that way by Nature to protect this member of the family *Phasmatidae*.

American Cockroach
Periplaneta americana

The cockroach family is the only living group of insects known to have existed in Carboniferous times—200 or more million years ago. Fossils of early American cockroaches have been found in coal beds in Pennsylvania, and in some areas such insect fossils are the only ones discovered. Except for the position of the wing veins there is little difference between ancient cockroaches and those of today.

This family is represented in North America by 55 species. Five of these are classified as pests by the Agricultural Research Division, United States Department of Agriculture. These five are the large Oriental, Australian, and American species, and two smaller ones, the brown-banded roach and the German cockroach. The last species is frequently called the Croton bug or the "water bug."

The American roach varies in color from reddish brown to dark brown. An adult measures one and one-half to two inches in length. It has a broad, flattened body, six long legs, and wings.

Each species has a preferred environment. The American cockroach develops in damp basements and in sewers. It forages for the most part on the first floors of buildings. And wherever there is dirt, these fetid-smelling insects thrive.

The eggs of a roach are contained in a pod. The American species carries her egg pod attached to the tip of the abdomen for a day or two before gluing it to an object in a protected spot.

The German cockroach carries her eggs around until they are

almost ready to hatch. She affixes the pods in a warm, dark place, and in only a day or two they hatch.

The eggs of the American cockroach hatch after an incubation period of two or three months. Though the young have no wings, they resemble adults in every other way except for size. One pod produces twelve young roaches; they take almost a year to become full grown, and during that year they go through a series of molts.

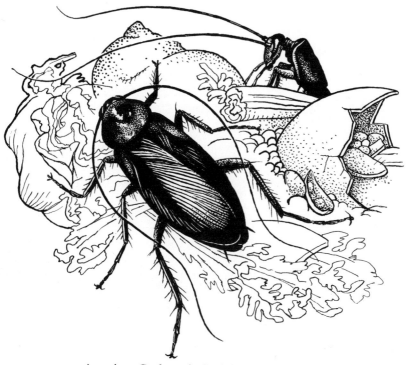

American Cockroach, *Periplaneta americana*

If conditions are ideal the roach is frequently found in all life stages: eggs, nymphs of varying sizes, and adults.

By day roaches secrete themselves in dark, sheltered places, but by night they come out to forage. And in their comings and goings, they carry filth on their legs and bodies; spread disease by polluting food; act as carriers for certain viruses which they transmit to animals; ruin food with their fetid odor; and damage fabrics and upholstery.

GRASSHOPPERS, CRICKETS, KATYDIDS, AND ALLIES 25

Roaches can be controlled by sprays and dusts. Most insecticides are recommended for general use, but some are restricted. As most are poisonous to man and other animals, they should be used as directed. Be sure to wash all exposed parts of the body after you apply any insecticide. And as the cockroach has survived from the Coal Age, keep in mind that you are dealing with an ancient enemy whose staying power is great.

2 TERMITES

Though the soft-bodied insects of this order are often called "white ants," this designation is not correct. These insects, wood-borers of proven ability, are not ants and not always white. Nor do they have the pinched-in waist between thorax and abdomen that distinguishes ants. The members of the order *Isoptera* are the termites—colony-living animals that inhabit multiple dwellings whose rooms are known as galleries. Termite colonies may be either in the ground or in wood—damp, rotten, or sound and dry.

Termites vary in size; some may measure one-third of an inch, while others may be as long as one inch. Frequently the large head has a hard outer layer known as chitin. The jaws are large and prominent and edged with teeth on the inner side. The four similar wings are long and narrow and are lost at maturity. The ankle, or tarsus, is usually four-jointed.

The metamorphosis which the termite undergoes is incomplete, and there is a wide variation in form that is known as polymorphism. Among termites this variation results in a caste system. A colony of termites designated as subterranean includes the winged reproductive adults, soldiers, mature workers, and nymphs. Termites classified as non-subterranean live in colonies composed of a king and queen (the reproductives), soldiers, and nymphs.

Throughout the world there are at least two thousand known

species of termites. Forty of these wood-destroying insects are native to North America. You can see all forty native species under glass at the United States National Museum in Washington, D. C.

On April 9, 1956, the Smithsonian Institution, of which the Museum is a part, received from the Department of Agriculture a collection of 230,000 specimen termites. The collection includes 1,286 of the known species. And it represents forty-six years of work on the part of Dr. Thomas E. Snyder—a retired entomologist formerly with the United States Department of Agriculture. When Dr. Snyder started collecting termites in 1915, there were only twelve identified species in the Smithsonian collection.

The subterranean species in North America are more numerous than the above-ground members of the order. Though the damage caused by the first species is greater in the South than in the North, localized termite infestations may occur in any state. Wood-dwelling termites are not so widespread as the other species, but there are enough in various areas to do considerable damage. These species destroy the wooden uprights and woodwork in buildings, the wooden frames of furniture, and other wooden products. All told, both kinds of termites are so destructive that in the United States the bill for damages chargeable to them amounts to $250,000 each day.

Most termites work under cover and a great many require contact with soil moisture. Some infest rotten wood; others prefer wood that is damp; still others like wood that is thoroughly dry. Probably the powder-post termite is the most common species living in dry wood, with its range a narrow coastal strip that starts in the neighborhood of Cape Henry, Virginia, extends south to the Florida Keys, west along the Gulf of Mexico, and all across southern Texas to the Pacific Coast. It then goes up the West Coast as far as northern California, where a break occurs until you come to an area in the vicinity of Tacoma, Washington.

Powder-post Termite
Cryptotermes brevis

The powder-post termite lives in wood that is dry and sound. It lives out its life span of two years and several form changes without ever having contact with the ground. Like all other termites, this species is social and lives in a colony. And each colony is highly regimented, for the members are divided into castes.

A colony of these insects includes the reproductives, or kings and queens, the soldiers, and nymphs. The reproductives may be differentiated from the good-sized wingless soldiers by their color. This may shade from light yellow to dark brown or it may be almost black. When it first becomes mature, a reproductive has branchlike appendages between the upper rim of the wing and the first long vein below. And when it is fully grown it measures about an inch in body length. The reproductives and their offspring are protected by the soldiers, who have powerful fighting jaws edged on the inner side with teeth.

When a powder-post termite of the reproductive caste first becomes an adult it has wings. It can fly only a short distance, however, unless it is carried along by the wind. As soon as reproductives find a place in which to start a new colony, they shed their wings. The males and the females pair, and immediately bore entrance holes in the dry, sound wood of their choice. In Arizona the reproductives frequently drill their entrance holes in dead cottonwood trees.

Once inside the site of their choice, the male and the female plug the entrance opening. The material for the paper-thin plug is composed of bits of excrement cemented together with a dark substance discharged from the mouth. Almost as soon as the termites have sealed themselves inside, the queen begins to lay her eggs. Usually one egg at a time is the procedure. The eggs quickly hatch into tiny white nymphs, and with their appearance a new colony is started.

The male remains with the female and continues to fertilize her, while the nymphs do the work of the colony. As the numbers in a colony increase, the size of the housing is enlarged until there are many new galleries. Nymphs keep these new rooms clean by removing all excreta and other dirt. Refuse is carried to unused galleries or pushed out through small openings in the wood. In addition to the disposal openings, the powder-post termite cuts other holes, including those to change humidity or temperature in the galleries and exit holes for colonizing flights—flights that take place either in the spring or in the fall.

Probably the powder-post termite can live its dry-wood existence because there are protozoa in the alimentary canal. Most authorities agree that the protozoa digest the cellulose in the wood and in this way the insect is nourished.

In addition to flights for colonizing, the powder-post termites spread in other ways. There is at least one instance in which they became established in a land that had never known a termite!

Pitcairn, remote South Pacific island, is far out of the usual sea lanes. Some 4,000 miles west of Valparaiso, Chile, the island was settled in 1790 by mutineers from H. M. S. *Bounty*. About a century and a half later, descendants of the mutineers ordered a church organ to be shipped in from New Zealand. The shipment carried a complement of termites. And according to a December 1955 report, the insects were eating the Pitcairners out of house and home.

"Nothing," the report commented in conclusion, "can be done now to stop their ravages."

Among subterranean termites one of the more common is the eastern subterranean termite (*Reticulitermes flavipes*). There are four castes in a colony of these insects: the reproductives and the winged ones; the pearly-white blind workers; the large-headed soldiers with strong biting jaws; and the nymphs.

One way to detect the presence of subterranean termites is by their earthen tunnels or runways on foundation surfaces. The insects build runways to get to the wooden parts of a building, and when this has been accomplished the workers in a colony start their endless boring. They chew out galleries that go with the grain of the wood, and, as the insects work, they do not stop to push outside the sawdust. They eat it.

Termite, *Reticulitermes flavipes*. Upper panel: soldier above worker. Lower group: left, winged adult; top center, nymph; bottom center, king; right, queen

A second way that you can be sure termites are in the neighborhood is by the swarming of certain winged adults—sexually mature males and females. Late in the spring or during early summer these termites acquire four silvery wings, all of which are of equal length and usually measuring twice the length of the body, to which they are loosely attached. These winged members of the colony are known as the "first reproductives." They differ from other members of their colony in that the outer body wall, the "cuticula," is the color of a chestnut or else ebon black.

During the swarming season the winged adults leave the old colony as if by a prearranged signal. An area may be clouded with them as they fly off in search of a suitable spot in which to establish a new colony. A swarming flight may be either short or long, but no matter the distance the insects always alight on the ground. Now they are ready to shed their wings, and this is made easier by means of the humeral suture. Curved and transverse, this suture is at the front of each loosely attached wing. Sometimes you can find quantities of shed wings on the ground in the vicinity of a recently established termite colony.

The length of a termite wing is a feature by which you can mark the difference between this insect and the ant. The ant's wing is only about as long as the body. Another way of knowing one insect from the other is by the differences in the bodies. The termite does not have the pinched-in-waist effect of the ant (another pest insect of another order, the *Hymenoptera*).

To control termites, destroy any connection, earthen tunnel or runway, between a colony and the wooden parts of buildings. A connection can be blocked so that the insects cannot reach the building; or the soil may be poisoned.

But to check the inroads of the ground-dwelling termite or the related wood-dwelling species, it is wise to consult an expert—either a private company specializing in the extermination of these pests or the Division of Insects Affecting Men and Animals, U. S. Department of Agriculture. The specialist will go into immediate action on your behalf while the Division will advise you on a course of action to take against termites, of which the Smithsonian Institution has 250,000 under glass—the best place to have them.

3 CICADAS, LEAFHOPPERS, APHIDS, and ALLIES

I n this order, the *Homoptera*, the insects vary so greatly in size and appearance that it is difficult to believe all of them have enough characteristics in common to make them so closely related. Some look like miniature pears or peaches, while others resemble minute oysters with the shells closed. In size some are no larger than a pin point; others have the proportions of a dime; and then there are those with a wingspread of 4 inches and a lengthwise measure of 3 to 4 inches.

There are nearly twenty families in this order, whose name is derived from *homo*, the same, and *pteron*, a wing. Not all of these insects have wings. But most winged members among the *Homoptera* have two pairs. The front pair is clear or leathery, and usually longer and narrower than the hind pair. When one of these insects rests, the wings are folded rooflike over the back. The mouth parts are designed so that the animal can pierce and suck.

The young, better known as nymphs, resemble the adults in every way but size. Maturity for insects of this order is achieved by a metamorphosis that is incomplete, for no radical change occurs in form as the nymphs pass through successive molts. The intervals between each molt are known as instars, and each one of these sees the insect somewhat larger than it was before. The increase in size is gradual; a change in color often takes place; and the acquisition of wings is typical of certain adult forms.

The *Homoptera* and the insects known as the True Bugs (*Hemiptera*) number some 55,000 for the entire world. In America north of the Mexican border, there are more than 8,700 species for both orders.

Periodical Cicada
Magicicada septendecim

The only place in the world in which you will find the periodical cicada is the eastern half of the United States. Here the insect makes its startling spring appearance after a years-long interval underground. In the South the interval is usually thirteen years, whereas in the North it is apt to be seventeen years.

In days gone by, the superstitious thought the periodical cicada was a harbinger of war. The reason for the belief is the distinctive marking near the outer ends of the front wings. This mark, a characteristic of the species, has the appearance of a heavily inked W, and comes from a darkening of the veins at these spots.

The periodical cicada, mistakenly called the "seventeen-year locust," is further distinguished by a predominantly black body; reddish legs; nearly transparent wings patterned with orange veins; and red eyes. And when it is fully grown, this large relative of such other sucking insects as aphids, scales, and leafhoppers, is nearly one and five-eighths inches in length.

In the spring a brood of these insects emerges from underground tunnels in which it has passed the greater part of its life. A single brood sometimes numbers as many as 40,000. The surface of the soil under a tree is punctured by an equal number of holes; they are often so close together that there are 84 to one square foot of soil surface. The brood comes out of the ground all at once, as if by a predetermined signal. The emergence takes place at night and during April or May.

The periodical cicada is still a nymph when it comes out of the ground. Once clear of its underground environment, the nymph heads for an upright object. A tree seems to be the preferred goal, but if a nymph cannot reach a tree, it goes to a branch or shoot of a bush, a weed stalk, or even a blade of grass. And when hard

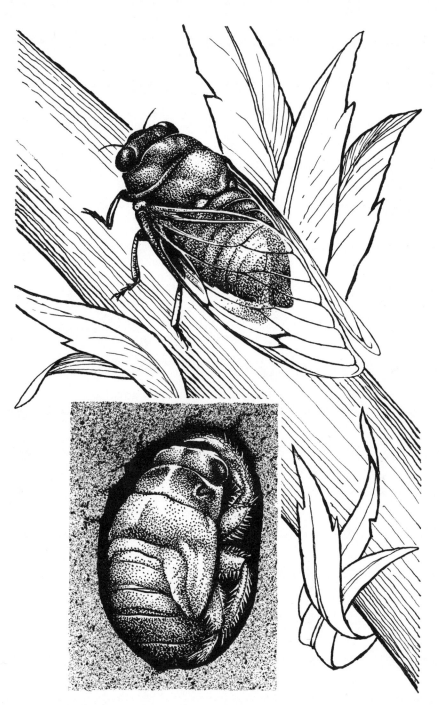

Periodical Cicada, *Magicicada septendecim;* adult above,
larva in burrow

pressed for an upright to cling to, the creature uses a fence post or a telegraph pole while undergoing the final metamorphosis.

Once it secures a firm hold on its resting place, the nymph is ready to shed its enveloping sheath. This skin splits down the middle of the back, and by a dint of hard work the nymph struggles free. The process may take less than an hour, but sixty minutes is the usual time. Now the cicada is free and an adult. But it is still soft and white, and another few hours must elapse before the outer covering hardens and becomes dark. After these transformations take place, the insect is mature and ready for its adult life of five or six weeks.

Of course in any given brood there are casualties. Often a great many eggs do not hatch; some nymphs die underground; and still more die in the process of shedding the last skin.

One week after it becomes an adult, the periodical cicada mates, and a few days later the female starts to lay her eggs, which may number 400 to 600 in all. To make a "nest" for her eggs the female manipulates an organ on the end of the abdomen; this is a sawlike device with curved blades.

In a hind-side-to position the female punctures the bark of a twig with her "bit," then bores a little pocket. This is a repository for 24 to 28 eggs. They are placed in two rows. There may be 5 to 20 pockets in a single twig, and as the pockets are aligned, they occasionally form a slit that measures 2 or 3 inches in length.

Though the female seems to prefer the twigs of such trees as the oak, the hickory, the apple, the peach, and the pear, or the stems of grapevines, egg slits have been discovered in seventy-odd species of trees, shrubs, and soft-stemmed plants. Slits or punctures damage or destroy nursery stock and orchard trees—particularly the young, recently transplanted trees. Sometimes even older trees are harmed.

Eggs hatch within six or seven weeks. The tiny nymphs fall to the ground, into which they immediately burrow. As soon as they are 18 to 24 inches below the surface, the nymphs attach themselves to tree roots. They live on juices sucked from the roots. Here they stay for thirteen or seventeen years, and at the end of either period they are fully grown. A few weeks before they are to come out of the ground, nymphs starts to burrow upward. Burrowing ceases about one inch below the surface, and here they wait—like so many actors for the cue to bring them onstage.

The date of emergence is influenced by latitude and elevation. On the southern parts of the range, the periodical cicada often starts out of the ground during the last week in April; in some northern areas the insect does not appear until the last week in May. And in almost any year broods emerge somewhere on the range, to undergo the final skin shedding, to mate, lay eggs, and sing their "swan song."

The song of the cicada, produced only by the male, is an almost incessant racket that starts a few days after the insect comes out of the ground. It is made with inflated drumlike organs on the sides of the abdomen, and there are two strong muscles to activate the drums.

The cicada drums from dawn to dusk, and as the temperature rises, so does the volume of sound. Usually all that you hear is a sustained burring, the basic note, but if you listen carefully, you will be able to distinguish a variation in cicada sounds. The basic notes, often sustained for 15 or 20 seconds, are similar to *tsh-ee-EEE-e-ou*. The middle, capitalized portion is a loud, shrill sound. The cicada also drums out a mournful bar of music that ends on a low pitch. Repeated at intervals of 3 to 5 seconds, this tattoo lasts about 3 seconds. Another sound may be classified as a soft, short purr.

A cicada sings its song first by raising the abdomen to a rigid, horizontal position. It holds itself in this manner until a note ends. Then the body drops back in place to assume its usual somewhat drooping position.

The periodical cicada is kept in check to some degree by various birds—particularly those birds that live in areas where trees are in small, open groves or in the neighborhood of houses. Other insects and mites feed on the eggs, and a fungus disease kills some adults.

Though this insect does not apparently do any feeding damage to plants and trees, the egg-laying procedure does. And when broods are unusually large, 40,000 for instance, control measures are necessary. But for the homeowner it is easier to wait for these insects to disappear than to try to combat them, according to Alfred W. Mitlehner, Suffolk County Extension Service representative in New York. He offered this advice in 1957 when the eastern half of Long Island swarmed with the periodical cicada—a unique North American insect.

LEAFHOPPERS
Family *Cicadellidae*

According to the *Columbia Encyclopedia* the leafhopper is "any of numerous species of small leaping insects." The book goes on to say that this long, narrow insect with four wings is found throughout the world, and that almost all cultivated and wild plants are damaged by some of the 2,000 or so known species in a family known scientifically as the *Cicadellidae*.

Of the world's known species there are about 700 in the United States, parts of Canada, and northern Mexico. These come in a great variety of sizes and colors. Most are yellow, yellow-green, or green, and measure ⅛ to ¼ of an inch in length. But some of the Pacific coast region—near Hollywood, no doubt—are brightly colored and gaily striped. A few of these western species measure as much as ½ inch in length.

The leafhopper is a restive creature and, considering its size, covers in one hop distances of no mean length. This hopping is the reason the insect is occasionally called the "dodger." When it rests, the leafhopper folds the paired long narrow wings over its tapering back.

A sucking insect, the leafhopper damages plants by feeding on sap. As it feeds the insect exudes leftover sap that is known as "honeydew," a rather sweet-tasting substance on which ants and bees feed.

Three representative members of the family are: the rose leafhopper, a pale-green insect that causes leaves to whiten and curl and the tender tips to die; the potato leafhopper, an insect whose head is mottled with white and one that causes the edges of dahlia leaves and those of other plants to die (this damage is called hopper-burn); and the aster leafhopper, one of several species that transmit plant diseases.

Among all the leafhoppers in this hemisphere, the potato leaf-hopper (*Empoasca fabae*) of the eastern half of the United States and as far west as Kansas, and the related western potato leafhopper, of parts of the Southwest, are two of the most destructive. Both species attack potatoes and cause hopperburn. The tips of the potato-plant leaves as well as the sides curl upward, turn yellow, then brown, and finally become brittle. The insects also damage a number of garden flowers including African marigolds, dahlias, hollyhocks, roses, and zinnias.

The adult eastern leafhopper is wedge-shaped, pale yellowish green, and about one-eighth of an inch in length. Soon after reach-ing maturity, the female lays her eggs by means of a tiny ovipositor. She pierces the stems of plant stalks that support the leaves or punc-tures the larger veins of the leaves themselves. The minute punc-tures are the "incubators" in which the equally small eggs are hatched.

The eggs hatch in about one week. In its nymph stage, the insect is wingless. But after passing through an incomplete metamorphosis, of which there are five stages, it becomes a winged adult in eight to fourteen days. Eggs that are laid late in the season hatch the following spring, and nymphs that become mature late in the season overwinter as adults and appear in the spring, also.

On any area of its range there are usually two or more genera-tions of leafhoppers during each year. In the South these lively little insects are busy at their destruction all year round. In the vicinity of Washington, D. C., the insect becomes abundant in July, August, and September. During these months, it damages two crops of alfalfa—the second and the third. The leafhopper causes the alfalfa to yellow and to grow less high than it should. Sometimes young stands are so weakened by leafhopper depredations that the weeds and grasses take over the fields, and the crops are crowded out.

The time may come when the beet leafhopper (*Circulifer tenel-lus*), an introduced species, will be controlled to some degree by natural enemies. The beet leafhopper, called the "whitefly" in the

West, is the only known carrier of curly top—a destructive virus disease which affects sugar beets, table crops, various flowering ornamentals, as well as many other forms of vegetation.

The curly-top carrier is an insect of the arid and semiarid regions of the western United States, southwestern Canada, and northern Mexico. In such areas this ⅛-inch insect jeopardizes the beet crop every year. In 1924 the growers of sugar beets in southern Idaho planted 22,418 acres, but had to abandon 11,442 acres because the beet leafhopper did so much damage. Of the 21,389 acres planted to this crop in 1934, more than 18,630 had to be given up because of the inroads made by the insect. The harvest in those two years was 5.51 tons an acre for 1924 and 4.88 tons for 1934. In the years when the beet leafhoppers are few or wanting, the yield for an acre in this area is usually 16 tons.

The insect that annually threatens the beet-sugar crop in Idaho and elsewhere overwinters as an adult. Whenever there is a warm spell it becomes active and feeds by inserting its tiny beak into plant tissues to suck the juices. Late in the winter the female develops eggs so that she is ready to lay them by the time the various host plants have started spring growth. Though a female usually lays 300 to 400 eggs, it is a matter of record that the number deposited inside the tissues of leaves and stems may be as many as 675.

No matter how many or how few eggs a female lays, some never hatch because two egg parasites act as controls. These parasites have no common name, but their scientific family name is much longer than either of them. The name is *Trichogrammatidae*, and the family is defined as "consisting of minute insects that kill by infesting a host."

Since 1950, entomologists have resumed studies of these parasites and their effect on the beet leafhopper, basing their work on some that was conducted during the 1930's. The two most promising members of the family as controls of the beet leafhopper are *Aphelinoidea plutella* and *Abella subflava*. As the two have no common names, those working on an experimental control project refer to them as "Plutella" and "Subflava." The current study seeks to determine whether the spring emergence of the two parasites synchronizes with the egg-laying period of the beet leafhopper.

In the Berger–Twin Falls area of southern Idaho the parasites' spring emergence and the egg-laying period of the beet leafhopper are fairly well synchronized. But elsewhere this has not been so, for there occurs what entomologists call "poor space-synchronization of parasite and host in the spring." If this differential in time can be overcome, there will be greater control by the two parasites of the beet leafhopper—a pest of peewee proportions that damages most wild and cultivated plants.

Pea Aphid
Macrosiphum pisi

Among all the aphids that burden the earth, some appear more artful than others. One of these soft-bodied sucking insects, the pea aphid, is amazingly self-reliant. Less than a ¼ inch long, this light-green aphid has a form of reproduction that is known as parthenogenesis.

In layman's language this means that the female can produce young without benefit of fertilization, and does so with the greatest of ease. A female pea aphid is so adept at this sort of reproduction that at the end of a summer there may be thirteen or fourteen generations of these insects—distinguished by three pairs of legs and a body shaped like either a peach or a pear.

During spring and summer all pea aphids are females. They are born alive by a female that is known as the stem mother—a progenitor that was hatched from an egg. When the offspring of the stem mother are ready to reproduce, they bring forth wingless females like themselves. Later-in-the-season descendants have broods that are both winged and wingless. Eventually some of the winged ones leave the host plant on which they were born and from which they received nourishment. They fly to a new host, and in so doing they may move from Russian-thistle, the original host, to alfalfa, clover, or possibly vetch. This insect is not much of a flyer, but frequently the wind helps it to travel as far as fifty miles.

At the new plant more winged and wingless young are born. Toward fall the broods contain males and egg-producing females.

As soon as these end-of-season aphids mature, they mate, and from these matings come fertile eggs that hatch the following spring.

Tiny and black, the eggs are laid on the stems of alfalfa or on leaves that have fallen to the ground. They are held in place by a bluelike substance, and on the northern parts of the range any snowfalls helps to protect them. Thus in the North the pea aphid overwinters in the egg stage. Sometimes this insect overwinters in an active stage, as in the case of aphids in the Pacific Northwest.

Pea Aphid, *Macrosiphum pisi;* wingless adults, winged adult, and nymphs

But in the South it is usually out and about during most of the winter.

At the time of its hatching in April or May the pea aphid is in the nymph stage. At first it is a small-scale reproduction of an adult. This lack of size is quickly overcome by four molts in rapid succession that bring the insect to its adult form.

In 1879 the pea aphid was first discovered on some pea plants under cultivation in Illinois. By 1959, eighty years later, the insect has spread to every state and a number of Canadian provinces. Each year it usually reaches pest proportions in at least a dozen states. It damages all kinds of peas, including those grown for their flowers; alfalfa and clover; and vetch, a climbing herb with pink or purple blossoms, grown for green fodder and hay and as cover and a green-manure crop.

The pea and other aphid species, also known as plant lice, injure plants by sucking the sap from leaves, stems, blossoms, and pods. Some of these colony-living creatures attack the roots of asters or other plants, while a number ruin such flowering bulbs as those of the iris, crocus, and tulip. The damage is curled and stunted leaves, stunted plants, and shrunken partly filled pods of peas.

The pea aphid is also a vector—a carrier, that is—of several virus diseases of peas. One is the yellow bean mosaic and another is the enation mosaic. The second is particularly damaging to crops of peas planted late in the season. The pods become so roughtened and toughened that the viner cannot shell them, and as a result frequently as much as half the crop may be lost.

Some seventy parasitic and predatory insects help to keep the pea aphid in check. In warm, humid climates they are killed in great numbers by a fungus disease. And since 1900 the U. S. Department of Agriculture has been working on the commercial control of the insect. To date only three or four insecticides have been developed that check the inroads of the pea and other aphids on crops. Like all other insects the pea aphid and its kind will probably be with us until the end of time. And for ants, bees, and wasps, this is a good thing.

The sweet sticky "honeydew" exuded by the pea aphid often coats the leaves below a colony with a sheen that makes them look as if they had been varnished. Bees and wasps eat the honeydew on the spot, but ants tend the aphids caring for them like so many herders looking after cows. Honeydew is a fine auxiliary food for the ants, and apparently the ants know a good thing when they have it.

Citrus Mealybug
Pseudococcus citri

Each year more than fifteen million gallons of oil are used in the United States to compound horticultural sprays. One insect that is controlled by an oil spray is the mealybug. Of all these minuscule creatures in North America, perhaps the best known to indoor and

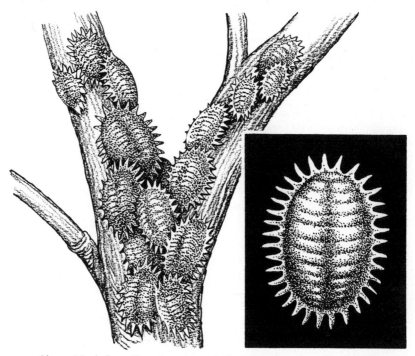

Citrus Mealybug, *Pseudococcus citri;* cluster on plant stem, adult
in inset, much enlarged

outdoor gardeners is the citrus mealybug. This pest measures no more than 3/16 inch at its longest. As a host it favors such potted plants as coleus, fuchsia, or begonia, to name but three of a long list.

All stages of the citrus mealybug may be present on a plant at the same time. The female, distinguished by an amber-colored body, lays her eggs in what appears to be a fluff of cotton. In a mass the eggs often number more than 300; they take ten to twenty days to hatch. The nymphs crawl away from the crevices of the basal parts of the leaf stems or from spots on the underside veins of the leaves. Somewhere along the main stem they settle down. Here they manufacture a covering that is waxlike in texture and white in color. Six weeks or perhaps even two months later the females in the group mature.

Two or three weeks after they hatch, the seldom seen, nonfeeding males of a brood make cocoons that have the appearance of tiny cotton snowballs. Then within a cocoon the male transforms into a winged adult that is no larger than a midge—an insect so small that it is often called a "no-see-um."

The mealybug inserts its tiny sucking beak into the tender parts of stems and leaves. This causes the part of the plant on which the insect feeds to lose color or to wilt. Eventually the pest-affected part dies.

The mealybug also coats the leaves of the host plant with a sticky substance known as "honeydew". A black mold thrives on the honeydew—also the natural food for some species of ants. Apparently the food is so well liked by the ants that these insects care for the mealybug. And sometimes the ants actually spread the pest to other plants, where it can make more honeydew.

In addition to oil sprays for large-scale control of the mealybug, other methods are used to keep it in check. To rid a house plant of the insect, wash the host with water, using as much pressure as the plant can stand. If there is no response to this treatment on either indoor or outdoor plants, a contact spray or fumigation may be the answer—but only after you have determined that the plant or plants in question can stand this type of control.

In agricultural areas the citrus mealybug and a closely related species, the citrophilus mealybug (*Pseudococcus gahani*, first discovered in 1931 in southern California), were major pests in certain areas. Now these two species have been brought under control. Both have been held in check by the Australian lady beetle—introduced in 1891 and known to many of us as the "ladybug" or the "ladybird beetle."

A new control for the citrus mealybug was introduced in 1951. It came from Sicily, and is an internal parasite with the scientific name *Leptomastides abnormis*. Though it has controlled the citrus mealybug in most regions, there are still some orchard areas in which the Australian lady beetle is released each year. At one time hundreds of millions of these beetles were reared and released to fight the citrus mealybug. The cost of producing the tiny controls was about $2.50 for each thousand.

Australia has supplied two other controls for the citrophilus mealybug. In 1928 two parasites were imported, and they were so effective that this mealybug was no longer the menace it used to be.

In this country and such others as Canada, Australia, New Zealand, and Fiji, the biological control of past insects is a continuing program. Some of the most harmful insects, in all about thirty, have been controlled in one or more countries by parasites or predators. And perhaps these are the best controls of all. For they were provided by nature for each plant and animal community of which man, though he is inclined to forget it, is an integral part.

San José Scale
Aspidiotus perniciosus

Before the slightest sign of green shows on the buds of the apple, the peach, or the pear, and other deciduous fruit trees in the Pacific Northwest, orchardists spray them with an oily pesticide. In the Northeast, however, most fruit growers do *not* spray while tree buds are still dormant, but wait until some new growth appears. But whatever the time of year or wherever the locale, the spraying is to eradicate a tiny bark louse that has been named the San José scale, belonging to one of several scale families known as the *Diaspididae*.

This scale is a member of a numerous family of sap-sucking insects with a world-wide distribution. It was accidentally introduced into California when a shipment of plants from China was delivered in San José. And today the colony-living insects named for this city are in practically all fruit-growing regions of North America.

The wind, the birds, and other larger insects are responsible for transporting this exotic—one that not only ruins fruit trees but also damages rose, lilac, and honeysuckle bushes, and such trees as dogwood, hawthorn, and mountain-ash. The fruits of these ornamental trees are fall and winter foods for some upland game birds; many songbirds; and one duck, the gaily colored wood duck. In addition fur, game, and other small mammals and some hoofed browsing mammals eat the seeds, fruits, twigs, and foliage of such trees. So the San José scale can have a profound effect upon the welfare of the plant and animal community in which it becomes established.

In northern fruit-growing areas, there are usually two generations of the San José scale in a season, whereas in the South there are apt to be at least three generations, perhaps four, or even more. The insect spends the winter on the host plant where it attempts to survive in all stages: egg, the newly emerged young—also known as crawlers, second-stage nymphs, and adults. As a rule only the second-stage nymph survives.

The San José scale hatches from an egg that the female deposits under her shell before she dies. A mature female is yellow and no larger than a head of a pin. Newly emerged young, the crawlers, are even smaller. As soon as one is free of the egg, it crawls to another spot on its host. If it is a female this spot is for a life-long stay. Almost at once it secretes a waxy substance for a protective covering. This is circular, about one-sixteenth of an inch in diameter, and is colored gray. Near the center is a slightly raised dot that is called the nipple. The male, smaller and somewhat oval in shape, has wings. At certain times of the year the male comes out from under its covering for short intervals. Perhaps these emergences are to ensure future generations, for the male does not feed during an adult life that is much shorter than that of the female.

There are some scale species in which several generations of females occur before the more usual reproduction takes place. A well-known entomologist was once queried about the way in which scale insects reproduce. He was more than momentarily silent before he said, "It's complicated. Let's let it go at that."

Though there seems little to be said in favor of scale insects, they have been and still are used to some extent commercially. In Central and South American various cacti are host plants for a scale insect (*Coccus cacti*) from which the natural dye, cochineal, is made. The dye comes from an extract of the bodies of the females only, and is contained in a pigment known as carminic acid. Today synthetic dyes color our silks and wools the scarlet reds that used to come from cochineal.

India, the chief source of shellac, has a scale insect that furnishes a natural product called stick-lac. It is caused by the feeding of a female scale. After sucking the juices of various trees, the females exude a resinous substance. Upon contact with the air, this hardens to form a protective covering for the female and her young. The twigs are scraped to harvest the scale "shells," and are then dissolved to remove the insects, twigs, and other foreign matter.

The residue, or seed-lac as it is called, is finally processed to make shellac. The shellac-producing scale also yields a red pigment similar to that of cochineal, and sometimes this too is used as a dye. But again, as in the case of cochineal, it has been widely replaced by dyes that are synthetic—a characteristic of the 1960's when the artificial has all too frequently replaced the natural and many people have forgotten that the origin of everything we have, or are, derives from the resources provided by Nature.

4 TRUE BUGS

If anything were to exterminate the enemies of the Hemiptera *we ourselves should probably be starved in the course of a few months.*

DALLAS LORE SHARP

Among entomologists the term "bug" designates only those insects in the order *Hemiptera*. This is one of the original Linnaean orders, and a large one in which the insects vary greatly in appearance. Though varied in size, color, and other physical characteristics, they all have one feature in common—mouth parts that are equipped for piercing, then sucking.

The piercing mouth part is a jointed organ that looks much like the beak of a bird. Called by scientists the labium, or rostrum, it contains the mandibles. These bristle-like jaws are in the front of the maxillae—paired styles of needle-like proportions that enable these insects to penetrate the tissues of plants or animals. An inner pair of styles, smaller than those on the outside, are the sucking mouth parts. These are grooved and so designed that fluids can be sucked through them. The inner styles also serve another purpose, for they let a bug inject saliva into the plant or animal on which it is feeding. This makes feeding easier.

Insects of this order date from the Lower Permian Age, approximately 215 million years ago. Maturity comes through a series of molts, and most adults have two pairs of wings. The composition of the pair to the front is a distinguishing characteristic of the order. Near the body they are somewhat leathery and thickened at the base; but the outer halves are thin, soft, and pliable. The formation of the front wings is the reason for the name *Hemiptera,* meaning half-winged. The wings to the rear are thin, soft, and pliable all over, membranous in other words, and are folded beneath the front wings. The wings of bugs overlap on the abdomen and distinguish them from such other insects as aphids, scales, and leafhoppers, whose wings are usually of a similar consistency throughout.

Though most of these bugs are plant feeders, their habits, ways of life, and environments are vastly different. Some few, including the water strider, are aquatic or semiaquatic. Others, such as the chinch and harlequin bugs, are land-living. One of the best known and least liked, the blood-sucking bedbug, is a house-dweller. A number of true bugs feed upon others of their kind. And as with any animal group, the insects of this order fall into the categories of good, bad, or indifferent.

Those that can be classed as indifferent are ones that have little effect on their particular plant and animal communities. An example is the spittlebug of eastern North America. Known, too, as the froghopper, this insect (*Aphrophora quadrinoata*) lives on various grasses and low-growing plants. If you see a froth on the stems of plants and the blades of grasses, you can be reasonably sure that it is made by the spittlebug to cover its eggs. Not all of these insects play a passive role in the plant and animal community. Such species as the pine, the Saratoga, and the meadow spittlebugs are pests—another division in the vast insect army against which we wage a constant war but one which we do not wage alone. For we have many insect allies, some of them in this very order. One is the masked hunter (*Reduvius personatus*). This flying insect, one-half to three-fourths of an inch in length, preys on several species of household and cereal pests.

Bed Bug
Cimex lectularius

Lodgings,—free from bugs and fleas, if possible,
If you know any such.
ARISTOPHANES, *The Frogs*

Aristophanes knew what he was talking about when he wrote lines on the difficulty of getting lodgings "free from bugs." Managers of hotels, motels, and other establishments that house transients are ever on the alert to check infestations of any bug. They are particularly on the alert, however, to check those of bed bugs, for this insect is one that gets from place to place by "hitching a ride."

Hitchhiking is necessary, for in its adult form a mature bed bug is wingless. Though it can and does crawl, the insect usually gets from place to place on the baggage and clothing of travelers; in shipments of household effects; in furniture, beds, and bedding handled by dealers in secondhand goods; and in deliveries of laundry and supplies of all kinds. All too frequently it is carried into various places open to the public by the actual guests and patrons.

The most common bed bug in the United States and the one with the widest distribution is the species whose scientific name is *Cimex lectularius*. Freely translated this Latin name means "a bug in a bed." A less widespread species, *C. hemipterus*, beds down in Florida and perhaps in a few neighboring states. In the South both species feed all twelve months of the year. In the North the more common bed bug feeds all year, too—provided the home of its host is well-heated.

Usually the food of this insect is the blood of a human host. Sometimes the reddish-brown bed bug feeds on the blood of other mammals or poultry. To feed it pierces the skin of the host with an elongated beak. As a rule most feeding is at night and as a rule most bites are painless to the sleeping victim. When it bites, the bed bug injects a fluid which aids the insect in obtaining blood, but also has properties that irritate the skin, cause it to become inflamed, or in some instances raise welts.

The size of a mature bed bug depends upon the amount of blood in its body. An unfed insect may measure ¼ to ⅜ of an inch in length, and the upper surface of the body has a crinkled appearance like that of crepe paper. After it has fed, however, the body is often so swollen and elongated that the insect looks like another creature. And instead of brown, the color when it is unfed, the insect is now a dull red. This transformation also adds to the illusion that you are looking at a different insect.

To fully satisfy its appetite, the bed bug needs three to five minutes of uninterrupted feeding. Then it leaves the host to crawl away to a hiding place—crack, crevice, underside of a mattress tuft or welt, or any other dark retreat that affords security. In such spots it digests a meal—a process that takes several days. If the insect is forced to go without food, it can survive at least four months and sometimes for as long as twelve months.

A bed bug hatched during warm weather can live for several weeks without feeding, and if it hatches during cool or cold weather, it can survive for several months with no food intake.

The egg from which the hardy bed bug hatches is white and about 1/32 of an inch in length. It may be one of 200 eggs that the mature female lays at the rate of three or four a day. This rate is maintained only when feeding conditions and temperatures are most favorable. The feeding must be regular and the temperature has to be more than 70° F. If the temperature is 60° to 70° F., the female lays only a few eggs; and at less than 50° F., no eggs at all are laid.

Temperature also governs the time required for an egg to hatch and the insect to mature. The time lapse between the laying of an egg and its hatching may be as short as six days or as long as twenty-eight. A newly hatched bed bug is translucent, nearly colorless, and about 1/32 of an inch in length. It has the same flattened shape as the parents, but has to undergo five molts before it reaches adult size. Warm weather or a well-heated house brings about maturity in four to six weeks.

There are often three or four generations of these insects in a single year. In homes or hotels that are overheated during winter, there may be even more. And with but one exception there are usually bed bugs in all stages of development at all seasons. The exception to this general rule is an unheated room in winter. Here only adults may be present.

If you do not see bed bugs or have not suffered their bites, you usually know when you "have them" because the insects secrete a fluid that has a musty odor. Though this is unpleasant, it cannot harm you unless you are violently allergic to it.

There are two ways to eliminate the bed bug: you can do it yourself by using a DDT compound or you can call in a professional exterminator. Today extermination of the insects that plague us is big business, particularly in large cities—happy hunting grounds for bed bugs and cockroaches.

Chinch Bug
Blissus leucopterus

Among Spanish-speaking peoples the expression *Tener sangre chinche* is used when speaking of anyone whose position can be described as "excessively unfortunate." And any grower of plants of the grass family who is plagued by the chinch bug is indeed unfortunate. For this minute insect, an outdoor relative of the indoor bed bug, damages so much corn each year that the financial loss in this country is estimated at $27,500,000. The yearly damage to wheat, rye, oats, and barley caused by this same little white-winged creature is estimated at $28,000,000.

Throughout the United States there are at least 175 species of chinch bug. Probably the most destructive is the one known scientifically as *Blissus leucopterus* which harasses agriculturists in eight key states.* And in the Northeast the hairy chinch bug (*B. l. hirtus*) can be the despair of the homeowner who takes pride in his lawn.

B. leucopterus is one insect that hibernates as an adult. In this form the creature has four white wings attached to a black body whose hairy covering is a silver-gray. The over-all body length is no greater than 3/16 of an inch. The preferred wintering spot of an adult is any native prairie grass that grows in a clumplike form. If such hideaways are not available, the insect winters in the bushes and grasses along fence rows, hedgerows, or the south and west edges of wooded lands.

The chinch bug does not leave its overwintering site until the days are sunny and there has been a constant temperature of 70° F. or higher for several hours. Usually the insect flies to any field in which small grain is growin, but there are years in which the spring flight has been directly to early plantings of corn or various sorghums.

* Illinois, Indiana, Iowa, Kansas, Missouri, Nebraska, Oklahoma, and Texas.

Soon after the males and the females arrive in a cultivated field, they mate. The average number of eggs laid by the female during the next three or four weeks is 200. She deposits each amber-colored egg behind a leaf sheath, on a root, or in the ground. In one or two weeks the first generation of the season hatches. There are two generations each year, but there may be more—provided weather conditions are favorable and the growing season is prolonged.

The nymph of the chinch bug is a minute, reddish-brown dot. It starts feeding at once by sucking the juices of the plant on which it hatched. As soon as the first host plant loses its succulence or starts to ripen, the nymph crawls to the nearest planting of corn or sorghum. The insects that move to a cornfield feed first on the outer rows, then as these rows wilt and die they crawl to the next, and continue this inward feeding movement until the entire field may be infested and completely ruined.

Crop rotation, early planting, and the use of hybrid corns and sorghums help to check chinch-bug infestations. But until the day comes when there are chinch-bug-resistant plants, effective biological controls, or successful man-made checks, the agriculturist may have to resign himself to a future in which he will be *tener sangre chinche* in some years.

STINK BUGS
Family *Pentatomidae*

Of the world's 4,000 or so stink bugs, some 300 occur in the United States. Most species are not strikingly colored but one exception to this more or less general rule is the harlequin bug (*Murgantia histrionica*). The basic black of this insect is splotched with orange, red, and yellow—the reason it was named for Harlequin, a gaily costumed character associated with *commedia dell'arte*, the pantomime so popular in Italy during the sixteenth century.

The harlequin bug was first discovered in Texas in 1864, but is now common throughout the South, and has extended its range well up into the Middle Atlantic states in the East and up the Pacific Coast as far as northern California.

Also known as the fire bug, the calico back or calico bug, and the collard bug, the insect is usually a year-round pest in the South. Here it feeds on various cole crops including kale, cabbage, and broccoli. Farther north the insect is active during winter, but only when the days are reasonably warm. Then full-grown nymphs and adults come out from under garden debris or from inside old cabbage plants to feed. Those on the most northerly parts of the range remain in chosen hideways during winter's most severe weather.

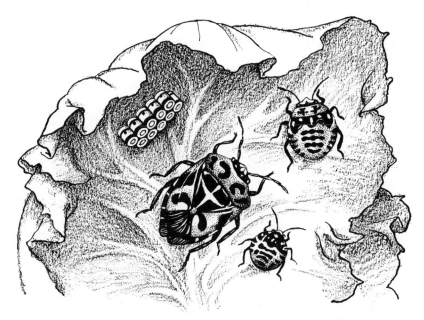

Harlequin Bug, *Murgantia histrionica*, on cabbage leaf; eggs at left, nymphs at right in various stages of growth

Early in the spring the harlequin bug comes out of its over-wintering spot to invade a field. After mating the female lays a double row of eggs on the undersides of leaves. Four to fifteen days later fertile eggs hatch, and six to eight weeks after that the insect is fully grown. During its nymphal stage, when it resembles the parents except for size, the insect feeds by sucking plant sap. Two or three weeks after the first brood of harlequin bugs becomes winged adults, a second brood is usually on the way. The feeding of both nymphs and adults causes the leaves of the host plant to turn brown. Eventually the plant itself wilts.

Other than dusting or spraying early in the season, the best way to control these bugs is to pick them by hand and drop them into a container of soapy water. You can also crush the double rows of eggs on the undersides of young leaves. This type of control must be done regularly if you want top-grade mustard or turnip greens, the turnips themselves, or unspoiled heads of cabbage.

Southern Green Stink Bug, *Nezara viridula*, on cotton boll; from left: nymph at fourth stage, adult, nymph at third stage

Five relatives of the harlequin bug are a definite threat to the cotton crop each year. Each of these pests is a stink bug and each has a range that varies from regional to all the cotton-growing states. The most brightly colored of the lot is the southern green stink bug (*Nezara viridula*). It is usually resident in the most southerly parts of the United States, but from time to time puts in an appearance north of its usual limits.

The southern green stink bug and kindred species hatch from tiny, somewhat barrel-shaped eggs that have hinged lids. The female lays her eggs one after the other in small clusters. They are always right side up and each egg is glued to the one next to it. Unlike many other insect eggs, these stink bug eggs are attached to the surface of the leaf. A newly hatched nymph is similar in form and habits to an adult, but has to undergo five molts before it becomes fully grown. And as an adult it overwinters by taking refuge beneath piles of rubbish when the weather is not to its liking.

At about the time the cotton is fruiting, the southern green stink bug arrives in the fields. The insect inserts its needle-like beak into a cotton boll, then sucks out the juices. A puncture may cause the boll to mummify, to drop off, or to be spoiled to such an extent that it cannot be picked. If an infestation is large and control is not successful, the yield may be cut in half and the grade of harvested lint and seed will be far from first class.

This insect and other cotton-destroying species can be controlled by various sprays and dusts. The burning of gin wastes is a precautionary measure that helps to check future infestations of such bugs—of which these five and most of the others are always in bad odor by name, nature, and behavior.

One member of the family that does not live up to the reputation of these five is the two-spotted stink bug (*Perillus bioculatus*). Though it excretes a nauseous odor from glands on the underside of the body, the two-spotted species is atypical because it is classed as beneficial. It preys on the Colorado potato beetle, and for so doing was called by Cornell's famous entomologist John Henry Comstock "a gallant fighter."

SQUASH BUGS
Family *Coreidae*

The squash bug family is a large one, and various species ruin such crops as squashes, pumpkins, and gourds on a range that includes the greater part of the United States, northern Mexico, and southernmost Canada. A good example of this family is *Anasa tristis*, a gray-brown insect with an elongated body.

This squash bug and its close relatives pass the winter as adults. Almost any protected spot serves as an overwintering retreat, but the preference seems to be a building into which it can crawl or a pile of boards under which it can squirm.

About the time the first runners of the squash, pumpkin, or cucumber begin to spread across the rich soil of your garden, the squash bug is ready and able to perpetuate its race. The bugs which mate at the start of a new season are virgins, for they are the only ones able to survive the winter. Once a mating is consummated the female flies directly to a patch of pumpkins, a hill of squash, or one of cucumbers. She lays clusters of shiny eggs on the undersides of the leaves of these vining plants. Some eggs take only one week to hatch, while for others the required time is two weeks.

The nymph is wingless, never longer than ⅜ of an inch, and one of two color combinations. It may have a bright-green body with a reddish head and matching reddish legs or a greenish gray body with the head and legs black. A nymph starts to feed at once, and, like the mature bug, it is a group feeder. A colony of feeding nymphs or adults sucks the sap from stems and leaves so thoroughly that the plants on which they feed soon wilt, turn black, and then become crisp. Young plants often die, whereas older plants are thrifty enough that only some leaves and runners are damaged. A nymph matures in four to six weeks, and there is only one generation each year.

You can trap these insects, hand pick and then drop them into a container of soapsuds, or with commercial insecticides spray and dust the plants on which they feed. English sparrows sometimes come to your aid by feeding on the squash bug. But a true predator is a tiny two-winged fly with the scientific name *Trichopoda pennipes*. Similar in appearance to the house fly, this insect lays eggs on the mature squash bug or one that is almost fully grown. Three or four days later, a maggot hatches from each egg. Of all those that hatch and bore into the host, only one lives to become fully grown. Two or three weeks may elapse from the time a maggot enters its host until it is ready to bore its way out.

The squash bug lives on in spite of the internal parasite. Little by little, however, the host loses the ability to function normally. The emergence of the parasite kills the squash bug. Leaving its dead host behind it, the maggot crawls to the ground and buries itself in the soil. It passes about two weeks underground while it pupates, then emerges to carry on the work of destroying more squash bugs —an example of the checks and balances established by Nature.

WATER STRIDERS
Family *Gerridae*

One August afternoon I watched some water striders darting back and forth on the surface of a streamside pool high up in the Bitterroot Mountains of western Montana, not far from the Nez Perce Pass. As I watched I thought once again what a pleasant summer pastime this form of observation is. As my mountain water striders skimmed jerkily back and forth, they brought to mind a flotilla of tiny sculls. For the insect's six slender legs are attached to a somewhat elongated body.

Probably at the very moment I was watching these bugs, other members of the family were sculling back and forth on quiet waters throughout the northern United States and eastern Canada. And undoubtedly another family group—those in the genus *Halobates*, were doing their sculling on the ocean's surface, for among the twenty or so species of these insects known for North America are some deep-sea forms. These marine striders frequently ride the waves hundreds of miles offshore.

The water strider rests on the surface with its short forelegs and long hind ones. The middle pair, set close to those in the rear, are the "oars." The insect stays on the surface because tension holds it in place. The weight of the waterborne creature depresses the surface slightly—just enough so that six concave lenses form. When sunlight dapples a pool on which water striders are performing, the lenses throw six circular shadow spots on the bottom.

There is a story to the effect that these bugs can be prevented

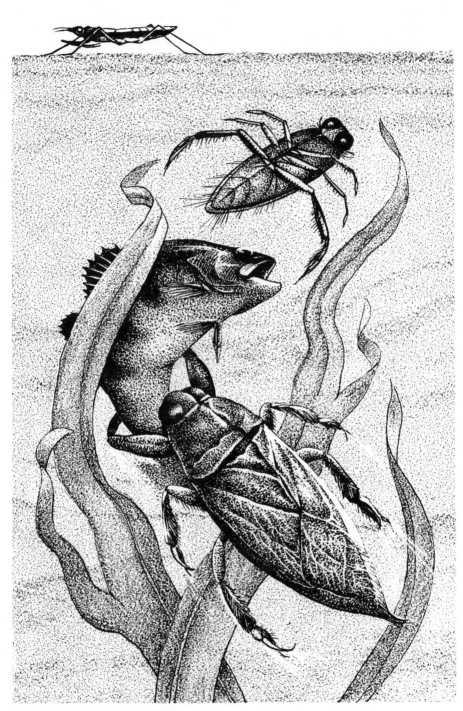

Water Strider, *Gerris marginatus*, on surface
Backswimmer, *Notonecta undulata*, in water at top
Giant Water Bug, *Lethocerus americanus*, catching fish

from forming the lenses. Presumably if some soap or sodium oleate is dropped into the pool used by water striders, there will be less surface tension, causing the insects to break through the surface film. If this be true, then the soap or sodium oleate procedure may be the way to catch the insect. Usually the water strider sculls away with such speed that it is difficult to catch by hand.

The short, grasping legs of the water strider, brown on its back, white underneath, are for catching and holding small insect prey and other small creatures of the stream. And not infrequently the insect jumps from the water to capture various flies.

It is likely that the female uses the short, grasping legs to hold herself in place while she deposits her sticky egg masses. These may be attached to the stems of water plants or placed in plant tissues. Upon hatching, a young strider is so similar in appearance to an adult that it is almost a perfect miniature. From the hour it hatches until it dies, this bug spends the greater part of its life on water.

When winter ices over streams and ponds or the droughts of summer dry up these waters, the adult strider protects itself by hiding under rocks and logs or crawling beneath streamside debris. The only other time the insect leaves its habitat is during the mating season. And then only certain members of a colony fly away from the area in which they were born.

The dimorphic, the winged forms, are the ones to take to the air. These members of a colony emigrate during the mating reason in search of new water areas suitable for starting another colony. Such an emigration goes unmarked by most of us. For the mass movement of the winged water striders is at night—a host of tiny phantom ships sailing through the darkness like Wagner's *Flying Dutchman*.

GIANT WATER BUGS
Family *Belostomatidae*

Another member of many fresh-water plant and animal communities is a brown, flat-bodied bug with forelegs adapted for grasping and the middle and hind legs constructed for swimming. This insect is called the giant water bug because it is the largest species of our *Hemiptera,* with some known individuals measuring as much as 4 inches in length. In one form or another it is found throughout the greater part of the United States and most of Canada.

A representative member of the family is *Lethocerus americanus.* According to Comstock and other authorities this bug and its close relatives "are rapacious creatures." No matter the species, the giant water bug feeds upon any animal of its community that can be subdued, including snails, frogs, small fishes of many species and even fair-sized trout. In turn the predator is food for various ducks and herons.

To catch its prey, the water bug swims as fast or a little faster than the creature it is pursuing. When it is alongside or perhaps slightly ahead of its quarry, the fast-moving bug closes in and nabs the pursued with the forelegs. Curved like those of a crab, these legs are equipped with needle-like hooks at each end. The water bug inserts the hooks on either side of the victim's body. Held thus, as if by pincers, the prey cannot squirm free, and the predator is able to drain the vital life juices with its piercing-sucking mouth parts.

Because it destroys so many fishes, the water bug is often called "the fish killer." It has still another pseudonym: electric light bug, which stems from a predilection for bright lights. This liking is often the water bug's undoing and also an accidental control. Sometimes a number of these insects fly directly into an electric light and are killed by impact. Only the adult is able to indulge in this apparent liking for electric or neon glare because only the mature water bug has wings.

The insect overwinters either as a nymph or as an adult. It secretes itself under piles of trash, in mud, or sinks to the bottoms of ponds, lakes, or pools of other waters. Once the weather of a new season is sufficiently warm, the giant water bug comes out of hiding to mate, so that another generation of these predators is assured.

If you study a woodland pond or any other body of water in which there are bugs of this kind, be careful in your contacts with them. *L. americanus,* our most common species, *Belostoma fluminea,* and all the others inject a powerful digestive fluid as they bite. The combination of the bite and the fluid is painful or down-right excruciating if you happen to be allergic to the substance.

Two other bugs, of two other families, are also among the host of creatures that make up some fresh-water communities. One is the backswimmer (*Notonecta undulata*), unique among all other aquatic bugs. This insect has a back shaped like the bottom of a boat, and on the surface floats wrong-side-to. If you disturb a back-swimmer, it rows rapidly toward the bottom, using its long, fringed hind legs to make a getaway. If you ever catch a backswimmer, handle it with care. The piercing mouth parts are sharp enough to inflict a nasty skin puncture.

The second pond or pool inhabitant is the water boatman—an oval, grayish-black bug whose normal length is less than one-half inch. The hind legs are well adapted for swimming because they are long, somewhat flattened, and well fringed.

The scientific name of this bug is *Arctocorixa interrupta*, and as such it swims through its chosen environment in a silvery casing of air. The particles of air in the water through which *A. interrupta* swims constantly purify the air enveloping the body of the swim-mer. Stagnant water provides no such purification. The water boat-man of such an environment has to surface every so often for pure air.

Though this insect swims well enough, it spends much of its time secured to some sort of anchorage at or near the bottom. It holds itself in place with its long middle legs. If it momentarily relaxes its grip, the casing of air causes it to rise quickly to the surface. Occasionally the insect floats on the water, and frequently it uses the surface as a launching platform from which it starts a flight by leaping into the air.

These four water insects and such others as the water scorpions, the shore bugs, and those known as the toad-shaped bugs have parts in a complex community centered in and around a pond or other water areas. Life in such a community is like an endless chain in which the predator is often preyed upon.

Beetles are biters and chewers, having for this purpose strong jaws, working, of course, horizontally. The number of different kinds of beetles, alone, which have been examined, is about a hundred thousand.

So wrote John Monteith, M. A. in *Living Creatures of Land, Water, and Air,* a McGuffey natural-history reader copyrighted in 1888. Since the day Mr. Monteith commented on the number of examined beetles, there has been almost a threefold increase in the known, described species of these sheath-winged insects. In 1959 the number was more than 275,000 species, including a small brown one named the confused flour beetle.

Spoken of as *Tribolium confusum* by those who prefer scientific nomenclature, this little beetle is among the 26,676 species described for all the country north of the Rio Grande. *T. confusum* is one of the least desirable native species, for it is a pantry pest. It can, and all too frequently does, eat its own weight in food each week. Its larva destroys many times its own weight in food during the three or four weeks it takes to develop. The confused flour beetle, various other bran beetles, and all sorts of weevils ruin quantities of packaged and stored foods. The seasonal loss of wheat in storage caused by these particular insects in the Great Plains area may be as great as 10 per cent. And in the Deep South the damage to corn awaiting use or shipment is often at a monthly rate of 9 per cent.

Not all beetles (*Coleoptera*) are categorized as pests. Many native species and some imported as biological controls are allies in the constant, costly war to check the insect hoards that could be our ruination. In 1952 a special dispatch from Sacramento, California, regarding a beneficial beetle was received by *The New York Times*. Datelined December 4, it read in part:

A million imported Australian beetles were applauded today by state officials for cleaning out the weeds of 100,000 acres of rangeland in Humboldt County, Northern California.

The weed-destroying beetle that received "applause" is *Chrysomela gemellata,* a purplish-green insect about the size of a pea. It was brought over from Australia in 1949. The weed that the insect eradicated is known in our West as the Klamath weed—a plant that comes to us from Europe, where it is called St.-John's-wort.

As naturalized in North America, the European variety displaces desirable range plants, and poisons livestock. Animals that eat much Klamath weed become scabby, sore-mouthed, and unthrifty. Those animals with white or unpigmented skin areas become photosensitive after feeding on this weed. Upon exposure to the sunlight the white or unpigmented skin areas get irritated and sometimes even blister. Now the introduced beetle, in eradicating acre after acre of the pest plant, has given one of the perennial range plants a chance to become reestablished. Where the Klamath weed used to grow, a bunch grass is flourishing as in the past.

The physical characteristics of this introduced beetle and all other beetle species are: two pairs of wings, with the first pair greatly thickened to form a pair of "wing covers," under which the membranous hind wings are folded when the insects rests. The so-called wing covers, the forewings, meet in a straight line down the back and serve as a sort of armor. The mouth parts of these hard-bodied insects are, as John Monteith commented, constructed for chewing. All beetles, including the weevils, undergo a complete metamorphosis.

Among weevils there are many known as snout beetles. A typical snout beetle has a beak that is often as long as the body and sometimes twice as long. But just to make weevil identification more difficult, a few species have a short, wide beak. All, however, have a beak that is downward curving. There are more than 1,800 snout beetles in the United States.

Some entomologists include the "twisted-winged insects" in the same order (*Coleoptera*) with the beetles and the weevils. Others place these small parasitic insects in an order of their own, *Strepsiptera*.

The beetles, the weevils, and the twisted-winged insects, as groups and as individuals, are an integral part of the various plant and animal communities throughout North America. Though a few species are aquatic and some live in the sea, most are land-dwellers. They occupy every possible kind of habitat; some, for instance, are a part of the small animal life you find on the forest floor. These beetles are supported by decaying wood and in turn help to reduce it to soil. They are a part of the endless cycle by which everything returns to the soil.

Convergent Lady Beetle
Hippodamia convergens
(*Color Plate 1, facing page 80*)

In 1942 more than 61,000,000 bushels of wheat, oats, and barley were destroyed by the greenbug in the Great Plains area. The greenbug (*Toxoptera graminum*) is a little plant louse that feeds greedily on small grains. The insect could gorge at will because there were practically no lady beetles around to keep it in check. As an adult or in its larval form the lady beetle is a voracious eater of greenbugs. More often than not the insect, a member of the family *Coccinellidae*, eats its own weight in greenbugs or other soft-bodied insects each and every day.

Also called the lady bug or the lady-bird beetle, this beneficial insect is known to most of us by sight or song. The familiar orange or reddish-orange insect with its black-dotted wing covers is the subject of a well-known jingle. According to entomologists the jingle makes no scientific sense.

> Lady bug, lady bug
> Fly away home.
> Your house is on fire,
> And your children will burn.

Though these four lines are not weighted with scientific truth, there is reason enough for them to be a part of the folklore having to do with insects. Apparently they are a corruption that stems from a jingle that originated years ago in the Old World. Once the hops were harvested, the vines on which the conelike fruits grew were burned. And in the burning the larvae of many lady beetles, "*Coccinellid* children," and numberless aphids, *Coccinellid* food, were killed. Then somewhat in the manner of a Calypso singer a minstrel of the time coined this:

> Lady bird, lady bird! Fly away home.
>> Your house is on fire,
>>> Your children do roam.

> Except little Nan, who sits in a pan,
>> Weaving gold laces,
>>> As fast as she can.

Though the rhyming is considerably better in the two-stanza version, the lines themselves express no more scientific sense than those of the later date. But both pay tribute to an insect whose activity may be described as enterprising and indefatigable from the moment it is "born" until it dies. This is fitting, for most of the hundred or so lady beetles in North America are beneficial. One exception to an almost exemplary insect family is the Mexican bean beetle, a wayward sort of creature that fell into bad repute many geological ages ago.

To distinguish one lady beetle from another, count the polka dots on the hard wing covers. One species has only two spots; another has nine, four on each wing cover and the ninth, the basal spot up near the head; and still another has fifteen when you count the basal spot. Then there is the convergent lady beetle: three-tenths of an inch over-all, it has six spots to each wing cover and two whitish dashes on the back. The dashes almost meet or converge, the reason for both its common name and its scientific one, *Hippodamia convergens*.

The lady beetle overwinters as an adult. Sometimes the insect hibernates alone in any convenient stormproof crack. More often, the insect joins others of its kind until hundreds of them jampack one small area. In the East, they often hibernate under piles of trash. But in the West the convergent lady beetle and related species fly from the lowlands to high country for the winter. They swarm into the hibernating area where they settle by the hundreds of thousands on every bushy growth. Once they have settled down they usually remain dormant from November until April.

The behavior of the lady beetle in the vicinity of Oroville, California, in the northeastern part of the state, is to the advantage of the Greenbug Control Company, a business that sells lady beetles at the rate of 135,000,000 a year. The buyers are agriculturists who use the insect to help check such pests as aphids, mealybugs, and pink bollworms. In Florida, Oklahoma, Kansas, and Texas the bollworm often ruins the cotton crops, and the company once shipped 39,000,000 lady beetles to Texas where they were used to help check the bollworm.

Pickers employed by Paul Harris, the manager, work in pairs to collect lady beetles in the mountains. To fill a gallon container a man has to collect at least 135,000 insects. (About 30,000 are needed to control the pests on one farm acre.) The pickers work for about forty-eight hours straight, then return to the plant. Here the beetles are put into cold storage. They can be stored for about two months at a temperature slightly above freezing.

Lady beetles are shipped at night, for the heat of day makes them too active. They are sent in boxes filled with pine cones into which they crawl and which prevent them from being hurt in transit. As soon as they arrive the beetles are "cooled," so that they won't crawl or fly away. Then, as time or necessity dictates, the farmer or large-scale agriculturist releases his biological controls. When the season comes to an end each lady beetle goes flying off on her own way. But each one has left a new generation behind—the larvae that hatched from eggs laid earlier in the season.

In the spring the lady beetle lays thousands of eggs on plants. The fertile ones quickly hatch, and the individual larva is tiny and has a carrot-like appearance which is heightened by numerous little tufts. The lady beetle-to-be hatches with legs that are well-developed and an appetite that may be similarily described. It starts to eat at once, and feeds on other insects, the eggs of many pest insects, and some small spiders.

The incipient lady beetle seems to be in a hurry to mature, for its growth is rapid. When it reaches its final larval stage, it develops a somewhat ovate form. At this stage in its life the insect enters a quiet interval—a period when it hangs by its tail. Once this marking of time is over, it emerges as an adult, the *imago*. Now the lady beetle has assumed its final form, the one that is so familiar and the one described in *These Also*, an anthology of prose and poetry about various animals:

I have turned to Fabre for enlightenment, but he had nothing to say about this popular, miniature beetle. . . . and I much prefer to picture him swaying in a 'cowslip' then existing somewhat precariously in a scientist's test bottle. It is sufficient for me that it devours the greenfly on my rose bushes, that it will trickle confidently across the back of my hand, showing no symptoms of home-sickness, and that when it takes wing, splitting its horny domino of black, or of orange, into two parts in a manner somewhat startling to the human eye—not to mention the frail, pale under-sails of silk—I know that not fear, but the joy of life surges upon its birdlike soaring flight.

Mexican Bean Beetle
Epilachna varivestis

(*Color Plate I, facing page 80*)

The Mexican bean beetle is another of the lady beetles. But the behavior of this coppery brown insect with sixteen black dots on its back is not above reproach. In some areas the insect makes bean-growing almost or wholly impossible, for both the adults and the larvae feed voraciously on the pods and the undersides of the leaves. This feeding is often so extensive that the leaves are left skeletonized.

No one knows exactly how this beetle developed such a liking for vegetable matter. Formerly it was carnivorous, but it is possible, so scientists say, that the Mexican bean beetle and a few related species made a switch in food habits in a geological era long since gone. For this small family group of foliage-eating beetles is world-wide, and each member has developed a preference for a special plant. In Africa there are beetles that feed on plants of the cotton family only; in the Orient there are those that adhere to a diet of potato-plant foliage; and in Europe the representative of the group is an eater of such legumes as the pea.

Throughout the past few decades the Mexican bean beetle has constantly worked its way north. Today its range includes even parts of northern states. Here and elsewhere the insect winters in the adult, or beetle stage. It usually passes the dormant period in wooded areas adjacent to bean fields. When the spring weather is warm enough the adults come out of hiding. Almost at once the female lays her eggs on the undersides of leaves. Sometimes the eggs hatch in as little as five days, or they may take a full two weeks. The bright-yellow larva is decorated with numerous forked spines; those on the back look rather like coarse, uncombed hair. Immediately upon hatching the larva feeds on the underside of a bean leaf.

The Mexican bean beetle matures with surprising rapidity. After undergoing four instars—growth stages—from which it emerges each time a little larger, in 20 to 35 days, the creature is a fully grown larva. At this point in its development, it attaches itself to the underside of a leaf. Then for about ten days the larva is quiescent, the interlude of pupation during which structural changes take place and from which the imago, or perfect beetle, emerges. If the imago is a female she will be ready to lay eggs within two weeks. And the cycle that means the destruction of more beans and plants is ready to begin all over again.

Dusts and sprays to control the Mexican bean beetle have been developed through the years, and in the 1920's entomologists believed that they had discovered an effective biological check for this pest. A parasite (*Paradexodes epilachnae*), found in central Mexico, was imported and reared until there was a sufficient supply for release. At first the field colonies of *Paradexodes* seemed to find conditions here to their liking, and throve to such an extent that their numbers increased. During the first season of release the parasite sometimes destroyed at least 80 per cent of the Mexican bean beetle larvae in a given area.

It appeared that the beetle was doomed in the United States. But the following season field investigators learned that not a single parasite in the hundreds of colonies "planted" in nineteen states had lived through the winter. So without a natural control and in spite of dusts and sprays, the Mexican bean beetle is responsible for an annual dollar loss estimated at more than $5,500,000. This loss might be averted if way could be found to juggle the genes of the insect so that it would revert to its ancient habit of feeding on other insects rather than plants.

Japanese Beetle
Popillia japonica

(*Color Plate I, facing page 80*)

In 1916 a few Japanese beetles were discovered near Riverton, N. J. Eight years later this small shiny green insect with coppery wings was established almost everywhere within an area of nearly 2,500 square miles. Today its range is along the coast from Portland, Maine, south to the vicinity of Wilmington, N. C. In addition many states adjacent to those on the coast have what the United States Department of Agriculture calls "spot infestations." These beetle-plagued areas also occur in parts of the Midwest. Except for one area in southeast Iowa, spot infestations are confined to the eastern side of the Mississippi River for this member of the family *Scarabaeidae*.

So little was known about the Japanese beetle in 1916 that American entomologists took some time to identify the insect. When they learned what it was, these insect specialists found to their dismay that there was almost no information about the exotic beetle in entomological tomes. They did find out, however, that *Popillia japonica* was common on all the main islands of Japan. One reference commented that the insect was not considered enough of a pest to warrant undue concern. We quickly learned in this country that what was true in Japan was not necessarily so in the United States, for in time the yearly damage attributed to the Japanese beetle was estimated at $10,000,000.

The progenitors of the Japanese beetle in America undoubtedly entered the country as grubs—the only form in which the beetle could have survived the long trip from its homeland. Probably the grubs were secreted in the balls of earth around the roots of imported nursery stock, imported before the plant quarantine laws were in effect. As the grub of this beetle is a root eater, those that were shipped in had plenty of food on hand.

Many years later one Japanese beetle in its adult form arrived in this country. The all-too-familiar bright-green insect was discovered in a lively condition at the airport in Brownsville, Texas. It had flown in on a military plane that had come from New York, N. Y., by way of Panama. Someone recognized the insect invader as an enemy alien, and it was put to death before even a single *frijole* was threatened.

Since the Japanese beetle has become established in the United States, the insect has developed a liking for the leaves, blossoms, and fruits of more than 275 trees, shrubs, and plants. The appearance of the insects on their favorite food plants coincides with the first warm days of summer. In the South, therefore, it may be out by mid-May, whereas in the North it may not put in an appearance until July 1 or even a little later.

The beetle flies only during the day, and is particularly active when the weather is warm and sunny. It feeds on plants, trees, or shrubs that are in the sun: small fruits such as the grape, raspberry, and strawberry; large fruits such as the apple and the peach; and truck and garden crops, especially corn, whose silk is eaten as fast as it grows. In addition numerous ornamental shrubs, various vines, and any number of garden plants other than the bean are "fodder" for the insect, which also eats the foliage of a number of shade trees and the turf of lawns, parks, and golf courses.

A feeding beetle chews out the parts between the veins. In time the leaf has a lacelike appearance. When it feeds on fruit the beetle is usually joined by others, and the mass feeding so ruins a peach, apple, or other fruit that nothing remains for home use or marketing. And the consumption of corn silk prevents the kernels from forming.

The female interrupts her feeding every so often to leave the host plant. She burrows into the ground—usually the preferred ground is covered by turf—to lay a few eggs. She then returns to the host to continue feeding. This procedure continues during the four to six weeks of the insect's greatest activity.

The eggs hatch in about two weeks, and the grub stage in the life of the Japanese beetle is underway by midsummer. The length of a newly hatched grub is about one-sixteenth of an inch. Frequently grubs are so abundant that fifteen hundred are in one square yard of soil. The grub stage lasts about ten months, during which the beetle of the year to come feeds on the roots of available plants, with those of various grasses preferred.

As it feeds, the grub increases in size and passes through three instars—the stages between each skin-shedding, or molt. After the last instar the grub is fully grown. The head is hard and may be yellowed or even brown; the body color and that of the blunt posterior is white or creamy-white. In the soil the grub usually assumes a curled position with the head almost touching the blunt rear. Uncurled, a fully grown grub measures about one inch.

During winter the grub burrows deeper into the soil. But as the spring suns warm the earth, it worms its way almost to the surface. It feeds for a few weeks, then becomes inactive. This quiet period is the pupal stage during which the changes that produce the beetle take place. Now the cycle from egg to adult is complete, and the insect emerges from the ground to begin its destructive feeding in its New World territory.

Shortly after the Japanese beetle was identified the U. S. Department of Agriculture began a study of the insect. ". . . it was obvious," two Federal entomologists wrote, "that the beetle had found ideal conditions for rapid multiplication and was capable of causing great losses to many economic plants and crops." Though the fact that the insect could and did multiply rapidly was obvious, it was also puzzling. How was it possible for the creature to reach pest proportions here when nothing of the sort took place in Japan?

The contrast between serious pest here, not so serious pest there, was the clue that alerted the Federal government's entomological detectives to the fact that in Japan there might be a natural control or controls. From 1922 until the end of 1933 American entomologists searched in Japan and other countries for enemies of the beetle. The thirteen-year search was rewarding, for the detectives rounded up any number of parasites and predators that helped to keep the Japanese beetle in check in other parts of the world. A selection was finally made, and more than forty insect predators and parasites were shipped from the Far East, India, Australia, and Hawaii to this country.

Of the five species of imported parasites, two are now well established in beetle-infested areas. These are the spring Tiphia (*Tiphia vernalis*) from Korea and the summer or fall Tiphia (*T. popilliavora*) from Japan. The parasites are little wasps that lay an egg on the body of the Japanese beetle grub. The wasp maggot feeds on the grub, thereby killing it.

The spring *Tiphia* is the better control of the two. It parasitizes the grubs on which it lays eggs. The average parasitization is estimated at 41 per cent. Within the past two years it has been discovered that one of our native flies attacks the grub of the Japanese beetle. Ultimately this native predator may be an important biological control.

Insect parasites and predators are not the only natural factors that help to limit the numbers of Japanese beetles each year. Extremely dry summer weather prevents the eggs from hatching or causes the death of newly hatched grubs. Then there is the milky disease whose germs or spores cause the blood of the infected grub to look somewhat like milk. The organism of the milky disease is being spread by the U. S. Department of Agriculture. Some 137,000 areas were treated with the disease from 1939 to 1953. The sites treated were in 220 counties in 14 states and the District of Columbia. In some of the areas to receive the first treatments there has been a marked reduction in the numbers of beetles. Milky-disease spore is available from certain licensed individuals and companies that are approved by the U. S. Department of Agriculture.

Two predators that feed on the Japanese beetle are imports like the insect itself. The starling and the English sparrow, two of our most common exotic birds, have been noted feeding on the pest. The gull and domestic poultry devour large numbers of beetle grubs during the plowing season. Moles and skunks also include the grub in their diets, though these mammals are apt to damage lawns or other turf areas while digging for this type of food.

Lastly there is a cooperative federal-state regulatory program to keep the beetle from spreading beyond the range of its flight. The program of quarantines, inspections, treatment of nursery and greenhouse stocks before shipment has been effective. By 1954 no Japanese beetle had been discovered in any area that had not known it heretofore.

White Grub
May or June Beetle
"June Bug"
Phyllophaga drakei

(*Color Plate I, facing page 80*)

Although these insects are beetles, and attract our attention each year in May, they have received the infelicitous title of June-bugs. They are more properly termed May-beetles. . . . The larvae of the different species of May-beetles are commonly classed together under the name "white grubs."

Comstock and Herrick
(*A Manual For The Study Of Insects*)

The adult May beetle varies in length from ½ to 1 inch. It is a stout-bodied insect with slender legs and a head so small that it seems almost nonexistent. The color of the insect varies, and may be dark brown, light brown, or a light reddish brown. The underside is dull but the wing covers appear as if they had a gloss finish.

The insect hatches from a pearly white egg shaped like a small cylinder. A female may lay only fifty eggs or she may expel twice as many. Each egg is deposited beneath the soil's surface at depths varying from one to eight inches. An egg hatches in three or four weeks, and the creature that comes into being is the "white grub." It has a dark-brown head and usually lies in a curved position.

A grub first feeds on decaying vegetation, but soon starts in on living plant foods. In its second year, a grub does the most damage. Among the crops on which it feeds are corn, soybeans, and timothy. It also eats the tubers of potatoes and the roots of bluegrass, including that of pastures in the Northeast and some North Central states. Nursery stock is not immune from inroads of the white grub. Frequently this root feeding kills plants in the nursery.

In its third year a grub does not eat so voraciously, for it is approaching the time when it is to pupate. This interval occurs rather early in the season, and is passed in an earthen cell that is three to eight inches underground. By August, at the very latest September, the fully developed beetle emerges from the cell and almost immediately buries itself in the ground.

Well after March 21 the adult May beetle emerges from the soil. The female lays her eggs, and both the male and the female eat the various foods that sustain them in this form. Though the adult eats the foliage of any number of trees, it seems to favor a group of ten. Of these the ash, the pine, and the walnut seem the more favored. It likes, too, the leaves of blackberry bushes, and in plague years the insect defoliates trees not ordinarily in its diet and shrubs if usual foods are not available.

Artificial light is irresistible to the May beetle. In the evening it flies to an outside light or will bump endlessly against a screen, trying to get inside a house where a lamp is burning. This beetle is a clumsy flyer and bumbles along through the air as if uncertain of its course. When one eventually finds a spot to land on, it settles down. Then, as if hypnotized, it stares at the light as time tolls away endless minutes.

As the May beetle wings its way toward a light, there is apt to be another insect flying along, too. This is the Pyrgota fly—an enemy of the May beetle. The fly strikes in flight, for only then is the tender skin of a beetle's back exposed. The ovipositor of the fly is in effect a miniature stiletto. The fly jabs the beetle and inserts an egg almost at the same time.

The beetle thus attacked drops to the ground. Seemingly she recovers, for in a short time she joins other beetles around the light or flies off to mate or to eat the leaves from branches at treetop level. But now she is marked for death. In four or five days the fly egg will hatch, and the larva that comes from it will feed on the fats and fluids in the body of the host.

At the end of a week the female beetle is unable to leave her burrow. All the life-sustaining forces are gone. But the parasite does not leave the host. It starts feeding on the muscles and the vital organs. In a week or ten days from the time she was stabbed the beetle is dead.

The life cycle of the May beetle is not effectively synchronized with that of the *Pyrgota* fly. There is only one generation of beetles every three years, whereas the fly has a generation each year. When the flies emerge in a year when there are few beetles, many of the little parasites die because there are not enough hosts to go around.

Colorado Potato Beetle
Leptinotarsa decemlineata

The Colorado potato beetle was once restricted to the Rocky Mountain area. This bascially yellow insect, now a widespread, unwelcome emigrant, is about ⅜ of an inch in length. It is distinguished by five black lines on each wing cover and a series of polka dots on other parts of the body and is categorized as a leaf beetle and in a family known scientifically as the *Chrysomelidae*.

Within its original range the beetle fed on the nightshades and other species of wild potatoes. Now it has increased the range until there is hardly a potato-growing state without the pest. The reason for the successful emigration is the planting of potatoes. As soon as the settlers in the vicinity of the Rocky Mountains put in potatoes, the beetle came down out of its original habitat and took to the cultivated plant with the relish of a gourmand. The potato plants nearest the original habitat acted as "steppingstones" to those areas planted at an earlier historical date. Thus the insect spread out progressively until it is common in most sections of the country, and has managed to get itself transported to Europe as well.

The adult form of the Colorado potato beetle is the one that overwinters. The insect passes its period of suspended animation beneath the earth's surface. As soon as the weather is warm enough the adults emerge from the ground and fly to the nearest potato plants or other closely related species. Soon the female attaches clusters of orange-colored eggs to the undersides of leaves. An egg can hatch in four days and as a rule takes no longer than nine days. The larva, also called a slug, becomes full grown in ten to twenty-one days after four growth stages from which it emerges each time in a larger form. The insect burrows into the ground for the quiet interval of pupation. During the next five to ten days changes take place which transform the creature into an adult beetle. It then squirms its way to the surface, flies to a plant, and, if it is a female, feeds for a few days before depositing eggs. The eggs may be the first of two lots that account for a second generation in some areas.

Spotted and Striped Cucumber Beetles
Diabrotica undecimpuncta
Acalyma vittata

Charles Dudley Warner once wrote: "To own a bit of ground, to scratch it with a hoe, to plant seeds, and watch the renewal of life,—this is the commonest delight of the race, the most satisfactory thing a man can do."

But all too often this commonest delight is short-lived when your garden truck provides a banquet for beetles. Two that spoil any gardener's delight take their names from the vegetable on which they feed. These are the spotted cucumber beetle and the one that is striped. They are both distinguished by an elongated form that measures about one-fourth of an inch in all.

The head and legs of the spotted cucumber beetle are black and the wing covers are decorated with twelve black dots—six to each side. In its larval form the insect feeds on the roots of corn—a dietary quirk that causes it to be known during this stage as the "corn rootworm."

The yellowish-green body of the striped cucumber beetle is somewhat narrower than that of the spotted species. It is distinguished by sharp stripes, three in number and black in color. These stripes are lateral and the one in the middle is the broadest. This species eats holes in leaves and flowers in gardens east of the Rocky Mountains. Both beetles and related species in some western states feed on the leaves of bean, melon, and cucumber plants. And both also overwinter as adults, usually in uncultivated areas and generally protected by garden debris.

In many areas the end of the overwintering interlude coincides with the blossoming of the apple trees. At first the adult beetle feeds on wild plants, but as soon as the earliest cultivated seedlings appear, it moves into the garden to devour the more delicate plants. From time to time the female quits eating and crawls into any crack in the soil's surface. She deposits a few eggs, then returns to her feeding. When the grub, or larva, hatches, it begins to feed on plant roots and continues to do so for about a month. Then all activity ceases and the period of pupation begins, and is over seemingly almost before it started. For the changes that bring an adult into being occur rather quickly. Once the insect has assumed its final form, it emerges from the soil to continue the cycle that ensures future generations of cucumber beetles.

The two cucumber beetles are noteworthy in a dubious sort of way. At the very beginning of the 1900's, Erwin S. Smith and associate workers of the U. S. Department of Agriculture discovered what sets these two apart from all other beetles, and, for that matter, from all other insects. The insects are vectors, carriers, that is, of a bacterial wilt. The disease is most prevalent in the North Central and Northeastern states.

Young plants affected by it die rapidly with little or no indication that they are sick; plants with large vines wilt gradually without any yellowing of the leaves, and eventually die, and when old plants are first affected the indication may be the wilting of a single stem, shoot, or stalk. The wilt is caused by bacteria that plug the water vessels of stems and leaves.

The bacteria can only enter those plants wounded by feeding cucumber beetles. Not all cucumber beetles are carriers, but any one of them may become a carrier if it feeds on an infected plant. And it is the cucumber beetle that is responsible for the continuing survival of the wilt-causing bacteria. Each year some bacteria live on because the bodies of overwintering adult cucumber beetles afford the necessary protection from the cold. This method of infection and winter survival is the only known example in nature.

Checkered and Spotted Asparagus Beetles
Crioceris asparagi
C. duodecimpunctata

Asparagus is a plant of such antiquity that Cato wrote about it in a treatise titled *On Farming*. His directions for growing this long-cultivated plant are similar to those recommended in contemporary horticultural manuals. This Latin writer suggested sheep manure as a fertilizer, for besides enriching the soil it helps to check weed growth. Though one could hardly ask for anything more, it would indeed be wonderful if this fertilizer also had an insect-inhibiting property.

Any grower of asparagus knows all too well that there is more to growing the plant than enriched soil and properly drained and weed-free beds. There is an insect that has a predilection for tender young asparagus, that can eat it without the inducement of drawn butter or Hollandaise sauce. This insect, the asparagus beetle, came to us from Europe not long after the Civil War.

The first to arrive was the checkered asparagus beetle. No longer than $3/10$ inch, this species is an attractive-looking creature because its checkered brown back brings to mind tortoise shell. It was accidentally introduced about 1868. Some twenty years later the spotted asparagus beetle reached us. Its uniformly brown back is decorated with a number of spots—six black dots to each wing cover and another of the same color as the basal dot.

Some time in April or May the adult asparagus beetle of either species comes out of hiberation. The overwintering spot is usually old stalks of asparagus plants, garden debris along fence rows, or natural piles of debris in wooded areas. The pest usually puts in an appearance at about the time the first asparagus shoots, tender and pinkish, are pushing up from the crown through the earth. The insect starts feeding at once on the tender buds at the tips of the spears. As soon as the female has satisfied her initial hunger of the season, she is ready to lay her eggs. She crawls around the spears, pausing now and then to stud the plant stalk with tiny, bright black eggs; these are attached singly. Generally an egg hatches in about ten days.

The larva, $1/3$ inch long, is either olive green or dark gray. The larva appears well nourished; in fact it is so fat that it looks as if it might burst its skin. But fat or not, it immediately starts eating. It feeds on the buds, the stems, and, as the season progresses, on the feathery leaves of stalks that have branched and unfolded. Larval feeding lasts ten to fourteen days. It comes to an abrupt end when the creature drops to the ground into which it wriggles. It remains

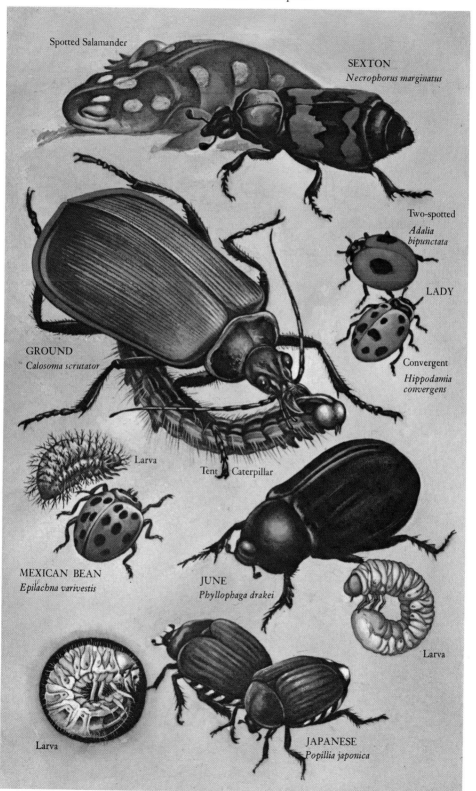

Spotted Salamander

SEXTON
Necrophorus marginatus

Two-spotted
*Adalia
bipunctata*

LADY

GROUND
Calosoma scrutator

Convergent
*Hippodamia
convergens*

Larva

Tent Caterpillar

MEXICAN BEAN
Epilachna varivestis

JUNE
Phyllophaga drakei

Larva

Larva

JAPANESE
Popillia japonica

beneath the soil for another ten to fourteen days—the interval of pupation. Then it emerges from the soil as an adult. If weather conditions are right—not too hot and dry—and the growing season is long enough, more than one generation of asparagus beetles may occur. These garden pests cause more damage to asparagus throughout a greater area than any other insect.

Both beetles have an enemy, a tiny wasp by the name of *Tetrastichus asparagi*, which is smaller than the shiny black eggs of the insect it preys on. The eggs are no larger than grains of sand, a size that makes this wasp a wee one indeed.

T. asparagi, whose trivial name is highly significant, is an Amazon in fact and feat. Year after year this warrior wasp lays unfertilized eggs. And the broods that emerge from the eggs of the spinster wasps are composed entirely of females. From the time of hatching until pupation only one week elapses, and the quiescent stage might be thought of as lasting no longer than a catnap.

T. asparagi takes double-barreled action against the asparagus beetle. She flies among the spearlike stalks until she finds one peppered with eggs. As she moves around on the stalk, she flicks her wings in typical wasp fashion and explores the plant's surface with her almost invisible antennae. Once an egg is located and considered promising, the little killer hoists herself onto it.

Then like a warrior about to do close combat with a sword, *asparagi* brings out her minuscule ovipositor, the egg-laying organ, at the rear of the abdomen. She plunges it into the egg, partially withdraws it, and then plunges it in once more—only this time the thrust is at a slightly different angle. She makes a number of these thrusts and semiwithdrawals. These maneuvers loosen the matter inside the egg.

When *asparagi* gives her *coup de grace*, she sheathes her ovipositor, gets down off the egg, and holds her mouth over the hole she made. She sucks until she has drained the liquid droplet from the egg. A day's feeding may be the contents of as many as five eggs. As most asparagus beds harbor numbers of these wasps, their combined feeding frequently prevents three-fourths of the beetle eggs from hatching.

Though *asparagi* feeds on the contents of the eggs laid by the asparagus beetle, the little wasp has another use for the glistening specks. Certain eggs are selected as "nests" for her own eggs—two or three of which are inserted by means of the ovipositor. The wasp eggs are placed right beneath the surface of the beetle egg or eggs. As she goes about her egg-laying, *asparagi* manages it with the utmost delicacy. She is careful to make sure that the contents of the host egg are not disturbed and that the opening made by the ovipositor is no larger than that of a pinpoint puncture.

Though the egg of an asparagus beetle contains an alien element, its development is not affected. A fat, apparently normal grub hatches, feeds upon the host plant, and does so for the next week or ten days. When it is a fully grown grub, it falls to the ground. At this point in its life the grub builds a shell-like structure in which to pupate. Such action dooms the grub, for the wasp larva hatched from the egg inserted by *asparagi* stirs itself with the building of the shell. It feeds on the life-sustaining elements of the grub and the feeding is so voracious that the grub is dead within a week.

The larva of the wasp lives on in the host shell for another week before it pupates. When the adult form is complete, the imago is ready to emerge from the "nursery" and work its way up out of the soil. Now it is ready to make safe the greater part of each year's asparagus crop. A gardening buff, one who believes wholeheartedly that you should never underestimate the power of the female, has nailed a plaque to the door of his tool house and potting shed. On it is inscribed:

> Gardeners love *asparagi*
> And her lethal quality.
> This little wasp, a sure-shot nemesis,
> Ends asparagus beetles during genesis.

FIREFLIES AND GLOWWORMS
Family *Lampyridae*

From start to finish the Glow-worm's life is one great orgy of light. The eggs are luminous; the grubs likewise. The full-grown females are magnificent light-houses, the adult males retain the glimmer which the grubs already possessed. We can understand the object of the feminine beacon; but of what use is all the rest of the pyrotechnic display. To my great regret, I cannot tell. It is and will be, for many a day to come, perhaps for all time, the secret of animal physics, which is deeper than the physics of books.

J. HENRI FABRE
The Glow-worm And Other Beetles

J. Henri Fabre, noted French entomologist, died in 1915, after years of observation on insects and the study of their behavior. During the years since his death we have learned something about the light flashed by the firefly and that emanating from other glow-in-the-dark creatures.

As recently as February 1959 scientists extracted for the first time the glow compounds from a South Seas fish, the *Kinme modoki*. The glow compounds of this fish and other animals including the firefly are (1), a substance known as luciferin that contains a small molecule and (2), an enzyme called luciferase. In the presence of the luciferase the substance with the molecule (the luciferin) decomposes to produce what N. J. Berrill of McGill University calls "a light of elfin quality akin to starlight, shining where or when no other light is seen, shining in answer to its own kind, a response of life to life."

In a general sense the luminescence or phophorescence of the fire-fly can be defined as "the property of emitting light without perceptible heat." When this phenomenon takes place in living organisms it is known as "bioluminescence." For a detailed account of bioluminescence, read *Living Light*, by E. W. Harvey. He died in August 1959, after having written 90 of the nearly 500 scientific papers on the subject of luminescence that have appeared during the past few decades.

The light resulting from the action of the luciferin in the presence of the luciferase may be a true yellow, or it may have a cast that is somewhat blue, green, or red. The color depends upon the species of firefly or lightning bug, to use the popular name for this insect— known, too, in some places, as the lamplighter. The intensity of the flashes and the intervals between flashes also vary with the species, and emanate from the light organs on the abdomen.

The greater part of the firefly family, the *Lampyridae*, is found in tropical and subtropical regions. The family is well represented

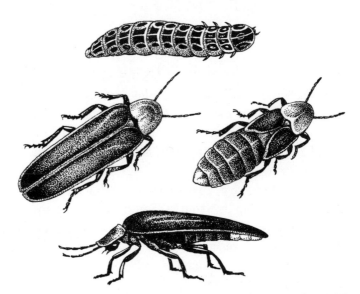

Firefly, *Photinus pyralis;* top: larva; middle left: male; middle right: female; bottom: side view of male

throughout the better part of the United States by some fifty species. One area in our country excepted from the extensive range of this soft-bodied insect is the region of the North Central states and those of the Rocky Mountains.

One species of firefly with which we are apt to be familiar is *Photuris pennsylvanica.* As an adult it measures about one-half to ¾ inch in length. The somewhat oblong body is pale gray above, but a sulphurous yellow on the underside toward the rear. And the paired feelers, or antennae, are long in comparison with the three pairs of short legs.

All fireflies flash a cold light, and that of our familiar species comes from the last segment of the abdomen. The tissues in this part of the body are extremely fat and, like those of other species, are composed of two sets of layered cells. Both layers contain a network of nerves and a number of thread-thin tubes for supplying air. The upper cell layer acts as a reflector composed of many individual parts, while the one below is the light-producing area. This may be defined as luminescent or photogenic. The air tubes supply the oxygen that makes it possible for the insect to produce the flashes that so impressed John Muir and his brother David when they first arrived from their native Scotland and came to south-central Wisconsin. John felt sure that his eyes were playing tricks on him as he watched the millions of fireflies above the meadow near their home, and asked his brother if he, too, saw the will-o'-the-wisp lights.

"Yes," David replied, "it's all covered with shaky fire-sparks."

The function of the light is thought to be a sex-attracting device. If you wish a demonstration of this, collect and imprison some adult fireflies in a glass jar. Then stand the container on your porch railing. In no time at all, other fireflies will be attracted to the flashes of the imprisoned insects, and will fly to the jar and hover around it.

Adult fireflies are not the only form of the insect to generate luminescence. The eggs and larvae of some species also glow, and this is true, too, of those females, which are wingless. The form lacking wings is known as a glowworm, and as such should be treated with the utmost care. Not that I am superstitious but it seems to me that lovers, young males, should be careful in the vicinity of glowworms if there is any stock to be taken in this legend: "If a man should kill a glow-worm, it will endanger his love affair, and may cause the death of his beloved."

The Encyclopedia of Superstitions explains the origin of this belief by saying that only the female glowworm has the luminous tail, which she uses for the purpose of attracting the male. Thus the legend that any male who puts out her light will have his own love affair go awry.

If this be so, then the killing of a glowworm is probably the only influence this insect has on man, for fireflies are of little economic importance. Yet the insects have posed a problem that scientists have been unable to solve. This riddle is the one of cold light—a phenomenon that may have "practical implications."

The diet of the firefly depends upon the species and the various stages of development. The faintly glowing eggs hatch in four or five weeks, and the larva begins to eat at once. It feeds on various soft-bodied creatures including snails and earthworms. Though a few eat vegetables, most are classed as carnivorous.

In its larval form this insect glows during the time it spends underground or in rotted wood and piles of rubbish. It also glows during the pupal stage, which lasts about ten days. The color of the luminescence during these stages is somewhat greenish, but when the insect is in flying form the flashes are a bright yellow-white.

According to Dr. Frank H. Johnson of Princeton University, the luminescence is "a useful tool in investigations of fundamental problems that apply to all living things. For example, it can be used in studies of the effects of drugs, heat, and cold, and antibiotics on organisms as a whole or on their various life processes such as respiration, reproduction, and digestion."

Sexton Beetle
Necrophorus marginatus

(Color Plate 1, facing page 80)

Not so many years ago the sexton of a church frequently had to dig graves in addition to his other duties. Today the digging of a grave is seldom a part of his job description, and though this custom is becoming another item of man's past social history, it continues to be very much a part of the behavior of the sexton beetle.

This beetle is a member of a family (Silphidae) that includes nearly one hundred species in America north of the Rio Grande. Most of them are carrion eaters. Necrophorus marginatus, whose name may be freely translated as "the body carrier," is a dark, bluish-brown insect. The somewhat cylindrical body is about one inch in length, and the forewings, or wing covers, are patterned in red. Now and then this patterning on some individuals is so large that the insect is more red than black—a color variation that might lead you to believe you have discovered a new species if you happen to catch one.

Known as the burying beetle in some localities, the insect is considered beneficial because it is a scavenger. Some authorities say it buries the carcasses of whatever wildlife dies or is killed on its territory. Other authorities of a more cautious nature comment that it is reported that the beetle inters the dead animals it finds—even those the size of a rabbit.

The sexton beetle is attracted to a carcass by the odor of death, which is particularly noticeable on a humid night. If the dead animal lies on soft earth, the beetle first on the scene starts to bury it at once. In short order a second beetle will fly in. The two, usually a male and a female, work together.

If a death occurred where the soil surface is hard, the insects move the body to a better burial spot, and according to John Henry Comstock, "A pair of these insects have been known to roll a large dead rat several feet in order to get it upon a suitable spot for burying." The insects use their six strong legs to tumble the carcass along. To get leverage, a beetle lies on its back, pulls in all six legs, then thrusts upward and forward. The impact on the dead body is like that of six small battering rams.

If no removal of the body is necessary the pair of sexton beetles bury it on the spot. They dig out the earth under the body and place this soil on top of the body. They continue to do so until the body is entirely covered.

Once the corpse is buried the female lays her eggs on it or in a little earthen chamber adjacent to it. The eggs hatch quickly, undoubtedly incubated to some degree by the nearby decomposing flesh. The larva, or grub, is bright yellow. It feeds on the flesh of the buried carcass.

The various stages of growth through which a larva passes are fast-paced. After being fed by its mother for several days, the larva is ready to pupate. It digs into the ground for this quiescent interval from which it will emerge as an adult. When the pupa has been transformed into a full-fledged sexton beetle, it tunnels out of the grave made for the carcass, and as soon as it "surfaces," it flies away to take up the duties imposed upon it by nature.

Whether you call it lucky bug, submarine chaser, or writes-my-name bug, it is still the same insect. These are all pseudonyms for a water-living creature best known as the whirligig beetle—an insect whose shape is like that of a flattened oval and whose lengthwise measurement is about one-half of an inch. Some of these beetles are bluish black but others have a decidedly brown cast to the underlying black. But the beetle of either color has a lustered effect, almost as if the wing covers had been dusted with flecks of copper.

The whirligig beetle lives up to its name. Apparently the insect never had any appreciable degree of what is called "directional sense," or else it was aborted aeons ago. For its movements never prove the geometric axiom that a straight line is the shortest distance between two points. It skims along over the surface of the water in a series of darting curves or semicircles that never seem to carry it forward and which have been described as "erratic."

Nature has seen to it that the beetle is well adapted for the life it leads as a member of stream or pond community. The front pair of legs are attached to the body in such a way that they extend forward; those in the rear are flattened so that they resemble small paddles. The rear legs are also fringed to offer as much resistance as possible to the water when the beetle forces them backward as a boatman uses his oars. The eyes, one on each side of the head, are divided into two parts. The upper half is above the water surface and the lower half is beneath water level. This permits dual vision, as it were; the insect can see what takes place out of the water and see, too, what is taking place in it.

The whirligig beetle seems to like the company of its own kind. You frequently see good-sized groups of them on the surface of quiet or running water, darting around one another in what appears to be an endless, pointless series of gyrations. Any disturbance puts an end to surface movements and sends the beetle into a deep dive. Sometimes it darts rapidly away in a zigzag fashion. Presumably it has another means of protecting itself. The odor of apple seeds is peculiar to the insect, and in times of danger the odor becomes much more noticeable. Apparently the aroma is not to the liking of some predators, for they quit chasing their prey.

Once a mating is consummated, the female lays one or many eggs. These tiny white cylinders are attached singly or in clusters to the submerged parts of aquatic plants. The larva that comes from the egg is slender, somewhat flat, and rather colorless. During the underwater part of its life, the creature breathes through gills that have the appearance of tiny tufts of feathers.

The first food is probably the larvae of the mayfly and of other more helpless stream creatures. When the time comes to pupate the larva of a whirligig beetle quits the water for the side of a pond or stream. On land it spins a tiny, jerry-built casing that has the consistency of paper and the color of moleskin. The beetle-to-be passes about a month housed in this drab, flimsy affair before the transformation from pupa to adult is complete. Then the adult breaks out of its gray casing and seeks water as quickly as possible. Upon reaching this usual habitat, it takes off over the surface in the whirling fashion that earned the insect its familiar common name.

Ground Beetle
Calosoma scrutator

(*Color Plate I, facing page 80*)

Calosoma scrutator is atypical among the thousand or so members of the ground-beetle family in this country. The quirk that differentiates this common beetle of the family *Carabidae* from all the others is an ability to climb trees.

Unless you are in the habit of keeping late hours outdoors, your chances of seeing the insect up a tree are slight. This good-sized beetle is one member of that part of the animal community that is up and about at night.

Placed lengthwise on a rule, *C. scrutator* measures about 1¼ inches. Held alongside of a color chart, you would have to rule out black or any color that is darkling—the name for one group of beetles. This insect is more brightly hued than most members of its family, and the full effect of the coloring can be seen when it rests. Then the hind wings are folded up and under the leathery forewings—the wing covers. These are green with rose-colored margins and they appear as if they had been lacquered.

Suitably enough the ground beetle overwinters in the ground. It may pass the dormant state either as a pupa or as an adult, and the coming of spring awakens either of them. Now the pupa has to undergo the transformation that changes it into adult form, while the roused female has to lay eggs. These are sometimes encased in mud cells attached to leaves.

As soon as it hatches, the larva is up and about. Even in this form, the ground beetle can and does prey on other soft-bodied forms of insects such as caterpillars. Frequently its prey is the type that is inimical to man's interests. There are times when the larva actually hunts for its prey, and there are also times when it waits in a burrow for some creature to pass by.

During the larval stage it feeds voraciously and during this same period it undergoes two molts in two weeks. Then for an additional two weeks it becomes an inactive creature, a stage that is followed by a week in which it is a pupa.

At the end of twenty-one days, give or take a few hours, an adult beetle charged with energy comes into being. It may have a life span of as much as a year. By day it hides under stones and debris of all sorts; by night it comes out to scurry around in search of food. While hunting, *C. scrutator* occasionally takes wing to get from one place to another; less frequently it climbs trees to track down a fat caterpillar. A predilection for this type of food is the reason this beetle is given another name: the caterpillar hunter.

CLICK BEETLES
Family *Elateridae*

If you do not know a click beetle from firsthand observation, you are probably familiar with the insect from crossword puzzles. A species often encountered there is the eyed elater (*Alaus oculatus*)—a dreary-looking creature that is a grayish black. The almost monochromatic color scheme is relieved slightly by two oval black spots well forward on the body about opposite the forelegs, and from these eyelike markings comes the common name of this particular beetle. Like the other members of its immediate family, it has a flexible joint at the base of the wing covers.

The construction of the joint is such that it bends easily and with an action that is lightning quick. This is a convenient arrangement for the click beetle that falls or lands on its back. When one of these insects, sometimes called snapping beetles too, lands bottom-side up, it lies quietly for a minute or so, then activates the joint. There is a loud click or snap, and the eyed elater flips into the air.

Sometimes the first flip is successful and the flipper lands on its feet. At other times the maneuver has to be repeated again and again to get the desired result. Once on its six feet the animal scurries away. The course may be through grassy sod or over decaying wood—both habitats frequented by this beetle. Apparently bright lights are a lure, for it and other members of the family gather in well-illuminated areas.

The eyed elater passes the winter in a state of suspended animation, and does so either as an adult or an undeveloped larva. Late in the spring the adult emerges from its overwintering spot, feeds for several days, and then mates. Almost immediately thereafter the female deposits in the sod numbers of speck-sized eggs, white, yellow-white, or yellow in color. The larva that hatches has a hard round shell which is either yellow or brown.

In its larval stage the click beetle is known as a wireworm. As such it feeds on the roots and stems of various garden plants and those grown on a large scale by agriculturists. Control is necessary when the soil is really infested. It was discovered during one study that certain wireworms, the larval forms of the *Agriotes* beetles, infested a single acre at numbers calculated at 3,000,000 to 25,000,000.

The shortest time in which the click beetle completes its life cycle is about a year. However, the time span from hatching until death may be as long as four years. The larva pupates in a self-constructed cell some six inches underground. It stays within its soil-covered casing for about a month before it emerges as an adult —the form in which it is capable of clicking.

Boll Weevil
Cotton Boll Weevil
Anthonomus grandis

In Enterprise, a town in southeastern Alabama, you will find a monumental fountain on which is inscribed:

In profound appreciation
Of the Boll Weevil
And what it has done
As the herald of prosperity
This monument was erected
By the citizens of
Enterprise, Coffee County, Alabama

The monument and the inscription seem strange indeed when you think of the losses caused by the boll weevil, often also called the cotton boll weevil. Each year the insect damages cotton and cottonseed to an extent estimated at $203 million in the thirteen states, now the North American range of this particular member of the family *Curculionidae*, the snout beetles or weevils.

Originally this small beaked insect was not native north of the Rio Grande. No one knows whether its original home was Mexico or some of the countries farther south. But no matter its point of origin, the boll weevil emigrated from Mexico into the United States. The point of entry was in the vicinity of Brownsville, Texas, and the date of entry was about 1892. By 1894 the quarter-inch creature was established in six Texas counties. For the next twenty years it advanced its front 40 to 160 miles a year. The result of this forward push was that by 1922 the insect had infested more than 85 per cent of the states comprising the Cotton Belt.

The boll weevil was first identified by Boheman, a Swedish entomologist, who got specimens from Mexico. The insect is ¼ of an inch in length and horizontally it measures about a third as much. The color is influenced by age; it varies from light yellow to gray or nearly black, with the older weevil the darkest.

This insect is one that overwinters as an adult. Woodsy trash or almost any protected spot near cotton fields serves as a hideaway during the months that designate winter. As soon as the last frosts are over the weevils return to the fields. The insect likes to feed on the flower bud, known as the square, but also eats the bolls, or fruits.

Squares, too, are the preferred part of the plant in which to lay eggs. With her long snout the female makes a deep hole in the bud. She deposits one egg in each puncture. It takes only three to five days for the larva, or grub, to hatch. Then for another week or two the grub feeds on the square or boll in which it hatched. With the cessation of feeding, a grub turns into a pupa—a stage that lasts from three to five days. As soon as the insect becomes an adult, it cuts its way out.

An adult of either sex starts to eat at once—buds, blossoms, or bolls. Three or four days' feeding conditions a female so well that she is ready to lay eggs. As it only takes three weeks in the cycle from egg to adult, there may be as many as seven generations a year.

The punctures made in a cotton plant by the boll weevil with its long snout open up or widen. This causes the buds to yellow, die, and drop off. Small bolls damaged by the insect also drop off. Though larger bolls may be punctured they do not detach themselves from the plant, but the lint from them is cut, decayed, and stained brown.

If it were not for some climatic and other natural controls, the growing of cotton would be almost impossible. When winter temperatures are low or those in summer are unusually high, there are fewer boll weevils. Then, too, more than 90 per cent of the over-wintering adults die during the season; many survivors of the winter die before they can produce eggs; and during the egg and larval stages, birds and parasites and predators keep the population of boll weevils from reaching numbers that would be impossible to count. Direct control, that is, control with dusts and sprays, is used extensively. And except for two years (1898–1900), research to find ways to reduce the losses caused by the insect has been conducted by the U. S. Department of Agriculture and various state agencies.

One result of this research has been the adoption of a stalk-destruction program in Texas and Mexico throughout the Rio

Grande valley. The annual program cleans up one million acres used for cotton growing. All planting is completed by March 11 and all stalks are destroyed by August 31. Then cotton-plant debris, seedlings, and sprouted cotton plants are plowed under. This procedure makes a host-free interlude between crops, and as a result considerably less cotton and cottonseed is ruined by these weevils.

But weevil damage and the resultant losses in Coffee County, Alabama, have been overcome in another way. In 1915 the emigrating insect reached this cotton-growing region. The crop was ruined and so was the one in the following year. Then contrary to traditional agricultural practices of the area, the citizens of Coffee County planted such other crops as corn, hay, and potatoes. Sugar cane was planted, too, and a number of hogs were raised. The growing of the new crops and the rearing of the livestock changed the fortunes of the former cotton growers. But one other agricultural adventure was more profitable than all the others. Everybody planted peanuts, or goobers, as they are frequently called in the South. And reports have it that the peanut crop for 1918 brought in $5 million. When the memorial in the form of a fountain was up, one local writer commented wryly: "The erection of the world's famed monument to the Cotton Boll Weevil at Enterprise, Alabama, was prompted and inspired by pure motives, which inspiration and motives will live forever."

The boll weevil is but one of the snout weevils. Another member of the family is the bean weevil—a pantry pest by the scientific name *Acanthoscelides obtectus*. Housewives are likely to be familiar with the insect; it measures no more than one-eighth of an inch in length. The body tapers sharply toward the head and is marked by white. The bean weevil flies both outdoors and indoors. Outdoors the female lays her eggs in bean pods. Some of these beetles reach maturity during the growing season and bore their ways out of the pods. Others are brought indoors when the beans are put in storage. If the place of storing is cold the larva remains inactive, but if the temperature is comparable to that of summer, the larva develops, and the house may be full of these four-winged insects. Fumigation clears them out in a hurry.

Another snout beetle, the strawberry weevil, can ruin a bed of these fruits. It lays an egg in the bud of the berry, then girdles the stem so that the bud drops off. The apple is not free from weevil depredations, either. The apple curculio—the technical name for weevil is curculio—deposits its eggs in young apples. The fruits often drop to the ground, and are wormy—even if they grow large enough to be harvested. These and other snout beetles, the *Rhynchophora*, injure fruits, garden truck, and agricultural crops to an extent estimated at more than $500,000,000 a year.

Engelmann Spruce Beetle
Dendroctonus engelmanni

> Ten years ago the Engelmann spruce forests in the higher Rocky Mountains of Colorado were a sight to behold. . . . Tall, green, silent, majestic, . . . an important asset to our natural wealth and welfare.
> Today, on much of that ground stand millions of dead trees —graceless, lifeless, valueless. They will stand there twenty years more, ghost trees and tragic evidence of how fast and silently a tiny insect can do its damage. . . .

In part these are the opening paragraphs of "Four Billion Feet of Beetle-killed Spruce," by N. D. Wygant and Arthur L. Nelson in the *Yearbook of Agriculture 1949*. The insect that killed these millions of trees is the Engelmann spruce beetle—one in a large family of wood-boring or bark-boring beetles known as the *Scolytidae*. It is a hard-shelled beetle, sometimes reddish-brown or then again almost black, or perhaps even a color between the first two. It is comparable in size to the housefly, cylindrical in shape, and no longer than ¼ inch.

In its adult form the Engelmann spruce beetle starts to fly in June and July. After a trial flight or two it goes directly to standing green trees or those but recently felled. The insects pair off—one male and one female to a tree-destroying team. Though the female does most of the work in preparing a place for the eggs, the male raises some of the young that hatch, while she raises the rest.

The female bores an opening into the tree, then goes on to hollow out a thread-thin vertical tunnel between the bark and the wood. Known as the egg gallery, it is parallel to the grain of the wood. A square foot of bark usually contains six or eight galleries. The eggs in each gallery number a hundred or more, and are deposited in three or four clutches.

Three or four weeks pass before an Engelmann spruce beetle hatches. A recently hatched larva starts to feed on the juicy inner bark, and continues to do so all through the summer and well into the fall. As soon as cold weather sets in, the larva becomes dormant and passes this quiet interval in safety. The inner bark insulates it against the cold weather and the winds that whip the high country.

When it is again springtime in the Rockies, the larva resumes feeding. With the advance of summer, it becomes mature, transforms into a pupa, and undergoes those changes that create the adult form. The transformation is complete by midsummer, but the beetle does not emerge from its birthplace at once. It continues to feed on the inner bark. Toward fall some beetles leave the tunnels in which they grew up, and move down to the base of the tree. Here they bore into the bark under which they stay during the second winter of their lives. Other young adults stay where they were reared. Then, when the second spring of the life cycle comes around, they emerge and fly away to attack living trees in their vicinity—a procedure followed by those near the base of the "nursery" tree.

Within its own plant and animal community the Engelmann spruce beetle has a control. This is the northern three-toed woodpecker, a black and white bird that locates an infested tree, chips off the outer bark, then feeds on the now unprotected beetles. How great an influence this woodpecker exerts as a control depends upon the number of birds in a given locale. When the woodpeckers are abundant at least 45 per cent of a beetle brood is destroyed and not infrequently the destruction has been as much as 95 per cent. Stands of predominantly young and vigorous trees in areas where good growth conditions prevail are less subject to attack, for the insect prefers large mature trees.

Between 1942 and 1948 the Engelmann spruce beetle killed four billion board feet of stumpage. This could have been turned into lumber for 400,000 frame houses with five rooms to a house. The estimated value of live standing trees is $8 million, while the value of the products that might have been manufactured from these trees is $200 million.

The beetle was first noted in 1941 on the White River National Forest—a region of spectacular scenery, alpine lakes, and wilderness areas in Colorado. Nine years went by before the Federal Forest Service got funds for large-scale control. For the next five years (1950–1955) more than 2,870,000 gallons of insecticides were used. Nearly 1,630,000 trees were treated at an average cost of $3.25 each. Private timber operators cooperated by removing infected trees on their lands, and the three-toed woodpecker worked as usual. On New Year's Day of 1956 *The New York Times* reported that war on the beetle was gaining; in fact the paper went so far as to say that it was in the mopping-up stage. Though this campaign to eradicate the Engelmann spruce beetle has been successful, the insect is still a threat to forested areas in other sections of the West.

The Engelmann spruce beetle and such other species as the southern pine beetle, the eastern spruce beetle, and the more widely distributed Ips engraver are an ever-present threat to the woods and forests of America. They represent only a few of the many insects that threaten our welfare and a large part of our economy.

One of the many values of our woods and forests is that they act as water reservoirs because the foliage of the trees breaks the force of the rainfall, and, as the rain drips from the trees, the soil can absorb more water. That the woods and forests are important to our economy is shown by the revenue from our National Forests for these five years:

1945	$ 16,273,800
1950	34,484,598
1955	79,520,880
1957	111,588,594
1958	91,545,820

Because woods and forests act as water reservoirs and bring in so much revenue, you can see why it is necessary to manage them for maximum benefits and yields. Such management includes the control of insects. State and Federal agencies have programs to check insect damage; to study insect-borne diseases such as oak wilt; and to develop by forest genetics trees that are pest-resistant.

6 BUTTERFLIES, SKIPPERS, and MOTHS

The Caterpillar and Alice looked at each other for some time in silence; at last the Caterpillar took the hookah out of his mouth, and addressed her in a languid, sleepy voice.
"Who are you?" asked the Caterpillar.
                              Alice's Adventures in Wonderland

The question nonplussed Alice because she felt that she did not know who she was after so many changes in height. What was more, she felt that it was no way to begin a conversation. She might have countered with a question of her own. She could have said, "Who are you going to be eventually?" For a caterpillar is a stage in the life of any scale-winged insect—whether butterfly, skipper, or moth.

The ten thousand or so species of butterflies, skippers, and moths in North American pass through similar life stages. This is a complicated development known as indirect, or complete, metamorphosis and involves radical changes in form and structure. First, the egg is usually laid on the plant that will be host to the larval form of the insect; second, the larva or caterpillar that feeds on the plant to which the egg was attached; third, the pupa or chrysalis—the stage achieved after a series of molts and instars (intervals between molts), and one that is passed in some sort of casing; and, fourth, the adult, or imago, when the insect emerges from its casing, cocoon, or chrysalid as a perfect four-winged, six-legged creature.

Butterflies, skippers, and moths belong to the order *Lepidoptera*, a name that comes from two Greek words meaning "scale" and "wings." The wings are membranous and covered with tiny overlapping scales. No wider than a human hair, the scales come off as dust if one of these insects is handled, and the wings are then left clear.

The insects designated as *Lepidoptera* differ in physical characteristics and individual behavior. Butterflies and skippers have body structures and quirks of behavior that are peculiar to them. These peculiarities distinguish them from moths, and as a result the order is sometimes divided into two suborders. Though this classification is quite proper and the one used in the 1957 edition of *The Encyclopedia Americana*, it is considered outmoded by some authorities. You may accept or disregard this division as your inclination or training dictates. For those who like, or use, suborders, here they are. The butterflies and skippers belong to the suborder *Rhopalocera*—a term derived from two Greek words, and one that means "a club plus a horn." The scientific name for the suborder of the moths is *Heterocera*, signifying that their antennae, the horns, are "otherwise or different" from those of their close relatives the butterflies and the skippers.

The common name, butterfly, is the one first used to describe the various yellow species. Presumably someone thought of these insects as yellow flies despite the fact that a fly has only two wings whereas the butterfly has four. Together with the skipper and the moth, the butterfly is descended from a remote common ancestor—represented today by two families of moths, the *Jugates*, in form intermediate between primitive insects and those now on earth. The *Jugates* are a link with the past, in itself nothing more than a prologue to the insect world of today and one in which, if you care to, you can find pleasure and profit.

BUTTERFLIES
Order *Lepidoptera*
Suborder *Rhopalocera*

The wings of the butterfly are broad, and the colors of the pigments in the scales are red, yellow, black, and white. The blues, the greens, and the metallic iridescent hues are usually the result of refraction, and are more typical of tropical species. Generally speaking the scales are on both the under and the upper sides of the wings. Those on the forewings of some males are so arranged that they form tiny tufts or folds. These scales are known as "androconia," and have a special purpose. In connection with certain glands, the so-called alluring glands, they give off an odor that attracts the females. One butterfly that is distinguished by these specialized scales is the aphrodite fritillary (*Speyeria aphrodite*)— a brown, black-spotted species of the United States.

The antennae of the butterfly are located on the forepart of the head, and the tips are enlarged so that they form little knobs. This enlargement gives the antennae the appearance of tiny golf clubs held upside down. The antennae are multiple-purpose organs; they are used for tasting, touching, smelling, and hearing.

The broad wings of the butterfly are attached to a slender body. You can study the way in which the butterfly manipulates its wings, for it is active during the day. Pick a bright, sunny day for your observation; most butterflies are so addicted to light that many of them do not fly when it is overcast. After flitting over meadow or field or along a road, a butterfly settles down with its wings held vertically over the back or slightly expanded. This is one way of differentiating a butterfly from a moth, which usually holds its wings horizontally when at rest.

Monarch Butterfly
Danaus plexippus

During 1950 and 1951, Dr. Frederick Urquhart of the Royal Ontario Museum at Toronto tagged 3,000 monarch butterflies. He had been labeling this showy black-and-orange insect since 1938 in an attempt to see how far south it flew in the fall. His first attempts were failures, for a label that stays in place on a monarch's wing is apt to make the insect instable during flight.

Dr. Urquhart's work with the monarch was interrupted by World War II. He had a tour of duty with the Royal Canadian Air Force, during which he became well versed in the principles of aerodynamics. When he returned to his tagging experiments, he

Monarch Butterfly, *Danaus plexippus,* on milkweed; top left:
cocoon; bottom right: larva; two adults on flowers

decided to attach a small paper label to the leading edge of the wing, close to the body rather than out on the wing surface. He cut a tiny hole in the wing, then folded the paper label over the hole, and glued the paper to itself. He had learned by trial and error that the wing of a butterfly is practically adhesive-proof.

The 3,000 butterflies set free during 1950 and 1951 had labels attached in the new way. But results were disappointing, for this tagging brought only one reply, mailed some forty miles from Toronto.

Dr. Urquhart continued his tagging, though the results were not encouraging. The labels attached to butterfly wings were not staying in place during wet weather. By this time, due to publicity, a great many people were interested in the doctor's work. In 1955, 10,000 monarchs were tagged by 382 people interested in the project. Results were a little more encouraging. There were thirty letters stating where a tagged monarch had been found; some of them came from as far away as Virginia.

Still it seemed strange that of 10,000 labeled butterflies only thirty had been discovered and reported. Dr. Urquhart decided on two emergency actions: traveling and tasting. To conduct what was in fact a field experiment the doctor first went South, and he ate a number of monarchs in the field. His feeding on butterflies was to learn whether the insects actually secreted an acid fluid—a then common belief—presumed to be the insect's defense against predators.

The monarch butterfly, Dr. Urquhart learned, has no more flavor than dry toast. He also had additional proof that these butterflies were far from unpalatable to certain predators. The birds of the area ate monarchs as fast as they could catch them. In time the doctor learned why. The white paper label on the tagged butterflies spoiled the natural color pattern that apparently protected untagged monarchs from most predators.*

To counteract bird predation in 1956, Dr. Urquhart and his assistants tagged 20,000 monarchs—double the number usually

* For a detailed account of "Production of Form for an Optical Effect," see *Animal Forms and Patterns, a Study of the Appearance of Animals*, by Adolf Portmann, University of Basel, published 1952, Faber and Faber, Ltd., London.

tagged. By December of the same year the number of marked butterflies reported was 125. Some of these released after tagging in Ontario had flown all the way to Texas and the Gulf Coast.

You will find the monarch in any part of the country in which milkweed grows. This plant, the only food of the larva, springs up in any available growing area including vacant city lots. Therefore the butterfly is one that city dwellers can see.

The adult monarch is with us during most of the summer. Large and reddish brown, this butterfly has wings veined in black—a color repeated in the borders of the wings. They are amply dotted with many small white spots, and have a spread of three and one-half to four inches.

Even on the most northerly parts of its range there are apt to be several generations of monarchs each year. The last generation, the one that matures a little before cold weather sets in, is the one to migrate. In the fall the monarchs gather by the thousands at some favorite spot, settling down on a bush or a tree until it is covered with a fluttering canopy. Then all at once these native North American insects take off on their southward flight.

The monarch, also known as the king billy or milkweed butterfly, migrates from Ontario to Florida in about three weeks. Others fly to California. At the end of the migration the monarch passes the winter in hedges or other sheltered places, with the same spot often used year after year by succeeding generations.

In the spring, individuals start north. On the return to breeding areas, the monarch looks like a different creature. Gone are the brilliant colors of the year before; they have been replaced by an all-over dusty brown. On the trip north the female stops to lay eggs on young milkweed plants. She glues the tiny, ribbed eggs, somewhat greenish and cone-shaped, to the undersides of leaves.

Once a caterpillar hatches, it starts to feed on the milkweed plant. Feeding is interrupted for brief intervals, while the caterpillar sheds its too tight skin. By the time the creature is fully grown its green skin is banded by stripes of yellow and black.

Suddenly all feeding stops. The caterpillar seeks a resting place. This may be a tree trunk, a fence post, or even the underside of an immature milkweed pod. The pupa spins a little rosette of silk to which it glues its tail and from which it dangles head down. About twenty-four hours after it has hung itself up, the skin splits. If you discover a caterpillar in this condition, you will see that within the split skin lies the chrysalis. This is the form that contains all the vital organs and the newly formed wings and the sucking mouth parts— a life stage lasting eight to twelve days. At the end of this quiet interval, the chrysalis cracks, and in time an adult monarch struggles out. The colors are bright but the wings are limp and crumpled and the body seems unusually large.

The adult clings to the casing from which it just emerged. It has to wait for the body to harden and the wings to expand and dry. Fluids contained in the body flow into the veins of the wings to help with their expansion and thus the size of the body is reduced. Finally the adult monarch is ready to fly away, and heads north.

During the northward migration of the monarch, the females lay eggs. By fall the last generation reaches Canada. The stay there is a short one, for as soon as cold weather is at hand, these most recently born monarchs band together for the southward migration. Records show that a round trip may cover a distance of two thousand miles or more. The flight may be at the rate of twenty-five miles an hour and against headwinds of as much as forty miles an hour. It may be over a large expanse of open water about which the monarch is supposed to have a morbid fear. Nevertheless the monarch has emigrated to Hawaii, where it is one of the most conspicuous of the lowland butterflies.

Viceroy Butterfly
Limenitis archippus

The viceroy escapes many predators because Nature has made it a mimic. In pattern and in color it so closely resembles the monarch that many predators leave the viceroy alone on a range that includes every part of the United States except the Northwest. Actually the viceroy differs from the other species because its wingspread is about two and three-quarter inches over-all, and the color of the wings is more of an orange-brown or cinnamon-buff.

The veins and the borders appear to be outlined in black velvet and dotted with little tufts of ermine-white. A viceroy is easily distinguished from other butterflies by a black band on each hind wing.

The viceroy develops from a diminutive egg which, like those of other scale-winged insects, is shaped like a hen's egg. For the covering is hard and contains the food for the animal that is to hatch. The larva, or caterpillar, that develops within the egg eventually breaks out, and is a brown or olive-green creature with a body covered by wartlike tubercles. These small knoblike affairs make the skin appear rough and bumpy.

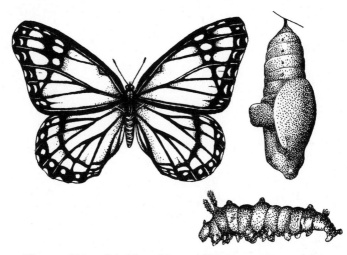

Viceroy Butterfly, *Limenitis archippus;* cocoon at right,
larva at bottom

As soon as it hatches the caterpillar starts to feed. It likes the leaves of such trees as the aspen, the poplar, and the willow. Feeding is interrupted only for the necessary four or five molts that bring it to the full growth of about one inch. Shortly thereafter the caterpillar is ready to pupate. Now it rolls itself inside a leaf that is attached to a twig. This retreat the caterpillar lines with a silky material. Thus protected from the elements, the creature passes the quiescent stage of its life when it is known as a pupa and its case is called a chrysalid—a name derived from *chrysos,* the Greek word for gold. And it is suitable for the viceroy and many

SILVER-SPOTTED SKIPPER
(underside)
Epargyreus clarus

PARNASSIUS
(female)
Parnassius smintheus

GIANT
SWALLOWTAIL
Papilio cresphontes

MOURNING-CLOAK
Nymphalis antiopa

ZEBRA
SWALLOWTAIL
Papilio marcellus

CABBAGE WHITE
Pieris rapae

other butterflies because the chrysalids (pupal cases) are often dotted with what appears to be little flecks of gold leaf.

All winter long the pupal case of the viceroy dangles from its twig. When the weather is sufficiently warm the following spring, the butterfly-to-be becomes active within its case. The false or pro-legs disappear, but the three pairs attached to the thorax are retained. These become the three pairs of the butterfly. To soften the hard casing that has protected it, the insect secretes a fluid. Then it pushes free—a wet young butterfly with wings that are soft, crumpled, and surprisingly small.

The first thing the newly emerged butterfly looks for is something to cling to. As soon as it finds a support it hangs itself upside down, holding on by its three pairs of feet. It fans its wings until they are hard, dry, and fully expanded. Now the viceroy is ready to become airborne and flit about the countryside with other butterflies, including the monarch that it so closely resembles.

Both species are members of the family *Nymphalidae*, whose front legs are not sufficiently developed to be of any help in walking. The feet have the appearance of little brushes, and for this reason the *Nymphalidae* are frequently called the "Brush-footed Butterflies."

Mourning-cloak Butterfly
Nymphalis antiopa
(Color Plate II, facing page 106)

The mourning-cloak seems unable to wait until winter is over. Sometimes it is found flying through wooded areas when there is still plenty of snow on the ground; frequently this purple-brown butterfly is out and about before there is any assurance that spring is here to stay. It is also one of the earliest-flying butterflies in England, where it is called the "Camberwell beauty."

The range of the mourning-cloak is the temperate regions of the world. It is found throughout North America, and south to Guatemala. Of all our butterflies that hibernate as adults, the mourning-cloak is the largest: in its adult form it has a wing span that may measure as much as 3½ inches. The forewings of the male are maroon and are bordered with a band as yellow as straw. The band on the upper side of the forewings is dotted with spots of blue, while the underside of the wings is a brownish black. The hind wings are similar to the forewings but have the barest hint of "tails." As a rule the female is similar to the male. Infrequently you will find a mourning-cloak that has an exceptionally wide wing border.

During June, July, and August you are apt to see the mourning-cloak in the vicinity of woodlands. Early in the season the female lays her eggs around the twigs of elms, poplars, and willows. Each egg is shaped like a tiny barrel and may be dark brown or black. The hatching of an egg depends in part upon the prevailing temperatures, and may take as few as six days or as many as sixteen.

The larva, or caterpillar, that hatches seems to be encased in black velvet. The body is covered with tiny spines, and is splotched with many white dots and a few that are red. By the time a larva is fully grown it measures about two inches. The larvae from a given egg mass often stay together, feeding on the leaves of the twig on which they hatched. This combined feeding can strip a twig or even a small branch of all its leaves.

The caterpillar of the mourning-cloak sheds its skin four times. It emerges from each molt somewhat larger, and by the time it has undergone the fourth molt it is almost ready to pupate. It feeds voraciously for a time, then stops all feeding, and attaches itself to a twig in a little brown case of silken texture. So protected, it hangs head down for at least a week and perhaps for two or more weeks. The pupa, or chrysalis, is dark brown with red points. During this period of quiescence, gradual changes are taking place in the body of the caterpillar. Once all the changes are effected, the insect works its way out of the chrysalid, and as soon as the body is hard and the wings are full-sized and dry, the now perfect butterfly is ready to flit off in search of nectar. It feeds by drawing up nectar through its long curled "tongue."

When the sources of the mourning-cloak's liquid diet are no longer available, the insect hibernates. In this country it seeks the safety of a tree hollow, but in Norway and Sweden it overwinters in wood stacks. When spring comes to Scandinavia, the mourning-cloak comes out of hiding. It feeds on the nectar found in the golden catkins of the broad-leaved willow. Then strengthened by its first meal or meals, the mourning-cloak quits Scandinavia to fly across the North Sea to England.

Cabbage White Butterfly
Pieris rapae

(Color Plate II, facing page 106)

The mating flight of this small white butterfly has been described as a "summer idyll that frequently passes unnoticed." Several males, glistening white in the sunshine, spiral upward in pursuit of a female—similar in appearance to the males, but with forewings marked with two black spots instead of one. When a mating has been consummated, the female is ready to lay her eggs. And such is the nature of this butterfly that in the North there are commonly three broods in a season while in the South there are sometimes as many as six.

The cabbage white lays one egg at a time on the undersides of the leaves of such plants as cabbage, broccoli, and mustard. Each yellow egg is shaped like a tiny flask and has twelve vertical ribs. An egg hatches in about one week, and the caterpillar, or larva, that emerges is green. Three stripes run lengthwise along the cylindrical body, that has a sparse covering of hair. The caterpillar is an enormous feeder, and often eats its way right into a head of cabbage. The damage it does to this plant and related varieties makes the larval form a serious crop pest.

This caterpillar feeds for two or three weeks, and in the meantime undergoes several molts, the last of which brings it to the full length of about one inch. Then it stops feeding just before it is ready to enter the pupal stage. As a pupa it is a slender green creature about ⅝ of an inch in length and shaped in a somewhat angular fashion. In its pre-butterfly form, the insect attaches itself to a twig with a loop of thread that is silken in texture. It does not hang head down, but remains more or less parallel to the twig around which it cast the silken loop.

The quiescent interval may be ten days or the entire winter if the insect is one from the last brood of the season. The creature emerges from its winter casing early in the spring—so early, in fact, that after its drying out period it is flitting around long before our two native cabbage butterflies are to be seen. One native species is the checkered white (*Pieris protodice*), sometimes called the southern cabbage butterfly; the other is the old-fashioned cabbage butterfly (*P. napi*, or *oleracea*)—known also as the mustard white and the gray-veined white. The two natives are not nearly so abundant as they used to be. Apparently *P. rapae* has driven them from much of their former range—areas in which various garden plants are cultivated. Now the two native species are to be found in uncultivated areas, feeding on various plants of the mustard family.

P. rapae, frequently referred to as the imported cabbage butterfly, was accidentally introduced from Europe. Its first appearance in the New World was at Quebec in 1860, and then in 1868 it was discovered in New York. Now you can net a specimen of the exotic anywhere in the United States and throughout the greater part of Canada.

Every so often there is a variation in the usual marking on the wings of the male and the female. Occasionally one lacks the black dots on the upper side of the hind wings, and is given the specific scientific name *immaculata*. Though the name implies that the butterfly is without flaw, fault, or error, this is not so. The feeding habits of the pure white one are no better than those of its black-spotted brethren. In fact, there is a verse extant that comments on the troublesome habits of *immaculata*.

> Though immaculate in dress
>   This species causes much distress.
> For it acts like all its kin,
>   Boring cabbages from outside in.

Painted-lady Butterfly
Vanessa cardui

Another migrant is the painted-lady. Sometimes this widely distributed butterfly migrates in throngs that are miles wide. In the spring of 1924 untold numbers of these butterflies made their fluttering way from Central America north into California and various areas of the Southwest. The flight lasted three days and passed a given point at a rate of almost six miles an hour. And the airborne column was reported to be at least forty miles wide.

Because the painted-lady has almost world-wide distribution, it is known, too, as the cosmopolite. A third name, thistle butterfly, is most appropriate because the insect feeds primarily on the thistle— a taste that endears it to farmers plagued by these prickly plants with lavender or purple blossoms.

As the painted-lady flits to a thistle, it is borne along on wings that have a spread of about two and three-quarter inches. The upper surface of the wings is brown with overtones of black, but highlighted by irregular streaks of bright orange. The underside of each front wing is a pale rose, but that of each rear wing is a purple-brown with an intermixture of white. And on the underside of each hind wing are four or five eyelike spots.

On its flight north the female lays eggs on such plants as the nettle, the burdock, and the sunflower, in addition to the preferred thistle. The larva, or caterpillar, is a dull-green creature mottled with black. It has a hairy head, a body with a yellow stripe on each side and sprinkled with a few tiny yellow bristles.

At spaced intervals the creature interrupts its enormous consumption of the leaves on the host plant to undergo one of several molts. After each successive skin-shedding it is larger. The last molt produces a fully grown caterpillar, now such a ravenous eater you might be led to believe that the creature knew it must soon fast as a prelude to pupation.

To prepare for this life stage, the caterpillar constructs a coverlet of tiny plant fibers and of silk unreeled from its own body. Then it fastens some leaves together around the casing it fashioned. This is the housing wherein occurs the transformation from pupa to full-fledged butterfly.

During this life stage the chrysalid may be one of three colors: cream, green, or bluish white. But no matter the color the markings are black or brown, and the little rough spots on the casing are frequently gold-tipped. In spite of differences in color at this time, the butterfly that finally comes out of the ruptured chrysalid is always the same hue and size and with like markings.

How the painted-lady passes the winter is an unsettled question. Some entomologists believe that it hibernates as an adult, while others think that each butterfly makes a solo flight south. Some must migrate or else there would be no return flight the following spring. On the other hand, local populations may build up to such numbers that a shortage of food induces emigration. Possibly this is true, for the mass migration of the painted-lady is occasional.

A close relative of the painted-lady is a butterfly of the New World—the American painted-lady (*Vanessa virginiensis*), known too as Hunter's butterfly and painted beauty. This can be differentiated from the more widely distributed species by the fact that the underside of each hind wing has only two eyelike spots instead of the four or five peculiar to its cosmopolitan relative. The caterpillar of the American species looks as if it were sheathed in black velvet, stitched together with gold thread and closed along the sides with small white buttons.

The universal painted-lady and the species found only in the more northerly parts of the New World are so similar in appearance that it is difficult to tell them apart in the field. But the red-admiral (*V. atalanta*), a close relative of both, is more readily identified. On each of the forewings there is a band of red, and on each hind wing there is a band of the same color. Another way to identify the red-admiral outdoors is by its behavior in the air. It is one of the few known insects that is capable of a gliding flight. While airborne it can make a speed of 8.8 miles an hour, pushed along by a wing-beat frequency that is ten times a second. The speed at which the painted-ladies travel is about six miles an hour.

All three butterflies belong to the genus *Vanessa*, and as all three are so closely related and so frequently pictured together, I like to think of the red-admiral as a gallant escort for the two painted-ladies—described in one old butterfly book as having "all the attributes of the eighteenth-century courtesan."

SWALLOWTAILS
Family *Papilionidae*

There are at least twenty species of swallowtails in the United States. Probably the first to be pictured was *Papilio glaucus*, the tiger swallowtail. When Sir Walter Raleigh was governor of Roanoke, one of his associates sketched this swallowtail—a striking yellow-and-black butterfly that exists in two forms. This is a peculiarity common to butterflies and one known as dimorphism.

In the North the female has wings that are yellow on both sides, and barred with black and bordered by this same color in which there is a sprinkling of confetti-like yellow dots. The southern form differs from that of the North in the color of the wings; they are black with a pattern that is barely discernible. The marginal band of the wings is dotted by yellow, and on each hind wing are orange spots and blue scales.

Both forms hatch from the same clutch of eggs. These are nearly round, except for a barely perceptible flattening of one surface that makes a base. The first choice of this butterfly among host plants for its larvae is the wild cherry. The larva that hatches is smooth-skinned, segmented, and green, and on the thorax there is a yellow-green eye spot edged with black.

The length of a full-grown caterpillar is often as much as two inches. The way in which the creature protects itself during this life stage is by the discharge of a sickening musk contained in little forklike scent organs. If you disturb one of these caterpillars, it shows all the symptoms of anger, for it shoots out the forks through little slits in the thorax and, as the musk is dispelled, the insect lashes the upper part of its body back and forth.

The extruded horns, the weaving body, and the general appearance of the caterpillar are enough to scare off any but the most ardent observer of insect behavior, and they usually make the animal safe for further development. When the time comes to pupate, the insect rests on its tail, held in this position by a silky loop of its own spinning and strung around the middle of the body. Now it takes on a form that looks something like a tiny cornucopia.

Eventually this protective casing splits and the actual butterfly appears.

For yet a little while it is quiet as the body hardens and the wings expand and dry. Then it takes off on its first flight, airborne at a speed of about seven miles an hour. And on its first day as a full-fledged butterfly and every day thereafter, this swallowtail is ready to settle down for the night at about six o'clock. It goes to sleep among grasses with the wings folded tightly, thus protected from the cold night air and much less conspicuous.

Zebra Swallowtail, Ajax Butterfly
Papilio ajax

(Color Plate II, facing page 106)

The larva of the zebra swallowtail is known as the "pawpaw" worm. This name is because the favorite food of the caterpillar is the leaf of the pawpaw, a tree of the central and southern United States. When it first hatches the caterpillar is a dull black, but it soon changes into a pale-green creature banded by several circles of yellow and one or two of black. If you move in on a pawpaw worm, it gives off a nauseating odor—probably a defense to keep away predators.

Though the caterpillar feeds all summer long, it does not feed all day long. The preferred time seems to be early in the morning and again late in the afternoon. Feeding of course is interrupted whenever the caterpillar undergoes one of its several molts. By fall it is fully grown, and after an interval during which it eats nothing, it becomes quiescent. In this third stage of life it passes the winter securely attached to a stem of a plant by a loop spun with its own silk and then cast around the upper part of the body.

Zebra swallowtails emerge from their protective casings at different times during the following year. There is an early spring form that has wings with a spread of about 2½ inches. The wings themselves are black and patterned in a pale green, and further brightened on each hind wing by two spots of peacock blue and a single large dot of crimson. On the hind wings of some individuals there is a second, smaller dot of this same crimson.

The "tails" extend back from the outer edges of the two hind wings. The first zebra swallowtails of the season have wings that measure about ½ inch; in the butterflies that emerge in the late spring or early summer, the tails are somewhat longer and the insect itself is slightly larger. The third butterfly of the season, the one that appears in midsummer, is not the brightest though it is the largest of them all. From the outside of one wing to the outside of the other, it may measure 2 7/10 inches, but the wing design is in no way different from the first two of the season. The author of *Animal Forms and Patterns*, Adolf Portmann, has this to say about the way in which the wing design originates:

. . . the two pairs of wings of a butterfly arise from two separate primordia in the caterpillar. The future design originates separately on each wing and while it is still in a folded state. Each part arises separately from the other, but is not independent of it. Directing mechanisms unknown to us control the banded design of the kite swallow-tail and of the swallow-tail butterflies in such a way that when the wings are opened, the banded pattern of the hind wings forms the continuation of the design of the front ones. The position of the wings in the living butterfly ensures this pictorial effect, . . .

Giant Swallowtail
Papilio cresphontes

(Color Plate II, facing page 106)

In the South the caterpillar of the giant swallowtail is called "orange dog" or "orange puppy" because it feeds on the leaves of citrus trees. In the North, where this butterfly is less common, the insect eats the leaves of the ash and the poplar. But North or South, the caterpillar of *Papilio cresphontes* is undoubtedly one of the ugliest of all butterfly larvae.

A full-grown larva measures about 2 inches in length, has a body ridged in orange and brown, and two little horns. The horns are fleshy and may be pulled in or shot out through a slit in the thorax. At the same time the horns are extruded, a rank odor is also expelled.

Though the giant swallowtail is a butterfly of subtropical North America, it is constantly extending its range northward. A few specimens have even been netted in Canada. The whereabouts of the insect on the continent determines how many broods a season there are. Probably one brood a year occurs to the north, whereas farther south there are two, and in the subtropics there may be three or four.

The insect passes through the usual life stages of all *Lepidoptera*. When it emerges from its protective casing there is an interval of quiet while the body hardens and shrinks and the wings expand and dry. Once these developments have taken place the largest of our butterflies is ready to flutter off in search of nectar. When it locates a flower and alights, this swallowtail holds on with its feet, then uncoils its long tongue and siphons off the sweet droplets—the concentrated sugar solution secreted by the petals—attention-attracting devices to lure insects for the purpose of pollination.

In its final form the giant swallowtail has wings that are velvety black on the upper surface, lemon-yellow underneath, and banded by a broad streak of yellow that starts on the hind wings, but loses continuity on the forewings where it becomes a series of dots. The outer edge of each wing is dappled in yellow, while the inner edge of each hind wing has a little crescent of red and an even smaller half-moon of blue. Though the tails of this butterfly are not so long as those of other swallowtails, the wingspread is by far the greatest, sometimes measuring as much as 5½ inches.

The wings of the giant swallowtail, like those of other insects, are extraordinarily efficient. The body of an insect weighs so little that it has no momentum, and so it is necessary for the wings to give lift as well as to pull forward. In a study of insect flight, Professor A. Magnan, College de France, reported that "the downward beat always takes longer than the upward beat." He also stated that either beat helps to support the insect and propel it forward. And so by lifting and pulling its unusually large wings, the giant swallowtail flits to and fro, a master of aerodynamics.

The swallowtails include a group, or subfamily, of white butterflies named the Parnassians. They are creatures of high altitudes and regions of extreme cold. In Asia some live at altitudes of more than 20,000 feet, or nearly 3¾ miles above sea level. In Russia others are found in the center of eastern Siberia, the coldest region on earth. But none of them are found beyond the Arctic Circle, whereas two

North American butterflies do venture to and beyond this snowy region. One is the well-known yellow swallowtail, that ranges from central Alaska north to and beyond the Arctic Circle. The second is another swallowtail, *P. machaon*, a species that flutters north of the Arctic Circle on this continent, and is found, too, in polar regions of Europe.

One of our best-known Parnassians is the mountain butterfly (*Parnassius smintheus*) (Color Plate II, *facing page 106*) that has a wingspread of 2 ¼ to 3 inches. The yellowish-white wings are so thinly scaled that they are nearly transparent. Both pairs may be marked with round red dots circled with black, and the tips of the wing veins are accented by tiny, dark triangles. To find this butterfly you will have to climb high in the mountains from Colorado to California, where the air is cool and sweet.

As a group the Parnassians seldom rise more than a foot or two above the surface of the earth. They fly only in the late morning and early afternoon, flitting back and forth during this brightest part of the day across grassy alpine meadows or drifting up and down mountain valleys with a fairly rapid though seemingly uncertain flight. As the afternoon wanes, the Parnassians that are still active fly more slowly until the cooling air makes them so torpid they are unable to fly, and have to bed down for the night.

Though the two types of swallowtails (*Papilio* and *Parnassius*), are dissimilar in appearance, they have two physical characteristics in common. Each has a type of wing veining peculiar to swallowtails, and each has larvae endowed with scent organs. These organs set swallowtail larvae apart from all other caterpillars, for they are the only ones so endowed.

According to the author of *Hawaiian Nature Notes*, E. H. Bryan, Jr., there are so few butterflies in our fiftieth state that the collector will be disappointed. Of the ten or so species found on these subtropical islands, only two are native. One is the Kamehameha butterfly (*Vanessa tammeamea*), named in honor of the king who ruled in 1816 when the first specimen was captured. The other, a "blue," by the scientific name *Lycaena blackburni*, is a small butterfly of forested areas.

These are only a few of the North American butterflies—some

common, others rare. In addition there are the snout butterflies; the nymphs and the satyrs; the metal marks; and the sulphurs that belong to the same family as the cabbage whites. These butterflies and those of regional and world-wide distribution have long tubular tongues for sucking nectar. As they feed, butterflies assist in the pollination of a great many plants—plants that could not and would not be pollinated in any other way.

Skippers
Family *Hesperiidae*

There are two thousand or so skippers in the world. Of this number nearly two hundred are native to mainland states and parts of Canada and Mexico. The characteristic from which these small *Lepidoptera* get their name is a rapid, darting flight that propels them forward in a series of mincing airborne skips.

The skipper usually flies by day, is frequently in the company of various butterflies. The body is heavier than that of a butterfly; the veining of the wings differs also; and the antennae, or feelers, are generally recurved, hooked, at the tips. Many rest in the same position assumed by resting moths, and hold the hind wings or both pairs of wings horizontally.

The larva, or caterpillar, of a skipper is almost always smooth-skinned, and can be identified by a large head and what has been described as a "thin neck." When the time comes to pupate, the larva makes a sort of rudimentary cocoon—an act that seems to indicate a closer relationship to the moth than to the butterfly. Then too, the pupa is rounded, and such a shape is more typical of the moth than the butterfly.

The skipper undergoes a complete metamorphosis that is similar to that of other *Lepidoptera*. From the egg comes a tiny larva; then molts occur each time the skin becomes too tight, at which point it splits to release a creature of greater size; when the larva is fully grown it suddenly stops feeding to enter the pupal stage, during which it seems in a state of suspended animation. Finally the moment comes when the casing cracks open sufficiently to permit the adult skipper its freedom.

At first the skipper is not ready to fly. The wings have to expand fully and dry thoroughly and the body must harden and assume its normal proportions. In its adult form the skipper has six well-developed legs. The predominant color of most of these insects is a dull brown with overtones of black; they often look so much alike that it is difficult to tell them apart. And though the designation is not particularly definitive, the North American skippers may be grouped as large, medium, and small.

Silver-spotted Skipper
Epargyreus clarus

(Color Plate II, facing page 106)

Among these insects the one known as the silver-spotted skipper is the handsomest. Its somber brown-black is brightened by a large silver spot on the under surface of each hind wing. Each forewing is banded with orange, and the body looks as if there were three V-shaped marks on it.

This skipper is one of the most widely distributed of all these insects. East and west the limits of its range are bounded by the shorelines of the two oceans. There are none in a part of the Northwest and in western Canada. But from the province of Quebec this skipper occurs all the way south to the Isthmus of Panama.

The female lays her tiny eggs on the upper surface of the small leaves of the various locusts. In less than a week the larva, or caterpillar, hatches. The large head is a reddish brown and distinguished by two spots of bright red, a color that is repeated in the first segment of its tapering body.

Almost as soon as it hatches the caterpillar cuts into one side of a leaf. Two parallel cuts are made to the edge of the leaf, but no cut is made opposite the outer edge, for the part still attached is to be used like the top side of an envelope flap. Once the initial work is completed, the tiny insect bends back the leafy flap. This is bound in place with silklike threads from the body of the builder.

You can always tell the leafy little tent of this caterpillar because it has a distinguishing architectural feature—a domelike top.

As soon as the caterpillar molts for the second time, it is forced to quit the first home, for it is far too big to fit in it now. The second dwelling it fashions is devised by using more of the silk from its body to stitch together two adjacent leaves. One end of this second home is left open. During the day the ever-enlarging caterpillar is inactive, but at night it crawls out through the open end of its home to feed upon the locust leaves that, like the feeding insect, are increasing in size.

After the final molt the caterpillar usually leaves its nest and the host tree, and inches its way to the ground. Once it has found some sort of shelter, the caterpillar spins a cocoon that resembles that of a moth, but one that is flimsier. When the cocoon is completed the caterpillar within becomes a chrysalis, and in time emerges from the ruptured casing a skipper complete in every way. At first the insect has a bedraggled appearance, but air and sunshine combine with natural processes to bring into being a creature capable of flight. Then the silver-spotted skipper is ready to become airborne, carried along on wings that have a spread of 1 9/10 inches.

Gold-banded Skipper
Rhaboides cellus

Probably the rarest skipper in the East is the one known as the gold-banded skipper. In the early 1830's a Georgia schoolteacher named John Abbot drew in color three life stages of the insect: the caterpillar, the chrysalis, and the adult form. Nearly one hundred years went by before anyone took a real interest in the gold-banded skipper. Then Dr. Austin H. Clark, a biologist who wrote *Nature Narratives* and other books on natural history, made a detailed study of the insect. Practically every fact known about it is the result of the Doctor's study.

The head of this caterpillar is a Chinese red, a startling contrast to the vivid green of the body. To serve as a retreat in which to rest and molt, the caterpillar stitches together cut or folded leaves, forming a shelter that looks like a tiny tent with a peaked top. Here the caterpillar rests by day, for it is a night feeder that likes the leaves of the button bush, a native North American flowering shrub, and those of the earth pea, commonly called the hog pea because the pods ripen underground like those of the peanut.

The chrysalid in which the insect changes form and structure is black and shining. It looks as if someone had glued tiny white cotton fluffs all over it. Once it has passed the allotted time as a pupa and has passed through the preflight interval, the gold-banded skipper is ready to skim over its range that starts in the vicinity of West Virginia and extends south to Mexico. As it spreads its wings for the first flight, they measure 6 inches from outer edge to outer edge at the greatest width. The color of the wings is a dark brown that lightens somewhat on the under surfaces of the front wings and is relieved on the upper surfaces of the front wings by a band of gold—a sort of hallmark that indicates the rarity of this skipper.

MOTHS
Lepidoptera
Suborder *Heterocera*

The New York Times once reported that a man in Hickory, North Carolina, came into possession of a thousand-dollar bill, such a rarity for him that he considered it a collector's item, and cached it in a metal box for safekeeping. By so doing he was to prove that pride cometh before fall, and to learn, also, that it is not always wise to lay up treasure on earth.

There came a day when the Carolinian wished to show the bill to friends. He threw back the lid of the box with a flourish, then went into a state of what must have been near shock. The bill was not its usual size because moths had eaten half of it. The dispatch did not specify. what kind of moth was responsible for eating five hundred dollars. But it belonged to one of the forty-odd families of moths native to America, north of the Rio Grande.

The mercenary moth and its kin belong to a suborder of the scale-winged insects known as the *Heterocera*. For the beginning naturalist the most practical way of distinguishing a moth from a butterfly is by differences in behavior and physical characteristics. Though there are a few day-flying moths, these plump-bodied insects are usually fly-by-night creatures. At rest the moth holds its wings in telltale positions that differentiate it from a butterfly at ease. Sometimes a moth folds the wings over the body, but at other times it holds them so that they are horizontal to the body.

The body of a moth is plumper than that of a butterfly; the head is small and sets close to the body; and the eyes, like those of so many nocturnal animals, are large and composed of many facets. Some species have simple eyes, the "ocelli," that are placed directly above the large compound eyes. No one knows with any exactness the function of the simple eyes, though they may "help" the larger ones that are for seeing. The large ones may be unprotected ("naked," to use the scientist's term) or they may be lashed. The hairs that form the lashes project from the points at which the various facets meet.

Generally the antennae of most moths differ from the clubbed forms of butterflies. W. J. Holland, author of *The Moth Book*, wrote that the antennae of moths have at least ten different forms. The simplest way to describe the antennae of our common moths is to say they are *not* clubbed.

Two of the most usual types are those known as "filiform," threadlike, or the ones that have the appearance of tiny plumes, "plumose." Some antennae are notched; others are curved; and still others have turns and twists that give them the appearance of fantastically designed skewers. These unusual forms have names of special significance. Antennae that are notched or which have little, knoblike enlargements are said to be nodose—an English version of the Latin *nodosus*, meaning knot. And on that part of the antennae known as the shaft there are usually scales on the upper side.

While in flight the wings of some primitive moth forms are not joined. But many of our more familiar North American moths have a yokelike arrangement that joins the two pairs of wings. This connection is known as the "frenulum," and is of two forms. A male moth has "a single, curved, hooklike projection that is attached to the hind wing," whereas the frenulum of the female is a projection of many tiny bristles. Either of these hooks onto or catches in a structure on the forewing named the "retinaculum"—somewhat in the way a hook catches in the opposing eye.

The wing structure, like that of the butterfly, is a framework of hollow tubes. These function as veins; serve in some instances as nerves; and act as ducts through which air is forced to expand the wings when a moth first emerges from its cocoon. The usual number of veins for each forewing is twelve, while the number for each hind wing is eight. The position of certain veins is one way by which moth families can be classified. Not all adult moths have wings, for some fully grown females have none. This characteristic sets them apart from butterflies, among which normal adults always have four fully developed wings.

The moth is another insect that undergoes a complete metamorphosis, radical changes in form and structure. Its first form is embryonic and represented by an egg. This is deposited by the female on the host plant best suited to meet the food requirements of the species. The eggs are curiously formed, variously colored, and frequently lined and ridged. Most are a single, solid color that may be white, pale green, bluish green, or brown. Occasionally eggs are mottled in such a way as to suggest a design. The most usual shapes are: cylindrical, lenticular, and spherical and hemispherical. Some, such as the eggs of the slug moths, are flattened and circular. All eggs have a minute opening known as the micropyle—from the Greek *mikros* (small) + *pyle* (gate, orifice). The opening permits the sperm to enter and fertilize the egg. The shape of the egg influences the position of the micropyle; on some it is on top but on those that are flattened or lens-shaped it is at the margin.

The second life stage is that of caterpillar. The variations in form are numerous; the color combinations are many; and the types of fleshy protuberances or hairy growths are so odd that the creatures are often grotesque in appearance. The large head, containing the spinneret, is attached to a body composed of thirteen segments. Sometimes the head can be drawn back, so that it is practically hidden by the folds of the first segment. The first three of these segments correspond to the thorax of the adult insect, and each has a pair of legs that match the legs of the final life stage of the moth, that of the perfect insect, or imago.

The number of times the caterpillar molts varies with the species. The usual number is five, but unusual caterpillars may molt only three times or as many as ten. Once the last molt has taken place, the creature is ready to pupate.

Pupation may occur in the ground or aboveground among fallen leaves or other natural litter. If the quiescent interval takes place in the ground the caterpillar forms an earthen cell; if it is aboveground the insect uses the spinneret to make a coccoon. The length of the pupal period varies with the different kinds of moths. When the hour arrives for the pupa to leave its earthen case, it squirms its way to the surface with power furnished by the abdominal segments. Some pupae encased in a cocoon are able to emerge by secreting a fluid from the mouth that breaks or dissolves the threads of the casing.

As soon as the moth emerges from the pupal case, it has to seek a resting place—a haven to which it can cling while drying out. This interval is rapid, and soon the perfect, six-legged insect is ready to fly away on its now strong wings.

The variation in the size of moths is great: the largest may have a wingspread of at least 9, perhaps 10½ inches or even 14 inches if reports about tropical species are true. Others are so small that the wingspread is no more than 1/16 of an inch, and such species and some others are known as *Microlepidoptera*.

The moths with which this section deals are a few of the representative species of North America, and are selected from the more familiar families including bell; clearwing; geometer; goat; miller; puss, silkworm, and smoky; snout; sphinx; tent caterpillar; tiger; and tussock.

Banded Woolly Bear
Isabella Tiger Moth
Isia isabella

(*Color Plate III, facing page 142*)

The reddish brown caterpillar with black bands and bristly hair that we know as the woolly bear was mentioned as long ago as 1608. In that year the *History of Serpents* by Topsell was published, and the author wrote the following description of the larval form of the Isabella tiger moth.

There is another sort of these caterpillars, who haue no certaine place of abode, nor yet cannot tell where to find theyr foode, but, like vnto superstitious Pilgrims, doo wander and stray hither and thither (and like Mise), consume and eat vp that which is none of their owne; and these haue purchased a very apt name amongst vs English-men, to be called Palmer-wormes, by reason of their wandering and rogish life (for they neuer stay in one place, but are euer wandering), although by reason of their roughness and ruggedness some call them Beare-wormes. They can by no means endure to be dyeted, and to feede vpon some certaine herbes and flowers, but boldly and disorderly creepe ouer all, and tast of all plants and trees indifferently, and liue as they list.

Yesterday's "Beare-wormes" are today's woolly bears, and Top-sell's comment that they "wander and stray hither and thither" is an apt description of this caterpillar's behavior in the fall. At this season you often see it crawling across sidewalks and highways in a manner that seemingly lacks purpose. But the fall movements of the woolly bear are to find a place in which to curl up as tightly as possible under some sort of protective covering. Overwintering spots may be under drifts or piles of leaves or accumulations of other natural litter or that tossed out by our society. Here it lies in a dormant state until the suns of a new spring make it sufficiently warm for the woolly bear to resume activity.

In the spring the woolly bear is also frequently in evidence as it moves this way and that in search of its first meal. If the insect locates one of our twenty native plantains, it should be "happy." Any plantain, including the lawn pests buckthorn and rippleseed, is in the diet of the woolly bear. It may meet some competition because plantain leaves are also well liked by cottontail rabbits. But as plantain is abundant in most sections of the country—even on poor, dry soil—the woolly bear should get its fill. It nips off bits of leaves with its strong biting jaws. The first meal and those that follow are large ones; the insect has to accumulate body fats to sustain it while undergoing pupation.

Some woolly bears never live until it is time for this "ordeal," for the insect, hairy though it is, is eaten by skunks. To make a woolly bear palatable a skunk rolls the caterpillar over and over to remove the hairs before eating.

After an interval of gorging, the now fat woolly bear ceases eating. This fast is followed by a period in which the creature becomes less and less active. Finally it ceases all movement, and seems to be resting for what is to come. Suddenly, as if recharged with life, the insect shakes off this lethargy, and starts a search for a place that will serve as a "hitching post" for its cocoon.

Suitable spots are the wide boards of old fences, the narrow slats of pickets, or the uprights of cedar-shake fences. The undersides of stones are also used. As soon as a satisfactory site is located, the caterpillar begins work on a cocoon. This is composed of the thread from the silk-producing glands and caterpillar hairs. The spinnerets are used to weave the cocoon that is spun around the body.

For two weeks, give or take a little, there is no outward sign that a moth is in the making. Then the cocoon splits, to release an Isabella tiger moth. Once free there is another interval of waiting, the final one, during which the body hardens and the wings dry. Now we have a moth with a wingspread of about two inches and one that in due time will deposit the eggs from which another lot of "Beare-worms" will hatch.

Once a mating is consummated the female is ready to lay her eggs on the host plant. Yellow and spherical, the eggs are deposited in many small patches, and there are instances when the number may be as many as one thousand. After hatching, the balance of the season is spent in eating and molting. By fall we may have a caterpillar whose black bands are so broad that little of the reddish brown shows, or the bands may be so narrow that the insect is more reddish brown than black.

The width of the bands used to be considered an indication of what was in store in the way of winter weather. Woolly bears on the northern parts of the insect's range—all of the United States, southern Canada, and northern Mexico—were anxiously studied. If the black bands were wide, the approaching season would be free of constant snow shoveling, stove tending, and bundling up every time you went outdoors. But if the bands were narrow, then the forthcoming winter was to be one of extreme cold, punctuated by intervals of moderation when there would be blizzards.

But as a weather forecaster the woolly bear is not at all reliable. When the American Museum of Natural History made its eighth annual woolly-bear census in October of 1958, those taking the count at Bear Mountain, N. Y., learned that the bands on seventy-four "bears" were not uniform. On some it was unusually wide, while on others it was so narrow as to be minimal. This lack of band uniformity led Dr. C. W. Curran, Curator of Insects and Spiders at the Museum, to comment: "The examination of the statistics indicates woolly bears are confused and not at all certain of the winter weather."

Tobacco Sphinx Worm and Moth
Phlegethontius sextus
Tomato Sphinx Worm and Moth
P. quinquemaculatus

(*Color Plate III, facing page 142*)

Dr. F. A. Urquhart, Curator of Entomology at the Royal Ontario Museum of Zoology, describes the moths of this family as "rapid-flying moths, with spindle-shaped abdomens, and narrow strong wings; antennae tapering at each end; usually large."

The five-spotted sphinx moth and the one with six spots are members of a family usually called hawk moths, but known, too, as hummingbird moths; like the bird from which they take the latter name the adults hover before open blossoms, then thrust their long tongues into the flowers to siphon off the nectar. As they feed, fluttering from one garden flower to another in pursuit of their sweet liquid diet, they act as pollinating agents.

In *The Yearbook of Agriculture, 1952*, discussing pollination by native insects, George E. Bohart writes:

The so-called hawk-moth orchids [there are thirty-odd North American species including the rein-orchis and the fringed orchis] . . . exemplify the many intricate modifications possessed by orchids to insure pollination by specific kinds of insects. In these flowers the nectar, lying at the bottom of a long narrow tube, is accessible only to the long-tongued moths. While probing for nectar, the moth brings each eye against a sticky disk to which a mass of pollen is attached, and flies away, carrying masses on its eyes. The masses (*pollinia*) then bend forward on their stalks in such a way that, when the moth inserts its proboscis into the next flower, they fit perfectly against the stigma and adhere to it. From the presence in Africa of an orchid of this type, with a nectar tube 12 inches long, there is inferred the existence in that region of a hawk moth with a tongue equally long.

Neither the tomato sphinx moth nor the tobacco sphinx moth has a tongue that measures a foot. Nonetheless they do their share 'in pollinating a flower such as the honeysuckle. The scent of the flower is heaviest in the evening and, as this is the time when the two moths fly, they are attracted to the spurred flowers. But the good work that they do as pollinators is often "undone" by the insect in its larval form as it feeds on the leaves of truck or garden vegetables.

The tomato and tobacco sphinx worms may be brown or green, and the name of the caterpillar comes from the plant on which it feeds. No matter the color and no matter the name, there are always several lines in a diagonal pattern on each side of the body. Toward the rear and on the upper side of the body is an organ that looks something like a little horn. This organ gives the caterpillars another common name, horn worm. In the South the two insects have a regional name because the pupa is oddly shaped. An irregularity in the cocoon, known as the "free tongue case," also has the appearance of a horn, and is the reason the insects are known as "hornblower" below the Mason-Dixon Line.

The colors of the caterpillars, and the horn that looks like a plant joint, are such good aids in camouflage that to locate these insects is difficult. But leaves with holes usually indicate that one of these pests is around, and the cultivated ground beneath their respective food plants is always dotted with their droppings—bright green and pellet-shaped.

These two sphinx moths overwinter as pupae; the time of their emergence as moths is early in the summer. As an adult, one has five yellow-orange spots on each side of the abdomen, while the other has six similarly located spots. The wings may be either light or dark brown, though the hind pair is usually less dark than the predominant color. The rear wings are banded with alternating stripes of the same color, with a light band between two dark ones. Both the adult male and female sip nectar from almost any garden flower, and act as pollinators in fluttering from flower to flower. From time to time the female interrupts her feeding, and the pollinating incidental to it, to lay her eggs.

The eggs look much like tiny clusters of seed pearls, set off by the green of the leaves of the tomato or tobacco plants on which they have been deposited. And from the eggs laid by an insect that is beneficial as an adult comes a new generation that in caterpillar form is a garden and commercial-crop pest.

The use of the name sphinx for these moths comes from the position the caterpillar assumes at rest. It raises the forepart of the body, then draws in its hairless head—an attitude reminiscent of the Sphinx in Egypt. This name is more popular in England than it is in North America. The common family name used by most Americans is hawk moth, despite the fact that the scientific name for the family is *Sphingidae*. This is a word of Greek derivation applied to any "monster" considered sphinxlike in shape or nature to which has been added the zoological -*idae* denoting family.

Both the five-spotted and six-spotted sphinx moths are night-flying creatures. By day they sleep with their long tongues, tightly curled like fully wound watch springs, held up under their heads, and with wings folded.

Polyphemus Moth
Telea polyphemus

(*Color Plate III, facing page 142*)

Though this large brown moth with feathery antennae is confined to the New World, it is named after one of the characters in the mythology of the Old World. Because it has eyespots on the wings, the moth was named for the one-eyed giant Polyphemus, who was blinded by Ulysses on the way back from Troy to his own kingdom of Ithaca. Scientists have recently classified this moth under a new generic name, *Antheraea*.

This spectacular insect is found throughout the United States and south into Mexico. With such a wide range the host plant on which the female deposits her bun-shaped eggs varies with the locale. You may find individual eggs or clusters on leaves of the birch, the chestnut, the maple, and also those of the wild rose. In northern states there is only one brood each season, but on the southern parts of the range two broods a season are usual. Holland describes the caterpillar as "altogether a beautiful object, so far as coloration is concerned." The color of the body is either a bright green or a green that has a decidedly bluish cast, and it is creased like an accordion. After its allotted number of molts, the caterpillar is ready to spin a cocoon.

The silk used by the Polyphemus moth to weave its cocoon is not continuous and, as a result, no one has been able to unreel the threads. The cocoon itself is of greater density than that of the one spun by the luna moth—another member of the family *Saturniidae,* the giant silkworm moths. The cocoon of Polyphemus is attached to a twig or rolled up in leaves. After the actual spinning takes place the caterpillar within releases a fluid that permeates the cocoon's fibers. Shortly after coming in contact with the air the fluid dries and gives the cocoon a chalk-white appearance. This protection makes it possible for most of these moths-to-be to survive winter. Then in early summer the adult emerges, a glorious creature whose wingspread may measure more than five inches from one outer edge to the other.

An oddity of Polyphemus is that as an adult it does not feed at all. The fat stored within the body nourishes it so that there is time enough for the female to mate and lay her eggs. Often there is so little time in her adult life that as she deposits her last eggs in clusters, she dies and falls to the ground beneath the plant that will be host for the next generation.

Throughout its range and within given areas, there is sufficient variation among these moths to create races native to a region. From time to time there is a melanistic individual, one whose wings are black on the upper surface. Less frequently one of these moths will be albinistic—all white or nearly so. Rarely an individual occurs that is a hermaphrodite. When such an aberration occurs, the division between the sexes shows with the wings on one side marked with characteristics of the male, while those on the other side will be similar to those of the female. But the normal adult is a beautiful creature, utterly unlike its namesake of which Virgil wrote: "A horrible monster, misshapen, vast, whose only eye had been put out."

Luna Moth
Actias luna

(*Color Plate III, facing page 142*)

In a photographic story about the Luna Moth, titled "Pale Empress of the Night" (*Pennsylvania-Angler*, November, 1952), J. Casey thus described the adult male:

A lovely ermined-furred body, curveous and beautiful, straw-colored dense feathery antenna, legs and feet delicately orchid-toned, harmonizing with the lavender band on the front margin of the fore-wings, . . . wings of pale green, seemingly adorned with flashing living gems, the eyespots transparent, but surrounded with rings of pale yellow, blue, and black.

Small wonder the Luna, easily distinguished from other silk moths by the long crisp trailers, is considered the most beautiful insect in America.

Though the luna is found anywhere from Canada to Florida, thence west to Texas and south into Mexico, it is not so familiar as a great many other North American insects. It is a night-flying species that floats through the air—sometimes to the accompaniment of the hooting of an owl; or often to the soft rustle of the leaves as they stir in a gentle breeze; and regularly to the almost soundless activity of other nocturnal animals including the tiny white-footed mouse.

Because the range of the luna moth is so extensive, there is a great variation in the food plants on which the female deposits her bun-shaped eggs, either singly or in clusters. In addition to the persimmon, the hickory, and the walnut, the host may be the sweet gum.

Star-leaved, straight-trunked, the sweet gum is a plant of the Coastal Plain and Piedmont sections of the southeast. It is usually abundant on its natural range, but as a food source is little used by other animals. A few songbirds, some upland gamebirds, and one species of waterfowl, the mallard duck, eat the seeds. Among small mammals only the chipmunk seems to enjoy the seeds that come from the ball-like fruit heads, and of mammals classed as fur or game, the beaver and the eastern gray squirrel are the only two that eat the seeds or gnaw the wood. So the caterpillar of the luna moth has little or no competition as it feeds on the leaves of the sweet-gum tree. Neither does it deprive other, more valuable wild creatures of food, and it offers little in the way of competition to those that use the tree. Most broods are not large enough to do much damage.

The greater part of the life span of the female is a sort of prolonged infancy from which she is freed for a few days of winged activity. During the period in her life when she becomes airborne, she mates, and if you happen to find a female after her nuptial flight is consummated, she will be a sorry-looking creature. The coloration that was once so breathtaking is gone; the delicate wings are torn and broken; and the life force seems spent. But in spite of her battered appearance, she still has enough energy to lay her eggs. As soon as the last tiny, shiny bluish-green egg is affixed to the leaf of the host plant, she dies.

There is an interval of seven or eight days from the time an egg is laid until the caterpillar hatches. The tiny, dark-green creature comes out of its shell with a voracious appetite. During the first forty-eight hours of its life, the infant insect is reported to devour so much food that its intake is 86,000 times its weight. It eats round the clock, stopping only long enough for each of the eight molts. After the final molt, the caterpillar is fully grown, and may measure lengthwise as much as three inches. Now its color is pea green and the body looks as if it had been accordion-pleated. Each of these pleats is dotted with ruby-red spots, but there are no spots on the head—a brown that matches the color of the feet. The colors, the body structure, and the markings appear to be functional; certainly they help to conceal the insect as it assumes an inverted position on the twig from which it feeds.

About a month after it hatches, the caterpillar is ready to make a cocoon, and the first indication that the time is near is a diminishing appetite. The gluttonous feeder is replaced by a nibbler that in turn gives way to a faster. Lastly, the luna-moth caterpillar, like some mammal hibernators, empties the digestive tract. Now the creature is much smaller than it was, and the green has a brownish tinge. This prepupal stage is marked by great activity as the insect moves about in search of a place for its cocoon.

A cradle-shaped affair, the cocoon is fashioned by stitching together leaves with thread from the silk organs in the head. Once the leaves are in place and have been reinforced with other leafy particles, a silken cocoon is spun within the casing. The silk for the cocoon originates in a pair of organs that act as "holding basins" for a liquid, jelly-like substance. There are ducts from these basins that unite in the mouth—a point at which they become the spinneret. As soon as the liquid is ejected from the spinneret and comes into contact with the air, it hardens. This caterpillar usually spends a full twenty-four hours to make the cocoon in which it overwinters.

In some areas the adult luna moth emerges about May Day. At first it is an unprepossessing creature—bedraggled, apparently misshapen, and so weak that it has difficulty in locating a perch on which to cling. About an hour has to pass before it is ready to fly, borne aloft on wings that some people believe look like the crescents of a waxing or waning moon. Perhaps this is one reason this moth was named for the Roman goddess Luna, but it was not reason enough for Thoreau—a fact that he noted in his *Journal* (Summer), June 27, 1859:

. . . P. M. To Walden. . . . I find an *Attacus Luna* half hidden under a skunk cabbage leaf, with its back to the ground and motionless, on the edge of the swamp. The underside is a particularly pale, hoary green. It is somewhat greener above, with a slightly purplish brown border on the front edge of its front wings, and a brown, yellowish, and whitish eye-spot in the middle of each wing. It is very sluggish, and allows me to turn it over and cover it up with another leaf, sleeping till night comes. It has more relation to the moon by its pale, hoary green color, and its sluggishness by day, than by the form of its tail.

Eastern and Forest Tent Caterpillars
Malacosoma americanum
M. disstria

In June of 1952 hordes of orchard, or eastern tent caterpillars, swarmed over the tracks of the New York Central Railroad at Pitcairn—a town in St. Lawrence County, N. Y. Estimated in the millions, the caterpillars halted a Diesel locomotive and a string of empty ore cars for thirty-five minutes.

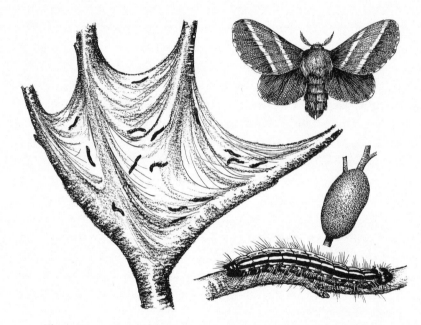

Tent Caterpillar, *Malacosoma americanum;* tent nest of larvae on wild cherry tree at left; adult moth, egg cluster, and larva at right

The insects covered the tracks, and caused the wheels of the locomotive to spin—creating the illusion that the Diesel was on a treadmill, for the crushed bodies made the tracks so slippery that the engine could gain no traction. The locomotive was detached, the tracks were sanded, and finally the engine was hooked onto the cars again, and managed to get rolling once more.

The train-stopping creatures were the larvae of a small, stout-bodied moth that flies at night. In its caterpillar form it is often a serious pest in apple and cherry orchards, though its preferred host is the wild cherry.

A closely related species, the forest tent caterpillar, was also a troublemaker in 1952, though it had been on the march toward destructiveness since 1947, when a small stand of aspen south of Sault Ste. Marie was stripped of all leaves by this insect. During the next five years there were more and more localized spots in which the trees were defoliated. By 1952 these spots had merged until all the forested areas at the eastern end of the upper peninsula of Michigan and the northern tip of the lower peninsula were infested by millions of hungry caterpillars.

By the time the crawlers, often mistakenly called "army worms," were ready to spin their cocoons late in June of 1952, they had stripped leaves off trees on more than 1,132,000 acres of forest lands. The Michigan outbreak was a fraction of the general outbreak that occurred on some fifty million acres in the lake states and Ontario, Canada.

The forest tent caterpillar is one of the insects classed as defoliator. Each year it and other similar insects damage well over a billion board feet of saw timber.

The adult forms of these two pests are small, stout-bodied moths whose colors vary from light to dark brown. The moth of the orchard tent caterpillar is distinguished by two light but distinct lines on the forewings. In its adult form the forest tent caterpillar is generally darker, and each forewing has two dark lines while each hind wing has only one line. The most marked difference between the two is in the larval stage. The orchard tent caterpillar actually builds the gauzy, weblike structures that are all too familiar on fruit trees early in the summer. But in spite of its name, the forest tent caterpillar does not build any web.

The moth of the orchard tent caterpillar deposits her eggs in a ring on the host plant. She coats the eggs with a substance that glistens like varnish in the sunlight. As soon as the egg is laid an embryo starts to develop, and continues to grow until it is nearly ready to hatch. Then comes that interval of arrested development in the life of an insect known as the "diapause"—a period of dormancy that sees the caterpillar safely through the winter.

The weather of the following year influences the time of hatching. If spring is advanced the caterpillars' emergence from the egg mass is early in the season. If the weather is not warm until late in the season, it may be early summer before the insects are ready to build the tent from which they get their name.

At intervals synchronized with their ever-increasing size, the caterpillars enlarge their tent by manufacturing more of the gauzy, weblike material. Sometimes a tent is so large that it covers an entire branch or several branches, and sometimes, too, every leaf on the tree will be eaten by the "tenants."

When the caterpillars are fully grown they leave the tent, and the departure marks a change in their way of life. Their gregarious days are over and each takes up a hermit-like existence after it finds a spot suitable for the cocoon it spins. Each member of a brood remains a hermit in the cell of its own making until the following June or July. Then the cocoon splits, to release an adult moth—a reminder that soon more caterpillars will be coming.

Apple Worm
Codling Moth
Carpocapsa pomonella

(Color Plate III, facing page 142)

The same temperature which causes our apple-trees to burst their beauteous blossoms releases the codling moth from its pupal tomb, and though its wings are still damp . . . , they soon dry and expand under the genial spring-day sun, and enable each to seek its companion . . . The moths soon pair, and the female flits from blossom to blossom, deftly depositing in the calyx of each a tiny yellow egg. As the fruit matures, the worm develops. In thirty-three days, under favorable conditions, it has become full-fed; . . .

This commentary on the emergence of the codling moth and its subsequent behavior was written by C. V. Riley, American entomologist and founder and editor of *Insect Life* (1889 to 1894). Riley was born in England but became an American by adoption. And the insect about which he wrote so knowingly also came from abroad. Sometimes known as the codlin moth, it is thought to have been imported from Europe about 1750. It adapted to the New World so readily that now it is found in North America wherever apples are grown, and where there are no apples the fruits of the pear, the quince, and the English walnut are eaten.

The larva of the codling moth is known as the apple worm, and in the 1930's and early 1940's the insect ruined about 15 per cent of the apple crop each year. The damage to fruit during this period has been estimated at more than $25,000,000 for each year. This estimate is exclusive of the amounts spent in trying to combat the pest—set at about another $25,000,000. By 1944 a few desperate orchardists decided to try DDT in an attempt to control the apple worm. The first use of the insecticide was so successful that since that year losses have been reduced until they are rarely more than two per cent and often less than one per cent of the annual crop.

In apple-growing areas on the northern part of the range, there is one full generation in a season and the partial development of another. On the southern limits of its range, there are three generations a season and a fourth is usually underway. No matter the generation, the damage caused by this "worm" is always the same, and almost everyone is familiar with it. The insect bores into an apple either from the blossom end or from the sides, then continues inward until it reaches the core of the fruit. It frequently leaves in its wake masses of pellets, coarse and brown, that may even hang outside the opening by which the insect entered.

In the North the caterpillar of the second brood, the one of the partially completed generation, overwinters in a cocoon that it secretes in a crevice in the bark. From time to time it spins the cocoon beneath anything that affords protection, but the site is always near a tree. In a winterproof spot and further protected by the cocoon, most of these caterpillars survive freezing temperatures and interludes of stormy weather.

The partially grown second generation of one season is responsible for the early appearance of the first adults of the succeeding year. The codling moth has a body that measures one-half to three-quarters of an inch in length, and wings that are streaked with light gray or brown. Each of the forewings is broad at the apex and narrow at the base, and when the insect rests it brings the wings together over its back in such a way that they resemble a bell. This is the reason the insect and other closely related species are called bell moths, and are in a family with the scientific name *Tortricidae*.

One of the Tortricids is a small caterpillar that uses seeds as hosts. Whenever the larva inside a seed changes position, it makes the seed "jump." Few people know the caterpillar within the seed, but many people recognize the seeds as the familiar "Mexican jumping beans." In Mexico the host seed for the caterpillar comes from the arrow plant (*yerba de flecha*) of southern Sonora and Chihuahua. The seeds which house these caterpillars are called *brincadores*, leapers or jumpers, and are frequently used as pawns in games of chance. One of these, a board game, has a chart divided into sections and carries the warning: Do Not Keep Beans Enclosed—They Breathe.

Another pest of fruit orchards is the caterpillar of the clearwing moth (*Sanninoidea exitiosa*). This insect is unlike many others in the suborder, for the scales do not cover the entire wings. The veins, the wing margins, and the body are scaled, and there is a tuft of hair on the abdomen. The wings are attached to a slender body, and have a spread of one and one-quarter inches. In flight the clearwing moth brings to mind an oversize bee. You can study this insect during the day as it flits around the lower branches of trees or in the vicinity of bushy plantings. You can also watch it at night, for after dark it flutters around outdoor lights.

The caterpillar of this moth is known as the peach-tree borer, one of the pests that burrows into living wood anywhere on a range consisting of the eastern two-thirds of the United States. If the borer does not kill a peach, it weakens the tree to such an extent that there is no fruiting. No one has been able to determine the loss in trees suffered by orchardists through the years or what the value of the peach crops might have been. But in attempts to control this pest during 1943 and 1944, the amount of money spent has been estimated at more than $3,000,000.

Gypsy Moth
Porthetria dispar

In 1957 state and Federal agencies appropriated nearly $5,000,000 for "the largest single aerial spray job ever conducted in the United States" to wipe out the gypsy moth caterpillar—a leaf-eating insect of Europe and Japan and one that is a threat to hardwood forests from northern Maine to those in the country dominated by the Ozark Mountains.

The gypsy moth is here and well-established because M. Leopold Trouvelot hoped to start a silk industry near Medford, Mass., where M. Trouvelot had settled when he emigrated from France to the New World. He set up a laboratory for entomological research in which he would attempt to crossbreed the gypsy moth with the mulberry silkworm (*Bombyx mori*). No doubt he believed the desired hybrid would revolutionize sericulture and bring him a fortune. But this was not to be.

In 1869 he sent to Europe for the material with which to experiment. Some historians say he ordered the eggs of the gypsy moth, but others state that he sent for cocoons. In due time he received specimens of one or the other stage in the life of this moth. While Trouvelot was working on the crossbreeding, some larvae got away from him. The insects found in the New England countryside an environment that was eminently suitable and one without any predators or parasites. During the next ninety years the exotic enlarged its range to include 38,000,000 acres in the northeastern United States.

The gypsy moth did not become established on this area by flying from one spot to another. The mature female cannot fly, and has to stay at the spot where she emerged in moth form until the day-flying male finds her. Once the mating is consummated, the female crawls to a well-shaded spot, and lays her eggs in lots of four hundred or more. Each egg has a hairy brown covering that may act as insulation for the embryo during the winter months. About May Day the egg hatches. By the middle of June the caterpillar is nearly two inches long; is dotted with matched pairs of red and blue spots; and is tufted with little hairy growths.

The caterpillar travels by means of these tussocks, for they "catch the breeze," and let the insect rise like a spiraling balloon. Spiraling lifts the caterpillar to an altitude of 2,000 feet, a height at which aerial cross-currents take over. The insect often rides the breeze for miles, and in all direction of the compass, before it drops to earth. A series of airborne emigrations brought the gypsy-moth caterpillars to Lansing, Michigan—the most westerly spot at which the insect had been found. It was detected almost at once, and promptly eradicated. According to federal pest-control agents the hurricanes of the past few years have helped the gypsy moth to emigrate, particularly along the eastern seaboard where it has been found in a number of regions that had never known the insect.

In addition to average winds or those of hurricane force, the dispersal agents, two other factors have been responsible in helping this exotic to become so well established. Natural controls were lacking, and without parasite or predator the gypsy moth was in no way restrained for thirty-six years—from 1869 to 1905. In that year the first biological controls were imported, but from then until now only a few have adapted to the New World. One of the most satisfactory is a European fly (*Compsilura concinnata*)—a parasite that kills the gypsy-moth caterpillar and also that of the brown-tail moth (*Euproctis chrysorrhoea*). This is another pest from Europe that also thrives in parts of New England. As a caterpillar the insect has some barbed hairs that are poisonous. If the barbs prick your skin the effect is similar to that of being "stung" by nettles, and the itching welts that result are known as the "brown-tail rash."

Frequently both species of caterpillars are killed by the wilt disease—a virus that affects butterflies and moths in the larval form as well as various true bugs and their allies, and some two-winged flies. The disease is polyhedroses, and an insect suffering from it grows weak, discolored, and eventually flaccid. By the time it dies the body contents are so disintegrated that they are mostly fluid.

Variegated Cutworm
Peridroma margaritosa

This was the most unkindest cut of all.
SHAKESPEARE, *Julius Caesar*

Any back-yard gardener who comes out early in the morning and finds the last one of his transplants sheared off, is likely to feel that the final cut was the most unkindest of all. The insect that does the cutting is the larval form of a brownish moth and several closely related species including the spotted cutworm (*Amathes c-nigrum*). These insects are common throughout the United States, and are distinguished by spots or stripes and a variety of colors, including gray, brown, and black. They often grow to a length of 1 ¼ inches. You seldom see one stretched to its entire length, for the moment the insect is disturbed it curls up as tightly as possible.

By day the cutworm hides beneath earthen clods or buries itself in the topsoil, but by night it comes out of hiding to feed. Such is its appetite that one *alone* can kill several plants in a night. Usually the insect feeds by cutting off small plants at or near the ground, and among the many vegetables it likes are the cabbage, the pepper, and the tomato. Flowering ornamental plants are not immune from cutworm attacks, and some on which the insect feeds are asters, carnations, and dahlias. In addition to those that kill by cutting are some that eat the foliage of chrysanthemums, dahlias, and sweet peas. Such cutworms are climbers and number among their kind those that bore into developing flower buds or fruits soon after they are set. A third group does not come aboveground at night, but remains in the soil to feed on the roots of plants.

Any cutworm is the larval form of the moths known as millers, night-flying species that belong to the family *Noctuidae*. As *noctua* is Latin for "owl," these moths are often called owl moths or owlet moths. As a winged creature the insect does no damage; its mouth parts are designed for sucking the nectar of various flowers.

Late in the summer the female deposits her eggs behind the leaf sheaths of any number of weeds or grasses or along the stems of like plants. The number of eggs varies with the species. If you have the patience to count them, you will find that some clutches contain only a few hundred but that others may number as many as 1,500. Though the egg period may be as short as two days, it is never longer than two weeks. By late fall the caterpillar that hatched so quickly is nearly as large as it will ever be. Cold weather interrupts the development of the cutworm, and for a winter refuge it burrows into the soil, wriggles under piles of trash, or squirms its way into the center of a clump of grass.

As soon as plant growth is underway the following year, the cutworm emerges from its overwintering spot, and resumes its cutting and feeding. By early summer it is a mature caterpillar and ready to pupate—the stage that leads to its final form. Both these life stages take place underground where the caterpillar prepares a cell or chamber in which to pupate and from which it emerges as a moth. Soon the life cycle of any one of these miller moths will start all over again, and there will be more cutworms to harass the home gardener or the man who grows vegetables for the market.

The moths in the miller family number about twenty thousand species, and their caterpillars are frequently referred to as "noneconomic" by those who refuse to call a pest a pest. Noneconomic is certainly euphemistic when used in connection with such pests as the various cutworms, the corn earworm, and the New Zealand armyworm, for these insects seem ever ready, willing, and able to take a cut of fresh foods or damage the sources of supply.

CLOTHES MOTHS
Family *Tineidae*

The clothes moths came to us from Europe, and each year the larval forms of these imports cause damage estimated at more than $25,000,000. The larva of the webbing clothes moth (*Tineola bisselliella*) and that of the casemaking clothes moth (*Tinea pellionella*) are responsible for most of the damage, though a less common third species damages furs of all kinds.

The larva of the webbing clothes moth, the moth of the illustra-

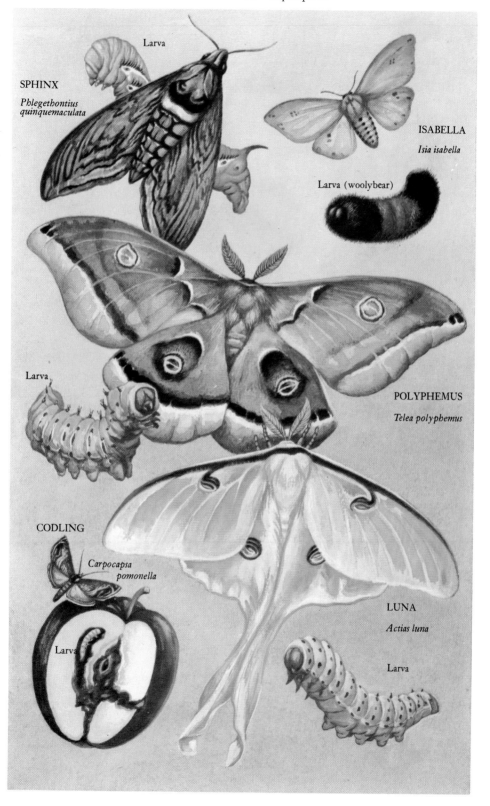

Larva

SPHINX

*Phlegethontius
quinquemaculata*

ISABELLA

Isia isabella

Larva (woolybear)

Larva

POLYPHEMUS

Telea polyphemus

CODLING

*Carpocapsa
pomonella*

Larva

LUNA

Actias luna

Larva

tion, makes a loosely formed web over the material on which it feeds. If the pasture is not green enough the tiny caterpillar wanders around on the material, trailing silken threads behind it until a new feeding area is located. If the new spot is satisfactory, the insect builds a thick canopy over it.

The larva of the casemaking clothes moth manufactures a home for itself in which to live but one which is mobile and goes wherever it goes. This cylindrical case is made of short lengths chewed from the material upon which the insect feeds, and is held together by silk the larva furnishes from silk-producing glands. The inside of the case is a decided contrast to the hit-or-miss appearance of the

Webbing Clothes Moth, *Tineola bisselliella;* larva at lower right

outside. Lined with pure white silk, the case is naturally enough smooth as silk. As the caterpillar grows, it adds to the house to accommodate its increasing size. The insect actually inserts little silken gores into the slits it cuts each time the case becomes too tight for comfort.

The larvae of these moths hatch from minute eggs deposited one at a time. The female selects a spot that will furnish food for the young as soon as they come out of the shells. Ideal spots seem to be those parts of clothes that are soiled and spotted as well as blankets and mattresses in the same condition. Such areas are apt to furnish the moths-to-be nutrients right at the start of their lives. The cracks and crevices of floors that are filled with lint or other accumulations that will serve as food are used, too.

From time to time the larva of either moth interrupts its feeding to molt. After the final molt, some additional feeding, and a quiet period, the now full-grown caterpillar builds a cocoon in which to pupate. This case is a silken sarcophagus in which the caterpillar undergoes the transformation—the breakdown of essential larval organs and their reassembly—by which it becomes a moth.

The webbing clothes moth has a reddish head and cream-colored wings that are unmarked. The case-making species is a yellowish-brown insect whose forewings are decorated with dark-brown marks. The four wings of these moths are much narrower than the four of other moths and many butterflies—a distinguishing characteristic of the insects whose young are reared at great expense to man.

Indian-meal Moth
Plodia interpunctella

There is nothing which seems to come amiss to its appetite, and it is, when established in house or store-room, a veritable nuisance.

W. J. HOLLAND, *The Moth Book*

Among insects that destroy grain and seed, none is worse than the Indian-meal moth, a small species, a member of the family *Pyralidae*, and a world-wide nuisance in its larval form. This moth is one of the insects that people once believed were spontaneously generated in grain. This belief is understandable, for many of the insects that ruin stored grain are unusually small, and go undetected until they are so numerous that the grain seems to have spewed them forth.

The larva of the Indian-meal moth feeds on dried seeds, nuts, fruits, and flour, water-ground meal, and an endless list of other food stuffs. The larva is a small white caterpillar that develops from a minute egg, and then passes through the other life stages common to all *Lepidoptera*. In its adult form, the Indian-meal moth has dirty-gray wings streaked with red, measuring about three-fourths of an inch over-all. The outer or hind parts of the wings are much darker than the fore parts—one way of differentiating it from the webbing clothes moth. Control of this insect depends upon on how tidy a housekeeper is, for as the *4-H Club Insect Manual* states: "It can be controlled by cleaning out all the old corn meal in the cracks and crevices of the pantry."

CATERPILLAR CONTROL BY BIRDS

Every butterfly, skipper, and moth passes through a larval stage when they are called caterpillars. This form is the one in which these insects are apt to be costly, economic pests. But Nature has provided a control. A leaflet issued by the Branch of Wildlife Research, U. S. Fish and Wildlife Service, states: "Probably more than half the food of 1,400 species and varieties of North American birds consists of insects."

Throughout plant and animal communities in North America the control of caterpillars continues year in and year out—provided, of course, man's impact on habitat does not destroy the things birds and other wild creatures need in order to live. This impact takes on a variety of forms; it can be the clearing away of protective cover; the residual effects of uncontrolled use of insecticides, pesticides, or too drastic predator and rodent-control campaigns; the drainage of wetlands and the subsequent loss of small water areas.

Those who study the diet of birds were amazed to learn how a single species kept in check the white-marked tussock caterpillar (*Hemerocampa leucostigma*). In times gone by this thread-thin caterpillar with its many white tufts was considered far too hairy to be in the diet of any bird. But in Washington, D. C., observers learned that when the insect was abundant, robins fed nestlings with the pests. In Massachusetts, English sparrows were responsible for the extermination of this caterpillar in certain small areas, and in Ohio the hairy woodpecker was an active, avid control. And when E. H. Forbush was in charge of a campaign to control the gypsy moth in Massachusetts, the birds of one area preyed on the caterpillars to such an extent that control measures were suspended for several years.

As long ago as 1858, J. W. P. Jenks was engaged in the study of the food habits of birds, now known as economic ornithology. He examined the contents of robins' stomachs in Massachusetts to determine their food habits and economic relations to agriculture. Late in the 1870's Professor Samuel Aughey of Nebraska published *Notes on the Nature of the Food of the Birds of Nebraska* in which he summarized thirteen years study of ninety different birds. This study involved the examination of the stomach contents of more than six hundred species. He was one of the first to work in a specialized field that continued to grow and won recognition by the Federal government through enactment of legislation for continued study.

Then in the 1890's, M. V. Slingerland of the Cornell Agricultural School wrote, ". . . by far the most effective aids in controlling the codling moth are the birds." The larva, or caterpillar, of the codling moth is the apple worm (*see*, p. 136), and birds as agents of destruction were noted by a New Hampshire observer, who made this comment:

Only 5 to 20 percent of the larvae survived the winter. An examination of seven trees . . . showed but 5 percent alive in the spring, 87 percent having been killed by birds, 4 percent by disease, and 3 percent by cold. It is quite evident that the birds, particularly the downy woodpeckers and nuthatches, are the most important enemies of the codling moth in New England. . . .

Today, economic ornithology, the interrelation of birds and insects, should be taken into consideration along with every other factor that affects the land and its plants and animals and, thereby, the world's welfare. For every individual is dependent wholly or in part on one or more individuals in its own community or those in another. "No man is an Island, entire of itself; every man is a piece of the continent, a part of the main, . . ." as John Donne wrote in his Seventeenth Devotion.

The way in which one individual depends upon another is exemplified in certain plant and animal communities of the South and Southwest. One insect in these communities is utterly dependent upon one plant that is typical of these areas. The insect is the yucca moth of the family *Prodoxidae* and the plant is the yucca—

known for its large panicle of white blossoms, and the state flower of New Mexico. The role played by each of these individuals in perpetuating the other is described by George E. Bohart in the *Yearbook of Agriculture 1952*.

It [the yucca moth] is no mere nectar sipper. At first, operating somewhat in the manner of the fig wasp, the female stabs the ovary of the yucca flower with her ovipositor and inserts an egg. That is common place insect behavior, but her next acts, though instinctive, seem to display careful planning and an uncanny knowledge of botany. She mounts a stamen, scrapes together a wad of pollen, carries it back to the pistil containing her egg, and thrusts it into the funnel-shaped stigma. She takes neither nectar nor pollen for herself but performs the only act that will guarantee the proper food for her offspring, the developing ovules of the plant. The yucca plant in its turn may lose a few seeds to the young worms—surely a small price to pay for such pollination service.

7 DRAGONFLIES and DAMSELFLIES

*Few people see the dragonfly in its native haunts except for
the fisherman and the naturalist, and it is often held in dislike
and fear by townfolk who occasionally visit the countryside.
. . . From my observation dragonflies seem to have their own
stretch of waterside and country byway and rarely go beyond
their chosen domain.*

HUDSON READ

In one form or another the dragonfly has been a member of North
American plant and animal communities for centuries on end.
During Paleozoic times what is now Kansas was the habitat of a
dragonfly that measured more than two feet. Proof of the existence
of such an insect came through the discovery of fossil remains a
number of years ago.

Of the world's 5,000 known dragonfly species, some 300 are
found within the United States. Not one of our twentieth-century
species equals the length of its primitive ancestor—one of the airborne creatures alive during the age of invertebrates and a few
early vertebrates. One of today's larger dragonflies, *Anax walsing-
hami*, has a wingspread of slightly less than 2 inches, and is a member of a family often referred to as "true dragonflies."

A foolproof way to identify a dragonfly is by the manner in
which one at rest holds its shimmering wings. They are held horizontally at right angles to the body, whereas the closely related
damselfly holds its wings together and at a slight angle above the
body. These insects are in the same order, but the dragonfly belongs
to the suborder *Anisoptera* whereas the suborder for the damselfly
is *Zygoptera*.

Ten-spot Dragonfly
Libellula pulchella

The ten-spot dragonfly belongs to one of the largest groups of these insects in the United States. It has a dark-brown body about two inches in length, formed somewhat like a prism, and with a lengthwise ridge along each slightly flattened side. The spots look to me more in the nature of bands than anything else, and in *The Insect Book*, Leland O. Howard described some species by saying:

> With many forms the wings are beautifully banded in brown, either in a series of cross bands or with large blotches which sometimes cover the basal half of the wings. . . . In some forms the wing markings are not dull brown, but become yellowish and in the very handsome and common *Libellula pulchella*, of Dru Drury, the brown spots alternate with milk-white spots.

You can see the ten-spot dragonfly in the series of still-water lagoons at Washington's Kenilworth Aquatic Gardens, or in natural pools where various rushes and water lilies grow. Hudson Read's observation about territorial rights is corroborated by Williamson, who says of the invasion of one dragonfly into the territory of another, "he is quickly hustled away by the rightful and irate owner."

After a mating is consummated the female lays masses of eggs, often so large that by count one was reported to contain more than 100,000. To lay her eggs the female flies low over the water, comes to almost a full stop, and hovers momentarily. While executing this maneuver, she dips the tip of her abdomen in the water and releases her eggs. (The eggs of various other species are inserted into the tissues of aquatic plants just beneath the water's surface.)

As soon as the egg hatches, the nymph, or naiad, starts to feed upon other small water insects, but as it grows the prey becomes larger and includes some tiny fishes. In its larval form the most outstanding feature of the dragonfly is the labium, the lower lip, an organ so modified that it is like a hinged mask studded with sharp teeth. The nymph folds this masklike flap back over the lower part of the face. When prey is close enough the nymph unfolds

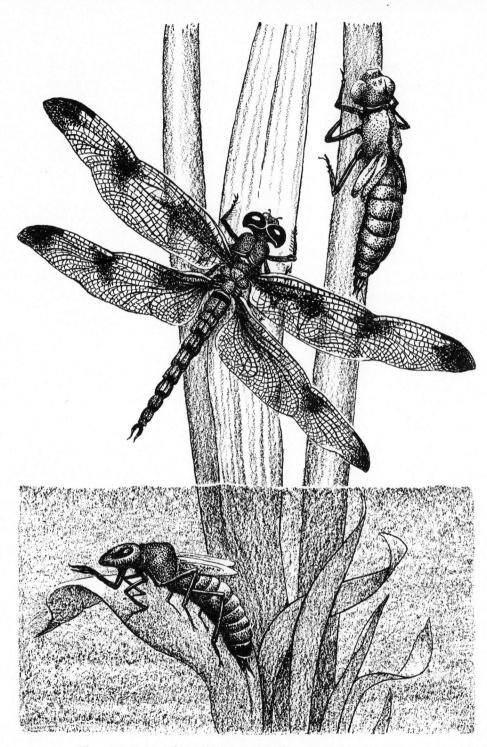

Ten-spot Dragonfly, *Libellula pulchella*; nymph in water, adult above, shed skin above at right the lip, shoots it out, and hooks the prey on the sharp teeth. With the prey so skewered the nymph then pulls it back into the mouth.

The movements of the nymphal dragonfly are possible because of the way it breathes. The apparatus for breathing is a series of tracheal branches that form any number of loops and penetrate the intestinal walls. From their location at the rear of the body, they are known as "rectal gills," and the water that is drawn in through them furnishes the necessary oxygen to keep the animal alive. This same water can be ejected with such force that the nymph is shot forward in a jerky fashion. It also moves from one place to another on the bottom of lake, pond, or stream by crawling.

The dragonfly nymph undergoes a series of molts—in the language of the scientist this is an incomplete metamorphosis. After the final molt it is broad and flattened, and in this form makes the ascent that takes it out of the water for the first time in its life. It overwinters in the soft bottom mud of the water in which the female laid the egg mass, or crawls into decaying bottom litter or any other protective material.

The nymph usually emerges from the water in May. Shortly before it comes out of the water it quits feeding, the feeding that has been in the nature of gorging ever since it first became active in the spring. It makes its way to the underwater part of a stem of some aquatic plant to which it clings motionless for several days. This quiet interval comes to an abrupt end as the nymph stirs, then makes its first upward move.

The ascent of the plant stem is so slow that the movement of the nymph is barely perceptible. Finally the head breaks water, creating a cat's-paw that is well-nigh invisible, and then, after additional inching upward by eighths, the time comes when not even the rear end is in the water. Now seemingly exhausted and still wet, the nymph clings with its sharp claws to the stem that was its ladder to a new life above water. This motionless interlude comes to an end when the creature starts to shiver like a mammal that has recently emerged from hibernation.

Now comes the indication that release from the nymphal state is imminent. A small slit occurs in the skin below the head, and ever so gradually lengthens in two directions—forward until it reaches a point between the eyes and backward until it is midway between the wing pads.

This slit is the door to freedom for the adult dragonfly. First the back heaves into view; next the big-eyed head is thrust out; then the long legs and the crumpled wings emerge; and finally the slender abdomen is hauled free. Nymphal shells such as the one from which the ten-spot dragonfly emerges and those of other species are often found in quantities along stream banks or still attached to the stems of water plants.

A newly emerged dragonfly is not active, for it has to wait an hour, perhaps two, and sometimes longer for the body to harden and the wings to color as well as to dry and spread. When Nature achieves these finishing touches, the adult is ready for its first swift flight.

The greater part of its short life as a winged creature is airborne. It hunts on the wing, spotting prey with enormous, all-seeing eyes that contain many thousands of facets, the sight units. It can contract and expand the muscles of the thorax so rapidly that the wingbeat is 28 to a second. With such a beat the dragonfly can attain a speed of more than 20 miles an hour. The big green darner, *Anax junius*, a high-flying species, hurtles along at 45 miles an hour throughout the United States, parts of Canada, and here and there in Alaska.

The dragonfly catches prey with its six long, reddish legs. It lets them down and bends them forward to form a sort of basket in which it catches quantities of flies and mosquitoes, its favorite prey. It is an enormous feeder; one under observation consumed 40 house flies in less than two hours.

The dragonfly hunts mostly on sunny days, and as it skims back and forth, wings ashimmer, it in turn is hunted by a number of birds including the swallow, the kingbird, and some small hawks. In addition to its enemies of the air, such water animals as frogs and fishes feed on the dragonfly.

Undoubtedly many egg-laying females are caught by these predators as they dip abdomens in the water—source of life for the insect that as an adult is known by such common names as darning needle, snake-feeder, snake doctor, horse stinger, or mosquito hawk.

Black-winged Damselfly
Agrion maculatum

"Demoiselle" is in world-wide use as a name for various species of wildlife. It is one name for the *pintano*, a black-banded fish of the coral reefs; the name for a small Numidian crane with long, flowing breast feathers; and also for the tiger shark, characterized by irregular bands and numerous spots. In the United States dem-

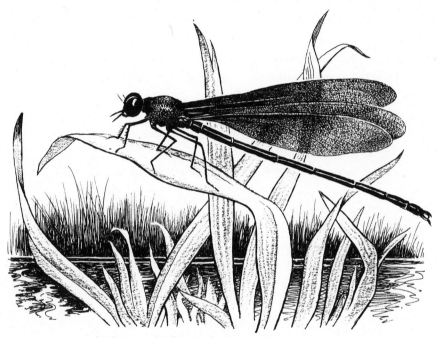

Black-winged Damselfly, *Agrion maculatum*

oiselle is the regional name of the Louisiana heron, and *Webster's New International Dictionary*, second unabridged edition, designates it also as "Any of numerous slender-bodied dragonflies of *Agrion, Calopteryx,* and allied genera."

Usually these insects have two pairs of wings of nearly equal size and bodies that are brightly colored. *Agrion maculatum* is a breathtaking sight as it flashes by on wings that look like black spangles cut from a single pattern, and measuring about 2½ inches from outer edge to outer edge. The body length is 1¾ inches and, except for a little black on the thorax, is a metallic green. An equally striking species in flight is the one known in Great Britain as the "blue-winged demoiselle."

The damselflies in tropical regions are large and seem to be in keeping with the lush vegetation. But those of North America are small—perhaps devised that way by Nature as more fitting for a temperate climate. Our damselflies are low-flying and frequent sluggish or still waters, where they dart along above aquatic plants of no great height.

Holding their wings vertically is not the only quirk peculiar to the damselflies. They fly through the air by hooking themselves together. The male grasps the thorax of the female when flying tandem—a practice during the interval when the female lays her eggs. Some species deposit eggs on bits of flotsam; others drop them on leaves; but some attach them on plant stems immediately beneath the water's surface. Males of certain species accompany females beneath the surface while they lay their eggs, but other males stay topside where they cling to the plant stem while retaining holds on their mates. The male that goes underwater with his coupled mate, surfaces first, flutters his wings several times, drags up the female, and then the two take off once more to continue the round of egg-laying.

The damselfly nymph is unlike that of the dragonfly, for it has a leaflike appendage at the end of the abdomen. The organ has three parts, and it is to the nymph what lungs are to us. With it the nymph extracts oxygen from the water. The gills also act as a paddle-propeller because of their action and location. If the nymph twists its body from side to side, the gills function like an oar that is used for sculling at the stern of a boat. At other times a nymph crawls around to get from place to place.

Before it becomes the flashing gaily colored insect that most of us are familiar with, the nymph has to undergo a series of molts. These ready it for the transformation into a demoiselle—a dancing fleck of color against the spatterdocks and pickerelweeds of its environment.

8 TRUE FLIES

Photographic studies of the drone fly, . . . clarified many points—among them the actual motion of insect wings, the method of steering and the way sudden turns are made by "feathering" one wing. Another discovery—useful to gyroscope research—is the role played by rapidly vibrating halteres of the drone fly. This pair of knoblike organs located behind and below the wings of every fly, vibrate as rapidly as the insect's wings and serve as gyroscopic stabilizers during its times of flight.

"How Flies Fly," *Natural History*
February, 1948

The drone fly is one of 85,000 insects in an order that is distinguished by a common characteristic—one pair of wings, and one only, as opposed to the usual two of other flying insects. The second pair has been so modified that they are the knoblike organs mentioned in "How Flies Fly." These halteres, as the knobs are called, are attached to the body with sturdy but thread-thin stalks; on large flies you can usually see them with the naked eye, but on small ones they are almost impossible to spot unless you have some sort of magnifying glass.

There are fifty families of flies in the United States, and they vary in size from tiny to those that measure nearly 2 inches in length. These insects have large eyes, barely visible antennae, and the mouth parts are designed for sucking, chewing, lapping, biting, and sponging. The body is thin and soft; the wings are membranous and as a rule lack color of any kind.

The life histories, behavior, and diets of these flies are also varied, and as with any other group of animals, there are the good, the less good, such as the crop pests, and the thoroughly bad, those that carry disease-producing organisms. Probably the most familiar species in this order, the *Diptera*, is the ubiquitous house fly—a pest whose potential for proliferating is an awesome subject to think about.

House Fly
Musca domestica

During the late 1950's The United Nations World Health Organization announced that if one female house fly produced 120 eggs on April 15, her family by September 10 could theoretically be 5,500,000,000,000 adult flies.

If all the offspring of one pair of flies survived, World Health continued, it would take only six months to cover the entire surface of the world with flies that would pile up to a height of 46 feet. And lastly, if you can take any more, one single fly has been found to carry 100,000 bacteria originating in human waste.

In its adult form this threat to our health and general welfare is a blackish-bodied insect of ½ inch in length. There are black stripes of greater density running lengthwise along the back, and the sides of the body are shaded in yellow. The single pair of wings are transparent, and in flight beat at least 20,000 times a minute. This frequency enables the insect to zoom along at a speed of nearly 5 miles an hour, and to travel 13 miles in 24 hours—the performance turned in by a marked house fly. A fly can land in practically any position—even upside down—because its feet are equipped with tiny suction cups. The large eyes are red-brown, and the mouth parts of this species are designed for lapping—one way to tell the pest from others that resemble it, for a biting fly indoors or out is never *Musca domestica*.

The house fly endangers the health of man and other animals because it carries disease germs in the digestive tract or on the hairy feet and legs. A fly carries the eggs of various parasitic worms; transmits typhoid, dysentery, and diarrhea; and has a part in causing cholera, yaws, and trachoma, among other diseases. Sinuhue, a physician to one of the early Pharaohs, wrote about flies as long ago as 2000 B.C. He commented on these insects in connection with a review of troops by an Egyptian general, and at the same time noted the physical condition of the soldiers.

When all were paraded, Horembeb stepped out from the dirty hut with his golden whip in his hand, and a servant held an umbrella over his head and kept the flies off him with a fly whisk while he addressed the soldiers. . . . Their eyes were sore from flies, and I reflected that soldiers in every country were alike.

The condition of the soldiers' eyes in Sinuhue's day was probably the same type of trachoma with which many present-day Egyptians are afflicted—a chronic conjunctivitis.

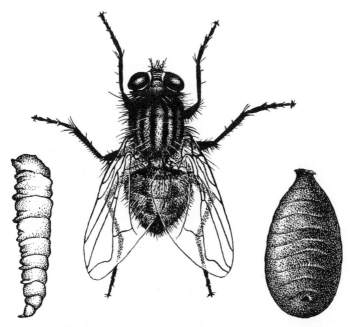

House Fly, *Musca domestica;* larva at left, pupa at right

During World War II flies were still plaguing soldiers. In *History of Entomology, World War II,* Colonel Emory C. Cushing states:

Diarrhea and the dysenteries have been ever-present camp followers of armies through the ages, and American soldiers were not to be spared these infections. . . . These two complaints either hospitalized or kept in quarters 523,331 soldiers during World War II. Not all the trouble from enteric diseases can be attributed to flies, but the more explosive and devastating epidemics were unquestionably started and maintained by indescribable plagues of these insects. . . .

My own observation about the house fly is that the insect does not set well on the stomachs of some Siamese cats. Poo-ying, my female seal-point, catches flies with winking quickness, and Sam-cat Chew, the male blue-point, is an equally adept flycatcher. Sam apparently has some natural resistance to house flies, for he is never sick after eating one, whereas Poo-ying is off her feed for days thereafter.

In the northern United States the house fly overwinters as a pupa or larva, but in the South or any warm region throughout the world the insect breeds the year round. The female lays her eggs in lots of about 125 each. Though the number of eggs is generally 500 all told, it is a matter of record that this insect is capable of laying as many as 5,000 eggs.

Animal manure seems to be the preferred place for the eggs to hatch, though other animal matter as well as vegetation is used—provided it is moist or in a state of fermentation. If the weather is warm the eggs hatch in eight or twelve hours, but if it is unseasonably cool the hatching time may be two or even three days. After feeding for four or five days, the all-white larva, or maggot, is ready to pupate. This stage in the house fly's life takes another four or five days, and after an interval that may last three to twenty or more days, the adult female is ready to lay her eggs.

Before the advent of screens the common practice of ridding a house of flies was to "shoo" them out. Shooing was a family affair, with each member armed with a cloth to flap like a regimental banner. Various members of the family would start to shoo from designated rooms, and keep on shooing until they converged at a single open door. Here with one final concerted flap, they would "show the flies the door."

For a number of years DDT kept us fairly free from flies, but today there is a strain resistant to this particular control. *Science Service* now reports that work is in progress to develop an aromatic bait that contains a liberal amount of an effective insecticide. Food odors attract flies, and this is the reason for experimentation on a poisonous but aromatic bait. The test bait is a by-product of a commercial starch manufactured from corn. And the use of this bait has shown that it attracts flies from as far away as a mile.

Fruit Fly
Drosophila melanogaster

An entomologist of distinction once remarked, "I can believe anything of an insect." Dr. Frank E. Lutz of the American Museum of Natural History proved that this remark was no understatement with regard to insect endurance. The Doctor wanted to learn whether insects could survive a trip to the summit of Mount Everest, where the atmospheric pressure is less than one third, 225 mm., than at sea level, 760 mm.

Lutz did not take any insects to Mount Everest, nor could he simulate all the conditions prevailing at its summit. But by means of a bell jar with a barometer inside and a vacuum pump he did provide two of the most important conditions—a decrease in atmospheric pressure and the consequent lack of oxygen. And the insects for the "trip" were fruit flies—those red-eyed little creatures that are a joy to the geneticist.

A number of these flies were put into the jar and then, little by little, the vacuum pump exhausted the air—an action that brought about a decrease in the jar's atmospheric pressure. When the barometer indicated a pressure equivalent to that of the tip of Everest, there was not the slightest indication that the fruit flies were affected. Additional air was exhausted until the pressure was the equivalent of eight miles above sea level. At this height the flies' activity was still unimpaired, for they continued to walk about. And like the band that played on, Lutz continued to pump until the pressure inside the jar was the equivalent of an altitude of 17 miles above sea level. Though none of the flies moved about, none died. And as soon as the pressure was restored to normal they became active, and apparently suffered no ill effects from the experiment—one of several in which they were used.

The tiny fly with which Lutz conducted his experiment is of world-wide distribution, abundant wherever fruit is decaying or fermenting, and also found in the vicinity of fungi or flowing sap. The insect has an amazingly short life cycle—ten days from egg to adult during normal summer temperatures. The eggs are minuscule and have two filament-like appendages as long as they are; the maggots, tiny and white, feed in the fermenting juices of decaying fruits, and sometimes in the top third of jars and bottles containing pickles. They undergo the change from maggot to fly within a puparium—a casing that has a pair of hornlike tubes through which the insect breathes.

Because the life cycle of the fruit fly is so rapid, the insect is used by geneticists to gain a greater knowledge of heredity. It can be reared readily on fermenting bananas or various artificially concocted cultures. Gregor Johann Mendel, the Austrian monk who pioneered in experimental work on heredity, was the first scientist to keep systematic records of great numbers of offspring for several generations. The account of his experiments and his conclusions were published in 1866.

One of the many biologists who have since followed Mendel's footsteps was Thomas Hunt Morgan of Lexington, Kentucky—the recipient in 1933 of the Nobel Prize in Physiology and Medicine. While Morgan was professor of experimental zoology at Columbia University from 1904 to 1928, he used the fruit fly for his "ingenious demonstration of the physical basis of heredity."

Before he experimented with the fruit fly, Morgan tried rats, mice, and plant lice without being able to get a pure strain. Then he heard that a geneticist at Harvard was working with the fruit fly. In 1909 Morgan sent for some, and in his laboratory they multiplied as fruit flies will. Finally Morgan had the insects by the thousands, all contained in neatly labeled bottles and set in rows along his shelves.

In the year that followed Morgan put his bottled flies to all sorts of tests. Sometimes the insects were subjected to temperatures low enough to freeze the ears and tail tips off opossums; at other times they were exposed to temperatures so high that a desert rattlesnake under the same circumstances would curl up and die. Bright lights were also beamed on the glassed and hapless little insects; and then there would be interludes of total darkness. Diets, too, were varied, and some flies were even exposed to an acid solution. The fruit flies withstood this particular type of "brainwashing," and no deviation from the norm occurred—the same old fruit flies with their large reddish eyes appeared in one generation after another.

But in April 1910 there was a break in the ranks, for "in a pedigreed culture of *Drosophila* which had been running for nearly a year through a considerable number of generations, a male appeared with white eyes." This atypical fruit fly, the first mutation, was exactly what Morgan had been hoping for. Immediately he made the white-eyed male work for him by breeding it with a regular red-eyed female. Then after letting them gorge on some fermenting banana, he popped his experimental pair into a bottle and stoppered it with cotton.

The first generation ran true to form—every last one of them was as red-eyed as the female. But this did not disappoint Morgan, for he did not expect results until the second generation. And he got them! In the "grandchildren," the eye combinations were:

One-third...Red
One-third...White
One-third...Mixed red and white

In the years that followed the first fruit-fly mutation, Morgan and his associates induced another twenty-five. These included insects with speckled wings, color variations, and some with no eyes at all. The study of fruit flies continued, and in time Morgan and his fellow workers learned that certain genes appeared in the males only, while others were solely in the females. They also found out that the genes of fruit flies appear in a regular order on the chromosomes—small bodies, usually definite in number, in the cells of a given species. The red-eyed gene, for instance, was always at the top of the chromosome, whereas the one that produced a speckled-winged species was regularly near the bottom.

Though the study of genetics began more than 100 years ago, it is not yet an exact science. One phase of it has received more attention than some of the others, and this is known as "linkages." Some characteristics are sex-linked, such as color-blindness and hemophilia, "the bleeding sickness," that affected two males of Spain's dethroned royal family to which it was introduced by Victoria Eugenie of Battenberg when she married Alfonso XIII. Victoria Eugenie inherited the gene—a sex-linked character—from her grandmother Queen Victoria, and passed it on to two of her sons.

At Purdue University Dr. Allen B. Burdick raises thoroughbred fruit flies. Raised under controlled conditions, these flies aid in the understanding of the mechanism of heredity. They are priceless to the biologist who uses them because he will not have to devote time "to disentangle the influences of heredity from that of environment."

As the fruit fly has helped in the past, so will it undoubtedly help in the future. Perhaps Dr. Burdick's thoroughbred flies will aid in solving some riddles of heredity that have nothing to do with linkages. One appreciative geneticist with a flair for the prankish has paid tribute to the thirty-or-more-generations-a-year insect by writing:

> Hail to thee, most fruitful fly
> That used to be so red of eye,
> For a cycle so damned short,
> That in a year we got a sport.

FLOWER OR SYRPHID FLIES
Family *Syrphidae*

A widespread old wives' tale has it that animal carcasses generate swarms of honey bees. This myth is part of the folklore of many lands including China and Japan, and is also referred to in the story of Samson in the Old Testament book of Judges.

The myth has more reason for being than many, for one species of syrphid fly, *Eristalix tenax*, closely resembles an extra-large honey bee. Known, too, as the drone fly, it breeds in carcasses, and as its resemblance to the honey bee is so striking, it is easy to understand why people thought swarms of honey bees were rising from a carcass when in fact the insects were drone flies.

Along with other members of a family that includes 2,500 species, the drone fly is also known as the hover fly. Probably you have seen one zoom up to a flower in your garden, brake, then hover in mid-air. Sometimes the insect seems to hang motionless above your annuals or perennials for so long that you feel as if it must be suspended by invisible wires. Eventually it does come in to a flower to feed on pollen and nectar. Look for the drone fly on bright, sunny days, particularly at high noon, for this is one insect that is not active on dark, dour days. As it visits first one flower and then another, the drone fly and others of its kind do invaluable service as cross-pollinators.

A predaceous member of the family is *Syrphus ribesii*. Its larvae and those of some closely related species devour enormous quantities of aphids. Together all these eaters of other insects constitute the most important group of predaceous *Diptera*. Some of them clean plant lice off the leaves of currant bushes in what seems like a trice.

In this large fly family the larval forms differ in appearance and habits to such an extent that five general types have been recognized. One of these types has larvae that live in ants' nests, and look so much like land shells that they have been described as such. And so completely deceived were a few early scientists that these larvae were actually given names designating them as mollusks. The functions of the ant-nest larvae (*Microdon*) are unknown, but those willing to hazard a guess believe that these syrphids secrete "a something" that is useful to the ants.

When you have reached the ultimate in insect identification and can recognize larval forms of syrphid flies, you might discover some in the nests of the carpenter ant or in those of the fire ant (*Solenopsis saevissima*)—a species introduced from South America.

During their earliest life stages, flies of the genus *Volucella* live in the nests of bumble bees. The larvae and the bees apparently live in perfect harmony, and scientists have had to discard a once-held theory that the larvae were parasitic. Now it is assumed that they eat food wasted by the bees, and eat also any bees that die or their excreta.

When the insect is ready to undergo the changes in form that will turn it into a fly, the last skin of the full-grown larva shrinks, hardens, and takes on an oval shape. This casing for the pupa is darker than the smooth, glistening skin of the active larva, and is the shelter in which the vital organs of the larva reassemble to produce the full-fledged fly. To escape from its shell, the newly winged insect pushes out the front end as if it were an emergency exit.

At least two species of syrphid flies are malefactors in the eyes of the gardener who likes to grow flowering bulbs. One is the narcissus bulb fly (*Lampetia equestris*)—a native of Europe which is now well established in the Pacific Northwest. The larvae of this exotic feed on narcissus bulbs. The second of these malefactors is known as the lesser bulb fly (*Eumerus tuberculatus*), and this one not only attacks those bulbs that flower as ornamentals but root crops including the bulbous onion.

As a family these flies are interesting to collect, and as a family they are relatively easy to catch with a sweep net as they hover above your garden flowers—flies in the clothing of honey and bumble bees, social wasps, and wasps of the solitary kind.

ROBBER FLIES
Family *Asilidae*

Robber Fly, *Promachus rufipes*, with captured Paper Wasp

The robber fly family contains nearly 3,000 species. All these insects are slender but strong, and have a miniature lance that is enclosed in a tapering beak. The robber fly jabs its prey with this lance, then impales the victim on the stiff bristles at the tip of the beak. In describing the entire family of robber flies, A. Fitch wrote:

These flies are inhuman murderers. They are the savages of the insect world, putting their captives to death with merciless cruelty. . . . Like a hawk, they swoop upon their prey and grasping it securely between their forefeet they violently bear it away.

One of these "inhuman" murderers is the species known as *Promachus rufipes*, a creature whose lengthwise measurement is 1 to 1 ⅜ inches. Any good that *P. rufipes* and other robber flies do is accidental, for the insects it captures during its darting flight are a miscellany. The diet includes beetles, dragonflies, and grasshoppers as well as butterflies, moths, bees, and wasps. And as the robber fly even preys on members of its own family, it is one of the true insect cannibals.

The robber fly has a complete life change. Its active life is interrupted by winter, which it passes in the ground as a larva or pupa. Actually so little is known about the four hundred or so species of robber flies in the United States that an entomologist of another era remarked: "The life history of some robber-fly is a great desideratum."

BLOW OR BOTTLE FLIES
Family *Calliphoridae*

One of the most familiar members of this family is the greenbottle fly (*Phaenicia sericata*), shown in the accompanying illustration. This insect is frequently referred to as "the greenbottle," and has a lengthwise measurement of ¼ to ¾ of an inch. The color of the body is such a shiny green as to be almost metallic—truly a reason for its specific or trivial name, *sericata*, meaning "to have a silk-like or satiny luster."

The life cycle and habits of the greenbottle are similar to those of the smaller, much less noisy house fly. The normal habitat of the insect is outdoors, but on occasion it enters a house when a storm is brewing or in search of a place to lay its eggs. Such provisions as meat and cheese are ideal repositories for the eggs. Soon a larva or maggot hatches, and develops so rapidly that long before winter settles down on the northern part of its range, the green-bottle-to-be is safely within a puparium.

An unabridged dictionary defines a puparium as "the outer shell formed from the larval skin which covers a coarctate pupa." In other

Green-bottle Fly, *Phaenicia sericata;* from left: larva, adult, pupa

words a much constricted larva (the coarctate pupa) is encased within its own outer skin—a skin now so hard and tough that it is practically frostproof.

The advent of spring and the warm weather that follows means the advent of a mature green-bottle fly. After it emerges from the puparium the adult feeds upon carrion and flowers, and during the course of the feeding a mating takes place. Once another generation of flies is assured the female is ready to lay her eggs on fresh or decaying meat, which is then spoken of as "blown."

Another species in this family is the blue bottle fly (*Calliphora erythrocephala*), which has been described by Leland O. Howard, U. S. Department of Agriculture entomologist, "as of rather dull color with black spines on the thorax." The blue bottle is a familiar insect of plant and animal communities of the West, where it is reported as preying upon the Rocky Mountain locust or western grasshopper.

FLESH FLIES
Family *Sarcophagidae*

These flies, closely related to the green-bottle, the blue bottle, and the screw-worm, have a scientific name that derives from "sarcophagous." The original meaning of this word was "An eater of human flesh." But today, zoologically speaking, it means "feeding on flesh."

The habits of the flies in this group are as diverse as the points of a compass. Some feed on decaying fruits and vegetables; others are parasites of living insects; and still others are parasites of various warm-blooded animals including man.

One of these flies is *Sarcophaga sarraceniae*, a gray or silver-gray insect that feeds on dead insects trapped by the pitcher plant. This is one of the world's carnivorous plants characterized by leaves shaped like pitchers, tubes, or trumpets. Most of the several known species of this flesh-eating plant are to be found in North America. Here they grow in bogs, swamps, or other areas in which they can get their "feet" in the water.

The pitcher plant traps insect prey that comes to feed on the nectar exuded by the leaves. An insect crawls into the mouth of the pitcher, tube, or trumpet to lap up the nectar, but when it has had its fill and is ready to leave, there is no escape. Down-pointing hairs around and beneath the lip on the inner surface prevent the insect from crawling out. And in its presumably desperate struggles to escape, it falls into the liquid contained in the pitcher. Some of the trapped insects are digested by the enzymes in this liquid, but others serve as food for *Sarcophaga sarraceniae*—exemplifying the belief of certain Scottish mystics known as "links," who held that "As nothing lives unto itself, it follows that each species reacts favourably, neutrally or adversely upon other forms of life."

MOSQUITOES
Family *Culicidae*

There are more than one hundred species of mosquitoes in the United States. These buzzing, night-feeding insects are a part of plant and animal communities from Alaska to the subtropical regions of our country and from the great coastal marshes of the East all the way west to desert country. Of these many mosquitoes the best known is undoubtedly the "house" or "rain-barrel" mosquito—named "peeping fly" (*Culex pipiens*) by Carolus Linnaeus, the great Swedish naturalist and originator of the binomial method of designating plants and animals.

The house mosquito breeds in standing water of any kind such as fish ponds, ornamental pools, rain barrels, or any catchall of sufficient depth to hold a little water. The female mosquito, the biting member of the family, lays her eggs during May or June. The eggs are laid one at a time or in boat-shaped masses that may contain 100 to 400 eggs. They are laid on or immediately beneath the surface of the water, and in one to three days the minuscule eggs hatch. The larvae of mosquitoes are known as "wrigglers" because they move through the water in a series of body jerks.

In appearance the wriggler has the shape of a miniature snorkel submarine because a slender tube, the siphon, is attached to the end of the abdomen. Every so often the wriggler thrusts the siphon through the water's surface; then, while the animal is held in place by surface tension, it siphons in a supply of oxygen. When the larva has the necessary supply of oxygen it wriggles away from the surface by a series of body jerks and descends to the bottom of the pond, pool, or other water in which it hatched. Here it feeds on plants so tiny that to see them you and I would have to use a microscope. If there is a film of oil (one control measure) on the water's surface, this means death for the wriggler, for the snorkel cannot pierce the film, and asphyxiation follows.

The usual larval period is a week to ten days—provided the weather is really warm. If the weather is unseasonably cold, this stage in a mosquito's life may be as long as three weeks. No matter the length of the larval stage, the little insect eats, grows, and molts. After the final molt, the one that brings it to the pupal stage, the mosquito looks like a comma (,). For the thorax, the body area that corresponds to our chest, is fat, whereas the abdomen is short and slender.

During the interval in which it is a pupa, the mosquito breathes by means of two little hornlike organs that are attached to the back of the thorax. As a pupa the mosquito reverses the position that was habitual when it was a larva. In its larval form the insect always remains bottom side up near the surface of the water, but in its pupal form the position is reversed. Right side up it rests quietly near the surface of the water, using its air tubes to bring in the necessary oxygen. Like other pupae, that of the mosquito does not eat at this period in its life, but unlike other pupae it does not always remain immobile, for if it is disturbed, it swims as fast as it can toward the bottom by jerking its abdomen. This downward progress is aided by a pair of leaflike organs attached to the end of the body.

Usually the life of a pupa is no more than two or three days. At the end of 24 or 36 hours, the pupal skin splits down the back to release a winged creature. As soon as the wings expand to their full size and become dry and tough, the insect is ready to spring into the air, using its discarded skin—the pupal case—as a float. Sometimes it takes off from the surface of the water.

A mosquito is able so to launch itself into the air because it is extremely light in weight and also because the tarsi, the forefeet, are covered with fine hairs. These enable the creature "to tread water" until it is ready to become airborne. The first to come out of the pupal shell and take to the air are the males, who hover above the spot where they emerged. Presumably they are waiting for the females to burst forth and become airborne so that they can mate.

After a mating is consummated the male lives at the most no

more than a week or so—a period during which he feeds on plant juices, and is seldom seen. The life expectancy of a female is a month, and during this time she feeds on plant nectar, her principal food, and from time to time either on human or other animal blood. Some authorities believe the mosquito needs blood in the way we need minerals and vitamins; that is, blood is a dietary requirement that keeps the mosquito healthy and the strain strong.

If a mosquito bites you, you know it is a female. That, of course, is the easiest way, though hard on the bitee, of distinguishing one sex from the other. The female is further distinguished by antennae and feelers, the palpi, so thin as to be almost invisible. These are on either side of the long and slender sucking tube, known as the proboscis. The nonbiting male has no such distinguishing characteristics. The antennae and palpi are plumose, plumed, so that the head appears to be decorated with bunches of tiny feathers. The bite of the female is effected with a little drill that can puncture many types of body covering—even the leathery skin of a frog or the overlapping scales on a snake.

In an attempt to learn why some people attract mosquitoes and others do not, Dr. W. A. Brown of the University of Western Ontario has been working with robot dummies and carbon dioxide —the heavy, colorless gas which is contained in the breath we exhale. The robots, dressed to look like men, were heated until they had the normal body temperature of 98.6° F., and then were saturated with carbon dioxide. Next, the two dummies were placed so that nearly six feet separated them.

Drenched with carbon dioxide the two robots had no appeal for certain species of mosquitoes. But when the gas was exhaled mechanically at the normal breathing rate for most human beings, the robots attracted mosquitoes to both their heads and bodies. The conclusions to be drawn from this experiment seem to be: hold your breath and mosquitoes will leave you alone.

Dr. Brown also learned during his mosquito experiments that the color and texture of the clothes we wear influence our mosquito appeal. The insects seem to prefer dark clothing, for as lighter and lighter color shades were used, fewer and fewer mosquitoes were attracted. And by the time white clothing was put on the dummies, the number of mosquitoes lighting on the robots was one tenth the number that landed on dark clothing.

At about the same time that Dr. Brown was conducting his experiments in 1958, a research group at Rutgers University, New Brunswick, N. J., disclosed that "mosquito appeal" can be measured by: (1) The chemical components of your exhaled breath; (2) The warmth your body emits.

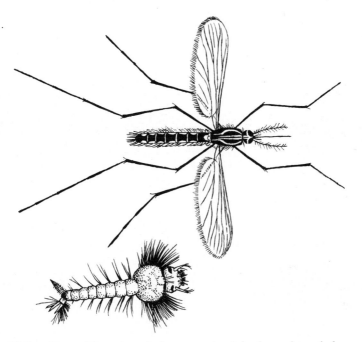

Yellow Fever Mosquito, *Aedes aegypti;* adult above, larva below

The warmth of a body is the means by which a mosquito locates a victim. According to Dr. Lyle E. Hagmann at Rutgers, a mosquito has a built-in heat-detection system in the tarsi, the front legs, that operates in a manner similar to a radar system. The tarsi-detectors receive the heat waves emanating from your body, and the mosquito flies directly to you. Presumably a thin person would be more attractive to a mosquito than a fat one, for a slim-Jim sort of individual has a higher metabolic rate. His energy and body consume food more rapidly than is customary with a stout or fat person.

Drs. Brown and Hagmann did their research with only a few of the world's 3,000 or so known species of mosquitoes. Among these various species, the ones classified as disease carriers are in the minority. Such a species is *Aedes aegypti*, the yellow fever mosquito. Epidemics of this disease were first identified during the seventeenth century, but no one suspected that a mosquito was responsible for the fever until the 1880's. Then Charles John (Carlos Juan) Finlay, an 1855 graduate of Philadelphia's Jefferson Medical College, settled in Havana to begin a life work on yellow fever. In 1881 he suggested that a mosquito was the carrier, and in the following year he specified the genus *Stegomyia*. The Reed Commission, directed by Major Walter Reed, U. S. Army Medical Corps, began a series of experiments that proved beyond doubt that Dr. Finlay was right in thinking a mosquito was responsible for the epidemics of yellow fever in tropical regions of the Western Hemisphere.

The disease was eradicated in the Panama Canal Zone and other areas through mosquito-control measures. Consequently with no incidence of the disease for a number of years thereafter, *A. aegypti* was thought to be the sole carrier of yellow fever. But in 1930 a jungle fever that caused many deaths in Brazil was identified as yellow fever, and it was learned that the source was another mosquito, *Aedes triseriatus*. So once again men like Walter Reed and his associates set to work to seek control measures to curb this new health threat.

Twenty-two years before the medical profession knew that a mosquito was responsible for yellow fever, it was discovered that one of these insects (*Culex quinquefasciatus*) transmitted filariasis —an affliction of the glands and limbs that causes them to swell and that may result in elephantiasis. By 1897, three years before Walter Reed's yellow-fever experiments, some of the mosquitoes that belong to the anopheline group were proved to be carriers of malaria. Twenty-odd species are now known to be vectors of this disease—one that affects some 250 million people a year, with most of those so stricken in India, where nearly 100 million people suffer from the disease. During the last three years of World War II, nearly one-half million of our troops at home and overseas were plagued by malaria.

During World War II, 92,649 cases of malaria were recorded for troops stationed within the continental United States. Today malaria in this country is at an all-time low. According to the Bureau of Vital Statistics there were only 132 cases here in 1957, and in the same year there was no incidence of yellow fever.

One of the world's most adventuresome bacteriologists was Dr. Morton Charles Kahn, who, time and again, tramped through South America's jungles on expeditions to study tropical diseases. One legacy that Dr. Kahn left the world is a trap that he and an associate developed in 1948 to destroy as many as 1,500 malaria-bearing mosquitoes in a night. The trap is equipped with a recording of the hum of a female, and when it is played it acts as a lure for the males, who fly in from miles around. They are killed when they come into contact with an electrified screen.

Certain species of both types of mosquitoes, anapheline and culicine, are carriers of various other diseases that affect man and other animals. Avian malaria, dengue fever, and equine encephalomyelitis are three transmitted by these insects.

Mosquito studies are being carried on all over the world. One group of scientists works at the East Africa Institute for Malaria and Vector-Borne Diseases—located at the top of a 3,000-foot mountain that thrusts up from the jungle of Tanganyika in Africa. Here, the director of the Institute, Dr. Bagster Wilson, and a small staff are studying *Anopheles gambiae*, considered the most deadly malaria-carrying mosquito in Africa.

In the eastern United States there are 33 million acres of freshwater and coastal marshlands. The coastal marshes are the breeding grounds for such giant mosquitoes as the salt-marsh (*Aedes sollicitans*) that can fly to towns and cities as far away as 50 and 75 miles from the marshes. In Delaware and New Jersey the first attempts to control marsh mosquitoes have been promising. The control is to manipulate the water levels so that the mosquito larvae are exposed to the sun and winds. Exposure to these elements kills the larvae, and at the same time tends to improve or preserve waterfowl habitat, whereas the use of insecticides or draining and filling are detrimental both to the waterfowl and their habitat—already suffering from man's ever-increasing encroachment.

Apparently the ecological niche into which mosquitoes fit in their own particular plant and animal communities is as a source of food for various other insects including the dragonfly, a few fishes, and a number of birds. In part this may offset some of the harm done by the insect whose name derives from the French *musket*, "little fly."

CRANE FLIES
Family *Tipulidae*

Sometimes the long slender larva of the crane fly is called a leatherjacket because its brown skin is so tough and leathery. Not infrequently the winged adult with its six long and slender legs is known as a "daddy longlegs," a name also used for the harvestman, an eight-legged animal of another order. In the past the daddy long-legs of the crane fly family were used to detect lost, strayed, or stolen cows. To locate a missing bovine by this technique involved cruelty to animals, for one of the insect's long legs had to be pulled off. As soon as a leg of this insect is detached, it slowly straightens out, and like the needle of a compass giving a lost person his bearings, the leg was supposed to point in the direction in which you should seek your missing property.

The crane fly is widespread, and among the thousand or more native species throughout the United States there is some variation. The one known as the range crane fly (*Tipula simplex*) has two forms: the male is winged, whereas the female is wingless. Generally the species on the northern parts of the range are the crane flies without wings. They look like large spiders, in spite of being closely related to the mosquito, as they crawl over the snow—a surprising performance when you consider that at this season hardly any insects are in evidence. So little is known about these wingless, winter-active forms that a detailed study of their life histories is in order for anyone who lacks an entomological project.

The best time of year to see crane flies is in the spring or fall. At either season these insects gather in great swarms, and "dance" only a few feet above the wet and watery areas in which they came into being. They bob up and down as if manipulated by countless invisible puppeteers, and frequently those gyrating above water land on the surface. They stay there without breaking through, held in place as water striders are held, by surface tension.

Once the adults have mated, the female deposits several hundred eggs in bogs, marshes, or swamps; along the shores of ponds, lakes, and streams; or in rotting wood or fungi. During their short larval stage, most crane flies do little harm, though some of the small species feed upon the leaves of such wild flowers as anemones and violets. The life of the larva is a few weeks, but that of a pupa is only a single week. A number of species overwinter in their embryonic form, the egg, but others pass this season as larvae.

Some crane flies should be in your collection of *Diptera*. As they are so numerous and so widespread, you should be able to catch at least one of these curious relatives of the mosquito.

9 ANTS, WASPS, BEES, and ALLIES

"An extensive and highly specialized order of insects, . . ."
Webster's New International Dictionary

A mong the more than 60,000 members of this order, the *Hymenoptera*, are such well-known species as the ants, bees, and wasps; less familiar ones such as the family of horntails and sawflies and the true gallflies; and also a number of tiny parasitic insects that go almost unnoticed but stand us in good stead because they control other harmful insects.

Though the order has been named membranous-winged, other orders of insects have the same type of wings. The differences between the wings of damselflies and dragonflies and those of the ants, bees, and wasps are in the veining. That on the wings of the damselflies and dragonflies is a small network, whereas there are only a few large veins and a small number of cross veins on the wings of ants, bees, and wasps.

The venation is not the unique characteristic of the wings of the *Hymenoptera*. What sets the wings of these insects apart from other insect wings is that they hook together to form a continuous surface. This is possible because the front margin of each hind wing is hamulate, furnished with a series of little hooks. And the hind margin of each front wing has a fold of skin into which the hooks, the "hamuli," catch. In a recently caught specimen of winged *Hymenoptera* it is extremely difficult to pull the smaller hind wings free from the larger front wings, though it can be done.

Not all members of this order have wings, and those that lack them are called apterous.

The mouth parts of these insects vary in form. The bee has a tubelike mouth in order to suck nectar from flowers, whereas the ant has jawlike mouth parts that permit it to pick up a seed, a crumb of bread, or other food and carry it away. And other mouth parts of these insects are for lapping.

There is usually some sort of sting, piercer, or saw on the abdomen of the females. The sting of a wasp or a bee is in reality a modified ovipositor, the organ for depositing eggs. Therefore if you are stung by one of these insects, you know it is a female. For males never possess ovipositors; a male honey bee, a drone, cannot sting you, but a worker honey bee will, for it is an undeveloped female.

The metamorphosis of these insects is complete. There are four life stages: egg, larva, pupa, and adult. Though there are solitary species, antisocial as it were, among the *Hymenoptera*, a great many are highly socialized, and live in well-ordered colonies. The ant has undoubtedly evolved the most highly developed social system.

The *Hymenoptera* is such a huge order that to make its classification somewhat simpler, it has been divided into two suborders and a number of superfamilies. The suborder for those *Hymenoptera* of a more generalized nature—those with the base of the abdomen broadly joined to the thorax—is the *Chalastogastra*. This name is derived from *chalastos*, loose, and *gastros*, belly, and the insects so categorized by this description are the various sawflies and the horntails.

The sawflies get their name because the female has a sawlike ovipositor that can make slits in leaves and stems into which the eggs are then thrust. One species of sawfly is the imported currant worm (*Pteronidea ribesii*). In its larval form it resembles a caterpillar and feeds on the leaves of currants and gooseberries by chewing holes in them. It overwinters either as a full-grown larva or as a pupa. If the overwintering form is a pupa, a silken case is spun for protection. The case is usually in a pile of trash on the ground where the larva has been feeding. When the weather is warm enough the following year, the sawfly bursts out of its case in the adult form.

When *Pteronidea* is in its winged state, it measures about ⅜ of an inch in length, and like other sawflies when at rest, it folds its wings flat over the back.

Two species of sawfly are well known and thoroughly disliked on two continents. In Europe and North America the larch sawfly and the European spruce sawfly have years in which they occur in great numbers. At such times they often defoliate acre after acre of coniferous trees. Our best-known species is the pigeon horntail, or pigeon tremex (*Tremex columba*). This insect is also among the largest of the *Hymenoptera*, for, exclusive of its egg-laying append-ages, this black and ocher-yellow creature may measure as much as one and one-half inches.

The other suborder of *Hymenoptera* consists of parasitic forms, and the ants, bees, wasps, and their allies. The name of the suborder is *Clistogastra*, from *clistos*, closed, and *gastros*, the belly. The dis-tinguishing characteristic of these insects is the fact that the second abdominal segment is greatly constricted. This constriction forms the pinched-in-at-the-waist look of ants and wasps. The slenderized abdominal segment or segments, known as the petiole, joins the rest of the abdomen to the thorax.

The ovipositor of these insects has at least three forms; for some it is used to bore holes in trees in which to place the eggs; for others, the parasitic forms, it is used to thrust eggs into the eggs and bodies of other insects; and for still another group, it is a sting connected with poison glands.

Of the host of hymenopterous insects, the late Frank E. Lutz once wrote:

What can one do with thousands of kinds of insects whose habits include such a range as leaf-eating, wood-boring, gall-making, being parasites, pirates, predators, architects, solitary, highly social, and so on?

Among the "thousands of kinds of insects" are some of the most interesting and least understood. These are the species that produce galls—the swellings on the tissues of plants that are familiar to many gardeners or to those of us who like to walk in the woods. The gall-making insects of the order belong to the family *Cynipidae*, and are sometimes referred to as guest gall wasps.

Two of the commonest galls made by *Cynipids* are the rose gall and the oak gall. Of the two, I am more familiar with the oak gall or oak apple. By fall these ball-like insect nests are brownish yellow and easy to spot, whereas in the spring or early summer they are greenish and not so easy to see. You will find them on the leaves or stems of various oaks. There are no exit holes in galls made by the *Cynipids*, and the adult gall wasp has to make its own way out of its spherical home when it emerges the following June or July.

As yet no one knows exactly how a gall forms, for it does not come into being until after the larva hatches from the egg laid upon a leaf, stem, or flower or in the puncture made by the female in the host plant. Therefore a study of galls and the insects that make them is a ready-made project for anyone wishing to undertake it.

Sometimes on a field trip you will find an insect that has been the victim of its own zeal. This is the female ichneumon wasp, a wood-boring insect that gets its ovipositor wedged so tightly in the wood it is drilling that it is unable to pull out. One of these wasps that is subject to this type of misfortune is *Megarhyssa macrurus*, the species in the illustration.

Whether immobilized or flying through the air with its tail-like appendages trailing behind, the ichneumon wasp rarely goes unnoticed. But a chalcid (*Brachymeria ovata*) is one of the seldom-seen insects of this order that stands us in good stead because it is a tiny parasitic control (Color Plate IV, *facing page 192*).

For more information about the parasitic *Hymenoptera* and other less well-known members of the order, beg or borrow such a book as *A Manual for the Study of Insects*, by Comstock and Herrick, or one that deals specifically with a subject, such as *Plant Galls and Gall Makers*, by E. P. Felt (see Appendix).

WASPS
Families *Vespidae* and *Sphecidae*

In 1869—when men were bold and women brave—B. D. Walsh, an American entomologist, wrote that some people were using the insect devouring propensity of hornets to a good purpose by suspending one of their nests in the house, thereby eliminating the common housefly. So long as the hornets were not meddled with, they did not meddle with the householders. He continues, however, by saying that he had never seen this take place though he had been told it did work!

JAMES A. CLARK, *Outdoor Indiana*

The hornets so used in 1869 are among the more than 2,500 species of wasps in North America. Of this number some fifty can inflict a painful wound by driving the needle-like ovipositor into the flesh. At the same time the wasp injects a fluid that causes a painful swelling. The wound may be so severe that the swelling lasts for several days, and in some cases requires a doctor's care.

Unfortunately the sting's the thing most of us associate with wasps. But many of these wasp-waisted insects, including the fifty troublemakers, are better neighbors than we realize, for they kill a great many destructive insects to provide food for their young.

The wasps most of us know are the ones that build nests in, on, or near houses. You will find their nests in attics; beneath the overhang of dormer windows or other protected spots on houses; in foundation plantings and trees shading houses; in stone walls or rock fences; and in the ground. The wasps that build in such places comprise three distinct groups.

One group includes the hornets and yellow jackets of the genera *Vespa* and *Vespula* (Color Plate IV, *facing page 192*). These black wasps, distinguished by a stocky build, may be marked with yellow or white. The lengthwise measurement of the queens is usually ¾ inch, while that of the males and the workers is about ½ inch.

The nests of hornets and yellow jackets are made of a material similar to papier-mâché. Originally the material used for paper-making was rotted wood or dead stems and leaves. Today many wasps use materials that are easier to get; they gather little chunks of paper and cardboard strewn across the countryside by the human litterbug. Whether the wasp uses traditional nest-making material or waste paper, the next step in preparation for actual nest-building is chewing. The wasp chews and rechews the mouthful of material it has gathered until it is a pulpy mass reduced to the proper consistency by generous amounts of saliva.

When the pulp is right for construction, the wasp spreads some on the chosen site—a branch of a tree, a gable of a house, or any other suitable spot. And from the foundation a nest is built. As a wasp works, it always moves backward so that it does not walk on the newly spread pulp. Apparently a wasp takes time out to inspect the quality of its work, for every so often the insect tests still damp material by touching it with the feelers. Presumably this is to determine whether the material will result in a nest of uniform thickness.

The nests of hornets and yellow jackets are usually large, globular structures in which there are any number of combs. If you study the ways of wasps, do not close in to watch hornets or yellow jackets at work, for they resent intrusion.

The second of the paper-making wasps is *Polistes*, the wasp with no common name and one that is slender, elongated, and measuring at least three-quarters of an inch or perhaps even an inch. These wasps may be black, brown, or red, with the various colors set off by a few yellow markings. *Polistes* is "peaceful" and, if you do not move in too quickly, will let you watch as it builds its papier-mâché home. This is a circular affair that looks like a chunk of honeycomb stuck in place so that the cells hang downward.

These two groups of wasps, the hornets and the yellow jackets and *Polistes*, have similar life histories. The perpetuation of the season-long colonies is assured in the fall when the females and the smaller males leave the nest for a nuptial flight.

Once a mating is consummated the male dies—the purpose of his short life has been served. The survivors of the nuptial flight, the now fertilized females, or queens, hibernate. A female may hibernate in a crack in a rock, under the loosened bark of a tree, or in a hole in the ground. And sometimes a *Polistes* queen will, if she can, secure herself from winter weather in your attic or basement.

When winter is well out of the way a queen emerges from hibernation. Her first duty is to locate the best possible nesting site, for it is a peculiarity of these insects that they never use an old nest. She flies thither and yon until she finds a spot to her liking. Here, using wasp papier-mâché she constructs a few shallow cells if she is a *Polistes* queen or starts the foundation for a large nest if a hornet or yellow jacket.

The queen hornet or yellow jacket lays a single long white and slightly curved egg in each cell, and when all are filled, she quits egg-laying for the time being. Each egg takes two or three days to hatch, and the grub that emerges is a grayish-white creature shaped like the egg from which it came. Helpless, the wasp larva hangs head down in its cell, a seeming violation of the laws of gravity. But a gluey secretion holds it in place by sticking it to the sides of the cell.

The queen has to rear her first brood without assistance, for she is the only survivor of last year's colony. Each day she feeds the workers-to-be freshly killed insects. The female hornet or yellow jacket gives her brood a diet of such insects as house flies, blow flies, and various moth caterpillars. A *Polistes* queen feeds her brood agricultural pests such as the armyworm, the larval form of a dull brown moth (*Cirphis unipuncta*) or the corn-ear worm. In some years the latter insect (*Heliothis zea*) ruins so much corn that the damage is estimated at $50,000,000.

The captured insect is chewed to mincemeat before it is fed to the young. This feeding lasts ten to twelve days, the period of the larval stage. As the grubs increase in size they fill up available cell space and depend less and less upon the gluey secretion to hold them in place. As soon as they are fully grown they spin little cocoon-like caps of silk over the cells, then transform into pupae.

A pupa of these wasps is as motionless as a mummy for twelve days or so and, like a mummy, it has a swathing. This is a thin, transparent membrane, a protective sheath that covers the pupa—at first a creamy-white replica of the parent. As the days go by, color appears in the wings, legs, antennae, and on the body itself. Then the hour comes when the membrane breaks, and an adult emerges.

The first brood of each season always develops into workers, whose destiny is to care for subsequent broods. This relieves the queen of all duties except egg-laying. Most of the wasps in the broods-to-come are workers—usually sterile females. The worker wasps are in complete charge of nest life; they care for all immature young; they forage for food; and they enlarge the nest to accommodate the growing colony—a colony in which most of the members will die as the season dies.

During the life of a colony there may be 15,000 workers if the insects are hornets or yellow jackets, but only a hundred or so queens and males. In a *Polistes* colony the workers may number several hundred, whereas the number of queens and males may be only two dozen. The difference in size between a colony of hornets or yellow jackets and that of a *Polistes* wasp can be accounted for by the number of eggs laid by the different species. A hornet or yellow jacket queen is capable of laying as many as 25,000 eggs, but a *Polistes* can lay no more than several hundreds.

The three groups of wasps known as the mud daubers construct cells of clay in which to deposit eggs. The construction starts early in the summer after the young males and females have left the nests in which they overwintered as pupae. As soon as a mating takes place, the female looks for a spot in which to build six to twenty clay cells for her eggs. Some of the larger species of *Trypoxylinae* make parallel cells that look like the pipes of an organ. And some of the males in this family are unique among *Hymenoptera* because they guard the door to the cell while the female is out hunting for food. This behavior on the part of male *Trypoxylinae* is apparently a big concession to domesticity and a great compliment to the female, for generally males have no further interest in "home-life" once they have mated.

The female catches about two dozen immature spiders, paralyzing them one at a time by stinging them. She stores this "fresh meat" in a cell, then lays an egg, and finally seals the cell with a clay cap. She may build as many as twenty cells, but as soon as the last one has an egg in it and is provisioned and properly sealed, she leaves for good. The larvae that hatch from the eggs feed on the paralyzed spiders. It is only a matter of a few days before they are ready to pupate. For this period of quiet they spin cocoons in which they remain for about two weeks. At the end of this quiescent interval they transform into adults.

A close relative of the mud dauber is the golden digger wasp (*Ammobia ichneumonea*), a black or reddish-yellow insect that measures nearly one inch in length and is distinguished by golden hairs (Color Plate IV, *facing page 192*). This wasp digs a burrow for its eggs and provisions the cache with a supply of paralyzed grasshoppers on which the larvae start to feed as soon as they emerge. The golden digger wasp is one of ten thousand or so different kinds of "solitary" wasps, which seem to prefer living alone. These solitary species have only two adult forms: fertile females and males. But even without any workers to help them, they seem to carry on well enough under the restrictions imposed upon them by Nature.

ANTS
Family *Formicidae*

Go to the ant, thou sluggard; consider her ways and be wise.
                                                    SOLOMON

Ants are the dumbest of all animals.
                                                    MARK TWAIN

Mark Twain also said, "It is difference of opinion that makes horse races." Whether you side with Solomon or tend to agree with Mark Twain the opportunities for studying the ant to determine the possibility of its wisdom or lack thereof are limitless, should you care to tackle an entomological project of this sort. For these highly social insects are cosmopolites, and throughout the world more than 3,500 described species live in colonies whose numbers vary from only a few dozen to as many as hundreds of thousands.

You will find these thin-waisted, long-legged insects in practically any environment you can name—from the arid floors of North America's five deserts to the green tops of trees in India, where the silk-building ants construct their formicaries. The ability of ants to maintain themselves here, there, and elsewhere may be explained by a remark of Frank E. Lutz, late curator at the American Museum of Natural History.

"Probably," he said, "the insects are not so much adapted to the environment as the environment is adopted by the insects."

Though many of these adoptive insects are black, there are also red, brown, and yellow species. Ants have the typical insect body of three distinct parts: head, thorax, and abdomen. The head is joined to the thorax by a thin "neck," and the thorax is connected to the oval abdomen by an extremely flexible "waist." In some species the waist is only one slenderized segment, but in others two segments have undergone a slimming process. The pinched-in part of an ant is the "pedicule," or "petiole," whereas the thicker part of the abdomen is the "gaster."

Usually the head of an ant is large and carries a pair of extremely mobile antennae that are elbowed and long. That part of the antenna from the head to the elbow is a single-jointed section known as the "scape," or "shaft." The second section from the elbow to the tip is a series of nine to thirteen joints, and can be referred to as the "funiculus," or "lash." And the tip of the antenna is likely to be slightly thicker than the rest of it.

The thickened tip allows space for the organs of touch and smell. These are known as the "touch bristles" and the "olfactory cones." The number of these specialized organs on each antenna depends upon the species. One with good eyesight such as the wood ant (*Formica*) has had by actual count 211 olfactory cones and 1,730 touch bristles on a single antenna. Ants with poor eyesight or those that are blind have a great many more touch bristles and olfactory cones.

A species such as the wood ant has two compound eyes and three simple eyes, the ocelli. Known, too, as eye spots, the ocelli come in threes and are located in a triangle between the large compound eyes. The compound eyes have a number of tiny facets which, working together, create a complete picture for the ant. This picture is similar to the ones we see on television screens and results when a succession of dots merge, creating a complete picture for the ant. This is important for ants with vision, for they use landmarks to find their way about on a territory.

The legs are jointed and end with the tarsi—the tiny clawed feet. At the outward end of the tibia on each front leg is a feathery-looking little appendage. This is the ant's cleaning apparatus, the little comb with which it keps the antennae free of foreign particles.

The mouth parts of an ant are dual-purpose organs and are composed of two sets of jaws. The first, or outer set, is usually shovel-shaped and equipped with tiny pointed teeth. These teeth are to the ant what our hands are to us. The insect uses them for a variety of tasks such as digging a tunnel, carrying out the colony's dead, bringing in food, and for countless other jobs. Inner jaws, a secondary set, are used for chewing, and they move sidewise against one another.

The abdomen contains a crop, also known as the "social stomach," and the true stomach. The particles of food with which an ant stuffs the crop are food for all, and can be regurgitated so that other members of the colony can have a share. Before an ant can benefit from any food in its crop, the insect has to pump a part of it into the true stomach, where it is digested by gastric juices.

In the abdomen are the poison glands from which the insect ejects a fluid that can cause acute pain, accompanied by a burning sensation. The ants with which most of us are familiar are various biting species, the formicine ants, which bite first, then use a built-in atomizer to spray poison into the wound.

Some of our best-known ants have adopted environments that greatly annoy man. One of these, a pest known to householders throughout the greater part of the world, is the Pharaoh ant (*Monomorium pharaonis*), also referred to as the brown, the little red, and the yellow house ant. In North America two other small ants qualify as household pests at various times. *Iridomyrmex humilis* came to us from Argentina and Brazil by way of New Orleans, where it was first discovered in 1891; the color of this exotic is brownish black and its length is no more than a 1/10 of an inch. Today the Argentine ant is a household and garden pest in the South. Then there is the little black ant (*Monomorium minimum*), sometimes a house dweller, but more often discovered throwing up tiny piles of sand in the garden or on lawns and golf courses.

Another imported ant is a serious pest in the Southeast. It, like the Argentine ant, comes from South America, and probably got into the country as a cargo stowaway. This reddish to blackish-red insect is the imported fire ant—a stinging species known scientifically by the resounding name *Solenopsis saevissima* v. *richteri*.

Outdoors the imported fire ant feeds on collard, cabbage, and okra as well as egg plant, germinating seed corn, and citrus trees. It frequently attacks newly hatched birds and the young of domestic livestock. Indoors it eats butter and other milk products, meats, and nuts.

The imported fire ant (the word "imported" is used to distinguish it from native fire ants) and its control are a real problem. The *Conservation Bulletin*, bimonthly newsletter of the National Wildlife Federation, recently reported:

Controversy over the federal fire ant control program, as administered by the U. S. Department of Agriculture in the Southeast, is in a stew—and still boils. More and more people are speaking out in opposition to the aerial application of lethal chemicals in controlling the fire ant because of proven damage to wildlife and other values.

Nature should eventually help to control the imported fire ant, according to a spokesman for the Alabama Polytechnic Institute, who says, "Because after any new pest explodes into a major infestation, it tends to level off. Natural predators learn to feed on it. Diseases chop down its too-thick populations."

While waiting for help from Nature, the U. S. Fish and Wildlife Service is "initiating new research as provided for by the 85th Congress in an attempt to ascertain the effects of chemicals used in the fire ant program and, possibly, to develop less destructive controls."

Though stinging and biting ants seldom cause anything but trouble, on occasion a biting ant serves a purpose that might be termed "pinch-hitting for a surgeon." In Honduras the bite of the leaf-cutting parasol ant is used by Indians to suture wounds. The soldier caste of this species is an inch-long insect with a heart-shaped head and enormous mandibles. When one of these ants bites, it is for keeps, as it never lets go.

If an Indian cuts himself badly, he draws the severed flesh together, then takes a live soldier parasol ant by the back and places it as close as possible to the wound. The ant immediately bites, drawing together the edges of the flesh on either side of the cut. Enough ants are used one after the other to close the entire wound. Then the Indian so sutured twists the ants' bodies until they come free of the heads. But the heads stay in place, for the soldiers will not relax their holds even though decapitated.

The life history of the parasol ant and those of other species throughout the world are similar. And one species in North America is a good example of the family life of the ant.

Black Carpenter Ant
Camponotus herculeanus pennsylvanicus
(*Color Plate IV, facing page 192*)

The black carpenter ant is one of our largest, measuring about ½ inch in length. It is also one of our most widely distributed ants, and occurs in woodlands throughout the North Temperate regions of the continent. In these areas it lives in stumps or fallen trees; in the heart wood of injured trees still standing; and sometimes even in the heart wood of healthy trees. It also damages telephone poles and the timbers of all types of dwellings. When I visited Seney National Wildlife Refuge on Michigan's Upper Peninsula in 1954, the porch of the guest cottage was so riddled with the galleries of these ants as to be unsafe. And in addition to the various types of forest trees and forest products it damages, the black carpenter ant has the unendearing habit of biting, as many a picnicker knows.

A colony of these ants may be sizable. Among the several thousand workers of varying sizes are a queen; a brood in all stages of development; and at certain times of the year numberless winged females and males. Each of these ants represents a caste, and as each caste has a definite function to perform, a colony of ants is a highly specialized organization.

The workers, the most numerous members of a colony, are sometimes called "ergates," a term that comes from the Greek and means a specific type of insect worker. The smallest workers, usually the first-born, are "macrergates," whereas the larger workers, those born after a colony is established, are "micrergates." For most of us it is more convenient to think of the colony of the black carpenter ant or that of any other species as having three main castes: worker, soldier, and reproductives.

A new colony of ants is in the offing when certain members of an established colony acquire wings. The winged ones are queens and males—the reproductives, that are now ready to leave the old, or native, colony. The leave-taking, or swarming, occurs at various times during the year and depends upon latitude and climatic conditions. A windless day and one on the sultry side seems to be the most favored.

On such a day the entire colony is thrown into a frenzy, and a sort of stampede takes place, for the nonflying ants go outside with those that are about to become airborne. The wingless members of the colony scurry around, climb up on plants and bushes as if looking for observation posts from which to watch the reproductives spiral into the air. Edwin Way Teale tells of a time in southern California when "so many billions of winged insects appeared over the Malibu Hills they formed a black cloud which was mistaken for the smoke from a forest fire. Rangers rushed to the spot and found the air swarming with insects."

The frenzy of a flight is described in *The Ants* by Dr. William Goetsch, Emeritus Director of the Zoological Institute and the Museum of the University of Wroclaw, Poland. This particular flight was at Punta Tragara on Capri.

I once observed a marriage flight which presented a profound spectacle of birth and death in nature. As the sun went down, the Italian house ants (*Pheidole pallidula*) began to swarm. From all sides appeared bands of little winged males; these bands quickly joined to form a light cloud which danced up and down over the blue seashore for the brief moment which was both the climax and the end of their lives.

Then came the much larger females. They rose heavily into the air; their wings are smaller than those of the males, and their movement was slowed by the masses of eggs they carried. At first the females flew about singly, but as soon as they noticed the swarm of males they hurried into its midst. Wherever the females appeared, a wild movement began. The males dashed headlong toward them; a mad whirl, and a male achieved his purpose. Joined together, male and female fell zigzagging to the ground, where after a short time the fertilization process was completed.

As soon as a mating is consummated the male dies. Now the fertilized female has to divest herself of her wings before she actually begins work on starting a new colony. Sometimes she rubs off her wings by bending sideways and pressing them against the ground or stones and stems of woody growths; at other times she bites them off; and in some instances the wings are shed bit by bit until the only evidence of them are little stumplike projections.

Once she has got rid of her wings the queen is ready to seek a place for a new colony. If she is a wood-dweller such as the black carpenter ant, she will gnaw her way into a rotting stump or other wood in the same condition. No matter the species and no matter the nesting site, the queen builds herself a small chamber—a closed retreat from the world in which to undergo a long fast while she lays a few eggs and rears her first small brood.

During this interval the wing muscles help to nourish her and her first young. Dr. Goetsch likens the wing muscles on the queen ant to the humps on camels, for like the humps they are storehouses of nutrients. A queen is nourished in a second way; not all the eggs she lays have a chance to hatch, for most of them are eaten by her.

The few eggs that hatch produce larvae that are grublike and without legs. Among the first larval forms of the ant, certain individuals are singled out for special feeding. These pampered ones are always the largest, and they are fed by the queen with the largest bits of food available. Consequently the larvae that have a priority on the most food mature quickly.

As soon as the larva matures, it is ready to pupate. Most of our common species of ants spend this quiet interval within a cocoon—spun like those of the caterpillars of moths and butterflies. (Such cocoons are sold in pet shops as "ant eggs," and are bought as fish or bird food.) The growth of an ant takes place between the time it hatches and the end of the pupal interval.

The first ants to emerge are workers, usually smaller than those to come from subsequent broods. They begin work at once by caring for the brood that is current, and within a few days assume other duties such as boring tunnels to the outside world, venturing forth to capture prey, and carrying prey back to the helpless members of the colony. This food not only nourishes and strengthens the larvae in the nest, but changes their color, too. For the ants-to-be are translucent from the diet of eggs on which they have been living. But the introduction of new foods in the diet gives the larvae color that may be that of honey or whatever else the workers bring in.

The first workers, the small ones, are short-lived, whereas those that develop subsequently are much larger and much longer-lived, often having a life span of as much as six months. But whether they are small or large the workers relieve the queen of all duties except egg-laying. Her one mating usually makes it possible for her to lay fertile eggs during a life that can be as long as fifteen years.

Among the workers are certain individuals that have extremely large heads and strong jaws. These ants are the soldiers in a colony. Their function is not to go forth to war, but to guard the home. The big head contains a thick skull covered by chitin—a hard, tough skin. A soldier often blocks an invasion of enemy ants by stoppering the entrance to the colony with its head. And with their strong jaws the soldiers tear to pieces the prey brought home by the worker ants—all of which have the best developed brain among the various castes of a colony. Here are a few measurements of the relative sizes of nerve centers in insect's brains as set forth in Adolf Portmann's *Animal Forms and Patterns*.

	Optic Centers	*Olfactory Centers*
	as % of the whole brain	
Moth (*Notodonta*)	51.2	13.4
Butterfly (*Pieris*)	79.5	2.3
Fly (*Musca*)	76.8	4.4
Ant (*Formica*)	9.9	18.1

Sometimes the soldiers join forces with the workers to care for the larvae, licking and stroking them, moving them about to give their charges the benefits of the best temperature and moisture conditions, or carrying them to safety in case of a raid by enemy ants.

The food of ants is varied and includes dead and living animals; plants and their seeds, fruits, pollen and nectar, and fungi. Among the honey-collecting ants of the southern United States and Mexico are certain members of the colony that act as vats. These ants hang in the nest and are filled with the nectar and honeydew (the sweet, sticky secretion of aphids) brought in by the workers. They are often filled to the bursting point, but are drained when hard times come to a colony as the members feed on the sweets stored in these living vats. A custom at some wedding feasts in Mexico is to serve honey-filled or nectar-stuffed ants as a delicacy.

The stories of ants and their actions are almost numberless and go back in time to the days of Herodotus, who wrote that ants in India dug gold for princes. One of the most recent stories concerning these insects has to do with the beggars at a Hindu temple in Shrirampur. The mendicants noticed that the offerings of sugar left by the devout were disappearing, and investigated to learn the reason. A line of ants was carrying away the sugar grain by grain, and in a nearby anthill several pounds of stored sugar were discovered. Whereupon, stated the *Times* of India, the beggars were so inspired by the industry of the ants that they tossed aside their alms bowls, and hired on as laborers at a construction job in the neighborhood of the temple. Reason enough to make Solomon smile, were he around today.

NATIVE AND INTRODUCED BEES
Superfamily *Apoidea*

The bees are humming at their work, dart here and there, enter the great scarlet and blue caves and canopied passages of flowers, . . . come out all powdered and scented like the courtiers of the last age, and yet all the while have a blithe sense that they are doing their duty, and gathering honey for the hive.

The Dial of Love, Walks In The Country,
And What We See There
Late nineteenth-century reader

The bees in North America that gather honey for the hive or individual use are the introduced honey bee and many of the 5,000 or so species of native wild bees. Most of these bees emerge from flowers all powdered and scented because they are robbers, bent on providing for their own neds. The booty they seek is the nectar and pollen from blossoms of numberless plants. And from the buds of various trees they collect a resinous substance with adhesive properties called "propolis," better known to most of us as bee-glue.

The nectar gathered from blossoming alfalfa, red clover, and other seed plants is turned into honey. The golden grains of pollen collected from the catkins of the flowering willow and other

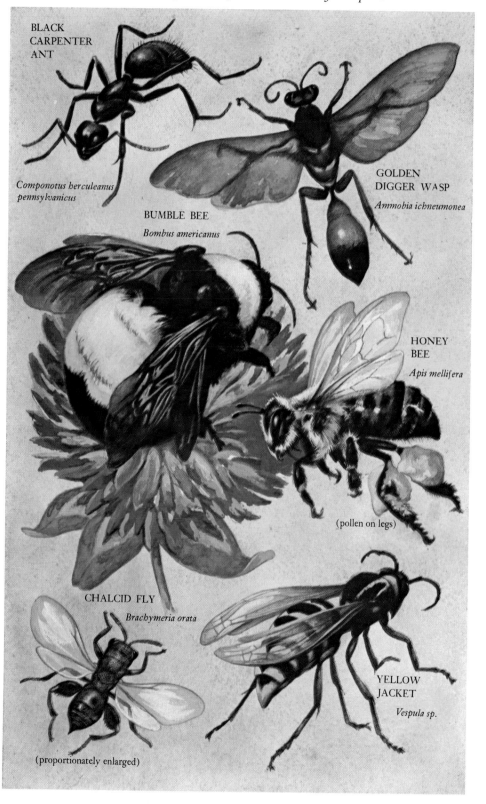

BLACK
CARPENTER
ANT

*Componotus herculeanus
pennsylvanicus*

GOLDEN
DIGGER WASP

Ammobia ichneumonea

BUMBLE BEE

Bombus americanus

HONEY
BEE

Apis mellifera

(pollen on legs)

CHALCID FLY

Brachymeria orata

YELLOW
JACKET

Vespula sp.

(proportionately enlarged)

sources are an essential food for rearing healthy broods. And the propolis, the waxy substance that oozes from tree buds, is a cement used during the construction of the comb.

In its quest for nectar and pollen the bee seems to be one of the pollinating insects that locates a blossom by using "a sense of numbers." Dr. E. P. Leppik of Augustana College, Sioux Falls, S. D., and associates of the Tropical Research Institute of the University of El Salvador have been working with insects that "recognize" numbers. They discovered that bees identify yellow flowers which are very much alike in size and symmetry merely by the number and arrangement of the petals; that is, they recognize patterns in flowers that have petals arranged in definite numbers. This is the way in which Dr. Leppik summed up his findings and those of his associates:

Bees *count* in the sense that they know if a nectar-laden flower has 1, 2, 3, 4, 5, 6, 8, 10, and 12 petals but not 7, 9 and 13, and that 3 and 5 have double meanings for them. Bees cannot clearly distinguish between marigold heads with 3 and 4 petals, two numbers that seem to be the limit of their mathematical ability, if such it can be called. Higher numbers are easily "remembered" if expressed in symmetrical structures.

In reporting upon his work, *The New York Times* commented:

To prove his point Dr. Lippik removed rays from Mexican marigolds, so that the number was reduced from 10 to 5, from 5 to 2, and so on. Marked bees either avoided the mutilated heads or were confused and visited both normal and abnormal flowers. If many flowers are mutilated, bees finally adapt themselves to the new condition. Scent is used as a guide when odor is intense. The removal of only a single petal is noticed by bees, but they will continue to examine all varieties of the flower so long as the nectaries are not removed.

Dr. Leppik believes that the reason for this arithmetical sense of pattern in pollinating insects is the quest of nectar and pollen. Nectar is not only hidden but protected by an elaborate floral structure. Hence a pollinating insect must be able to recognize a nectar-bearing flower at a distance to save time and energy. A flower is spotted as a whole, which means more than the sum of a flower's characteristics (size, color, symmetry, odor). . . .

As bees gather load after load of nectar from the flowers they recognize, the insects perform an invaluable service in their respective plant and animal communities. For they are the agents that pollinate the flowers, and by so doing ensure the production of seeds and fruits.

The hive bee, colonized in North America during the early 1600's, was at first used solely as a source of honey. Little thought was given it as a pollinating agent, for wild bees were still plentiful in those days to carry on such work. Though the hive bee is still the annual source of many millions of pounds of honey and two million or more pounds of beeswax, its value as a pollinator is now fully realized. This highly social insect pollinates at least fifty agricultural crops on which we depend, and in nearly all agricultural areas is now the most numerous flower-visiting insect. And so essential is the transfer of pollen from flower to flower that beekeeping must be carried on to maintain profitable agriculture.

In some areas the leaf-cutting bee of the family *Megachilidae* is the principal pollinator of alfalfa when this important hay-producing crop is in bloom. Most of these bees are somber-hued insects, being black, blue-black, blue-green, or purple. As a rule the undersides have a brush of light yellow or brownish hairs. These hairs are the devices provided by Nature for the collection and transfer of pollen from one flower to another—winged insurance for the agriculturist or nurseryman that there will be seed for future acres of alfalfa, buckwheat, or clover and for flowers such as marigolds, mignonette, and morning glories.

Another wild bee, the bumblebee, is responsible to a great extent for the pollination of red clover. The amount of nectar concealed in the blossom of this plant is small in comparison with the amounts offered by other flowers, and it is contained in a little envelope at the end of the long corolla tube. The length of the tube and the relatively small amount of nectar cause the honey bee a lot of work for a little profit. If flowers with easy access and greater amounts of nectar are nearby, the honey bee goes to them. But certain bumblebees have extremely long tongues and a predilection for the nectar and pollen of red clover—a combination that is fortunate because it ensures pollination of this important forage and green-manure plant.

The relationship between the long-tongued bumblebee and red

clover was demonstrated more than one hundred and fifty years ago in New Zealand. Though red clover was well adapted to this country, there was little or no seed production until the very last years of the nineteenth century. Then several species of bumblebee were imported, and these *fin de siècle* insects took to their new environment with gusto. In time their yearly numbers were such that the annual seed production of red clover increased until it reached a satisfactory quantity.

The hive bee, the leaf-cutting bee, and the bumblebee—insect friends of man—and a great many others are distinguished by the fact that they provide a store of pollen and honey for their offspring. Some species flout this usual pattern of bee life, for they do not lay up stores for their offspring, but appropriate those of their more industrious relatives.

Another distinguishing characteristic of the honey bee and some wild species is the true social habit. This is best typified by the honey bee which has a complex society involving division of labor and cooperation between parents and offspring. Those wild bees that lack an organized society usually nest by themselves, and for this reason are referred to as "solitary" bees.

Though nesting alone seems to be to the liking of such bees, they do not withdraw from the society if their own kind. Not infrequently you can find acre after acre in which their burrows are no more than one inch apart. An area riddled by burrows is called a bee town, and one in Utah occupied by alkali bees had an estimated 200,000 nesting sites.

A farmer in the vicinity of Prosser, Washington, has a high regard for the tiny alkali bee (*Nomia melandri*) because he believes this species is faster and more efficient in pollinating alfalfa than other, larger bees. Therefore he protects them from skunks and birds by placing little wire baskets over the patches of ground in which they nest. With no predators to cut down their numbers, the bees do such a thorough job of pollinating that the average yield of seed for each acre is nearly one thousand pounds, whereas the average yield on a statewide basis for ten years (1946–1955) was 397 pounds.

On a nation-wide basis we are indebted to these stinging insects on three counts: as a source of at least 242,000,000 pounds of honey a year; as a source of more than 4,450,000 pounds of beeswax each year; and as the pollinating agents of one hundred or so agricultural plants and endless wild and garden plants.

What manner of creature is a bee at once so beneficial and so capable of inflicting a painful wound?

The body, like that of the closely related wasp or any other insect, is divided into three main parts—head, thorax, and abdomen. The head has the organs of sight and touch and those for mastication and honey collecting. The two compound eyes are on each side of the head; the pair of jointed antennae, the feelers, are beneath the eyes and forward, and the mouth parts are adapted for several functions. For the mandibles—the horny, toothed jaws—can cut propolis into shapes for building, and can handle pollen and nectar; the proboscis is adapted to siphon the nectar from the blossoms; and the mentum sheathes the tongue, the "ligula."

The tongue is covered with hairs which are thought to facilitate the upward intake of foods—perhaps on occasion lapped with the tip from flat surfaces. The size of the tongue depends upon the species and type of bee. Three families of wild bees are classified as short-tongued and four as long-tongued. These categories are not hard-and-fast taxonomic rules. Among hive bees the tongue of the worker is twice as long as that of the queen or the drone—two members of the colony that do not help with the collection of nectar or pollen.

The two pairs of wings and the three pairs of legs are attached to the thorax. In the stratified society of the honey bee the thorax of the queen is an elongated oval; the shape for the drone is more truly oval; and that for the worker is foreshortened. The membranous wings are transparent, and hook together by means of tiny clasps on the front margins of the hind wings. When the name of the order *Hymenoptera* is used in reference to bees, you can think of it as meaning "wedded-wings." The six legs, jointed and extremely mobile, are covered with pollen-collecting hairs.

The third body part, the abdomen, is joined to the thorax by a waist—not nearly so narrow as the one found in ants and wasps.

And except for those species that are stingless, the female has an ovipositor or sting.

A part of the internal anatomy is adapted to help with the disposition of the nectar—drawn up through the proboscis. The nectar, basis for honey, passes into a short pharynx, and then into the honey bag, or gullet. Here are salivary glands whose secretion makes it possible for the bee to knead pollen into pellets. This secretion also helps the bee to create cells when it uses the bee-glue gathered from tree buds.

The bee also secretes other substances, and uses a do-it-yourself technique for the manufacture of wax used in construction of the comb. This wax comes from eight pockets on the under, or ventral, side of the abdomen.

Still another secretion is one with which many of us are familiar. This is a fluid, transparent, full of formic acid and other irritants, that the queen or worker bee injects at the time a sting punctures your skin. The poison comes from the venom bag located near the end of the alimentary canal.

The bee, unlike the wasp, leaves the stinger in the victim. The stinger should be scraped out at once to prevent as much of the venom as possible from getting into the wound. Cold applications relieve the swelling that results from a bee (or wasp) sting. After the swelling is reduced, applications of water and bicarbonate paste are the recommended treatment.

Some people are so allergic to the chemicals in bee venom that death results. *Science Service* reports that the familiar bumblebees and honey bees kill more persons each year than all the poisonous reptiles combined. In a study of bee stings conducted at The University of Würzburg, Germany, researchers found that two components of bee venom cause antibody formation in rabbits, but the test animals were unable to produce antibodies to counteract the highly poisonous ingredients in bee venom. Work is being continued, of course, in the hope of finding an immunizing agent to protect the highly sensitive person from the effects of the lethal part of the venom, known as "fraction I."

The life histories of our native and introduced bees are in four stages: the developing egg; the larva, or grub; the pupa; and the adult. To illustrate the life cycle of the bee, we have selected a native species and one that is introduced.

BUMBLEBEES
Genus *Bombus*
(Color Plate IV, facing page 192)

Though we call this large black-and-gold species the bumblebee, the British refer to it as the humblebee. Both names are fitting, for they come from the humming noise the insect makes in flight. This was noted by Nikolai Andreevich Rimski-Korsakov, the Russian composer, who gave the insect a form of immortality with his droning composition, "The Flight of the Bumblebee." Theoretically—as demonstrated through laboratory tests and wind-tunnel experiments—the bumblebee should not be able to fly. The size, the weight, and the shape of the body in relation to the total wingspread are supposed to rule out the possibility of flight. But with a fine disregard for the laws of aerodynamics, the bumblebee, all fuzz and buzz, continues to fly from the time the first queens come out of hibernation until the last ones crawl into sequestered spots in which to overwinter.

The derring-do of the bumblebee so tickled author Murray Banks that he quotes a verse about the flight of the insect in his book *How To Live With Yourself.*

> I like the joke on the bumble-bee;
> His wings are too small to hold him.
> He really can't fly, professors agree—
> But nobody ever told him.
> ANON.

The active season of the bumblebee may start as early as the first part of April or it may not begin until late in May. Seasonal activity is governed by its whereabouts on a range that includes all of the United States and southern Canada. The first queen bumblebees of each season often emerge from hibernation when the catkins of the pussy willow are heavy with their loads of golden-yellow pollen, or the countryside is splashed with the pink of apple blossoms.

A recently awakened queen is far from lively because her metabolism has not yet "thawed" sufficiently to permit the first normal activity of the season. This is to locate a nesting site for the new colony she will found. She flies back and forth over a given area in the manner of a pilot flying transepts, often skimming low over the ground in her search. Sometimes a queen alights on the blossom of an early-blooming plant and surveys the terrain in the immediate vicinity.

The preferred nesting site seems to be an abandoned meadow-mouse nest, though runways are also used. If such sites are not found, the queen builds a nest low in the grasses of her habitat or constructs one of sphagnum moss—a moss of wet and watery places. And on occasion—perhaps as a last resort—she digs into the ground and hollows out a small chamber which she then lines with bits of dried grasses and leaves.

Once a nest is in order, a queen brings in load after load of pollen and nectar. She collects pollen from pussy-willow catkins by crawling back and forth over them. Two sections on each hind leg are edged with long, stiff, and inward-growing hairs that catch and hold the pollen until the queen has a full load.

She deposits her supply of pollen and nectar, now in honey form, upon the floor of her nest. She also fashions a little waxen pot to hold an extra supply of honey. Now she is ready to lay a few small white eggs on the pollen moistened with honey. During the ten days it takes the larvae to become fully grown, the queen tends them like a hen fussing over a brood of chicks. As individuals reach mature larval form, each spins a paper-thin but surprisingly tough cocoon in which to pupate.

The queen remains in attendance during the quiescent interval of the brood, feeding from time to time on the supply of honey in the little waxen pot. At the end of ten days or two weeks, the cocoon ruptures and out pops a small worker bee. Each immediately assumes its duty in the colony so that the queen can devote the rest of her life to laying eggs.

The small worker is the bumblebee you see during the summer, whereas the one you catch sight of early in the season is large; she is the fertile queen that has overwintered from last year's colony. Late-in-the-season broods contain mating females and males, or drones—sluggards who live on the labors of the worker bees.

During the shortened days of late summer the mating females and do-nothing males take leave of their colony. These perpetuators of the race mate in the air. Now the fertilized females have a few days or weeks in which to fly around on a territory marked with signs that foretell a change in seasons. The males die, and back in the nest the old queen stops laying eggs. As the days of summer become fewer and fewer the number of bees in a colony decreases little by little. Finally all are dead including the old queen. Outside the nest the young queens are seeking places in which to over-winter. As the range of the bumblebee is extensive, the queens vanish from the scene throughout an extended period. In some areas no bumblebees fly after mid-July, while on other parts of the range some will still be out and about in mid-October. Finally the buzzing of the bumblebee in flight is stilled until the seasonal cycle changes once more with the advent of spring.

Unfortunately the number of bumblebees and other wild species is not so great as it once was. Man's encroachment on habitat is responsible for the decrease among the insects so helpful in the pollination of red clover, alfalfa, and other seed plants upon which we depend.

Hive or Honey Bee
Apis mellifera

(Color Plate IV, facing page 192)

For every tablespoonful of honey we eat, a single bee has to collect nectar from nearly 2,000 flowers. For every pound of honey offered for sale or used in the hive, a bee has to make at least 37,000 round trips between the hive and the sources of nectar. And to make the usual one hundred pounds of honey during an average season, the bees in a colony fly some 50,000 miles.

The insect that does so much flying was first studied in detail during 1737 by the Dutch savant Jan Swammerdam. In that year he counted the cells and bees of three straw hives, then three years later, René de Réaumur, French physicist and naturalist, counted 43,008 bees in a large swarm. The first honey or hive bees in North America were brought from Europe by early colonists. Upon seeing these semi-domesticated insects, the Indians named them "the white man's fly."

The usual number of honey bees in today's hive may number 50,000 to 80,000. Each colony has a caste system in which there are three types of bees separated into two groups. The first group includes the reproductives—the queen and the drones. The primary function of the queen is to produce eggs, and during her lifetime she usually lays 500,000 eggs, though estimates have placed the number at three times that. The second reproductive is the drone— a do-nothing male whose sole function is to be mated with a young queen for starting a new colony. As soon as a mating is consummated, a drone may quit the hive of its own accord, but more frequently it is driven out by the workers or killed within the hive. The drones that escape after a mating or a mauling usually manage to live until fall when they die with the first cold weather. The second group of a colony is made up of worker bees; these are sexually immature females who in the first two of their four life stages differ in no way from the queen.

The worker bee is the one all of us know, for it is the member of the colony that collects the pollen and nectar. Among workers some act as scouts, or foragers, in locating food sources; others gather only pollen; and still others have the exclusive duty of collecting nectar.

When a scout, or foraging bee, finds flowering alfalfa, dandelions, or white clover, to name but three of many food sources, it returns to the colony, and transmits its discovery to other workers by a series of "dances" as complicated as a quadrille. These dances are usually performed on the comb in the darkness of the hive, though now and again a dance is executed on the horizontal landing board attached to the hive.

Karl von Frisch of the University of Munich studied the dancing of bees within the hive, using a red light to which bees are insensitive. He learned that the movements of the dancers tell the other workers the direction of new pollen or nectar sources and how far they are from the hive.

A bee telling the whereabouts of new food sources by means of the "round" dance, makes two circles with the first danced in one direction and the second in the opposing direction. If you were to make a model for this dance, you would cut out a somewhat flattened figure 8 with loops of the same size. Once you had your cut-out, you would then fold one loop over the other but in such a way that the loop being folded would not fit true upon the other.

A round-dancing bee may perform on one spot of the comb for a matter of seconds—perhaps even for a full minute—before she moves to another section. On this part of the comb she dances again to give directions to a different group of workers.

The "wag-tail" dance is a true figure eight with the loops close to one another as in this 8, or farther apart as the lines from one loop to another are elongated. As she makes the lines between the loops the worker waggles her entire body from side to side.

During either of these dances the performer usually has a line of other workers following her. These follow-the-leader bees bring to mind a conga line or skaters playing snap-the-whip. They try to touch the dancer with their feelers; by so doing they may pick up the scent of the flower to which they are being directed, for the antennae of a bee are the organs of smell. And a bee's hairy body is well adapted for being impregnated by the scents of the flowers it visits. The body remains highly odorous unless the flight back to the hive is a long one. If it flies in from a distant source the scent is "washed" away by the air and the breeze until it is so faint as to be useless as a locating device.

The round dance is used to indicate pollen or nectar within a hundred yards or less from the hive. The wag-tail dance, the execution of a true figure 8, is for indicating food sources at greater distances from the hive. This dance, or rather the length of the lines run by the performing bee between the two loops, indicates whether a flight will be three hundred yards, three thousand yards, or three miles. No dancing takes place to indicate food sources beyond a limit of three miles, though bees often fly farther than that—even as far as seven or eight miles.

The wagging dance is also used to indicate the direction in which the alerted bees should fly. The direction of the runs made by the dancer in its figures are the signposts that guide the way. A bee dancing on the comb indicates direction by gravity, and according to von Frisch does so in the following style:

. . . upward wagging runs mean that the feeding place lies toward the sun; downward wagging runs indicate the opposite direction; upward wagging runs 60° to the left of the vertical point to a source of food 60° to the left of the direction of the sun and so on.

The number of trips made by a worker bee depends upon the abundance of pollen and nectar and the number of colonies in a given area. On its numerous daily round trips between hive and blossoming plants, a worker flies along at a speed that may reach 25 miles an hour. In order to push through the air a bee has to beat its tiny wings at a frequency of 250 times a second.

A worker usually visits only one species of flowering plant on its trips to collect pollen or nectar, and generally gathers either the one or the other from a single, small area. In a study of bee movements an investigator learned by watching marked bees that those working one day on a strip of buckwheat, 6 by 13 inches, were back on the same strip the following day. A bee working a blossoming bed of Shirely poppies has been known to make 47 trips between hive and poppies. The number of trips made by bees to collect dandelion pollen may be as few as eight or as many as one hundred.

The nectar of a flower siphoned by a bee is a concentrated sugar solution that contains the carbohydrates a bee needs. The various pollens supply the necessary proteins, fats, vitamins, and other food elements. At times the honey bee looks for salt or other minerals, and it carries water into the hive from various sources.

Pollen is fed to a brood of workers in larval form and also to young adult bees. Larval queen bees, however, receive special feedings of a substance known as "royal jelly." This highly nutritious food is produced for the most part by young worker bees, and the feeding of it to larval queens accounts for their large size. The older members of a colony feed on nectar or the honey which is elaborated from it.

Nectar is processed by the bee to make honey. First, it is converted into a sugary liquid containing glucose, a natural sugar, and fructose, fruit sugar. The conversion is possible because certain complex organic substances, the enzymes, in the crop effect a specific transformation of the nectar and while so doing accelerate the process.

The fluid that results is stored in open cells. When evaporation reduces the fluid to the proper consistency for honey, the bees seal these honey containers with a wax. The stored food, one of the oldest foods in the world, is compounded of 70 to 80 per cent sugar and 30 to 20 per cent water, minerals, and traces of acids, proteins, and other unanalyzed substances.

The amount of honey required by the usual colony of hive bees (55,000) each year is 400 to 500 pounds. The honey sent to market is that in excess of the requirements of the hive. As there are ten thousand or so nectar-yielding plants, the variety among honeys is great. The nectar of clovers such as alsike, sweet, and white makes a high-grade honey that is pale yellow. The honey derived from the nectar of buckwheat blossoms or those of heather is dark yellow or yellow-brown. And the sage honey of California is said to be similar to that gathered by the ancient Athenians on Mount Hymettus where the bees collected nectar from wild thyme.

The insect responsible for the honey of Hymettus and other varieties is given to swarming in late spring or early summer. Usually the old queen quits the hive and flies off, followed by thousands of workers. The swarm congregates on some sort of upright until scouts locate a site for a new colony. Frequently this is a hollow in a tree, an empty hive on the grounds of another beekeeper, or such an unlikely cavity as the police telephone box selected by the swarming bees of Karl B. Rector in Washington, D. C., during the early part of July 1958. If no cavity of any kind is available the swarm will start to build an unprotected comb.

Once it was a common belief that ringing a bell or beating on a tin dishpan would hasten the clustering of bees. Such is not the case, though it is still considered effective in some areas. There is an old, old superstition to the effect that if a marriage occurs in a family keeping bees the insects should be told of the ceremony, or they will leave the hive and not return. As recently as 1945 the *Daily Mirror* of London ran a picture of a country wedding, taken at the moment a girl in her bridal finery was bending over the hives at home and whispering: "Little brownies I am married."

Another superstition has it that bad luck is sure to befall the owner of the land on which a stray swarm settles. And if the swarming bees should alight on a once-living plant, death may come to some member of the owner's family. Writing in *Pastoril*, V, 1714, John Gay commented:

> Swarmed on a rotten stick the bees
> I spied
> Which erst I saw them Goody
> Dibson dyed.

All superstitions about the swarming of bees are bound to pass as the Age of Innocence has passed. And the unpredictability of swarming is passing, too, for beekeepers in Great Britain are warned electronically when a hive is about to swarm. A microphone-amplifier-analyzer system picks up the humming of the bees in an apiary and broadcasts it to the beekeeper. About half an hour before a hive is ready to swarm, the hum of the insects changes in tone. This warns the beekeeper to make preparations for preventing the loss of the swarm.

Shortly after the swarm departs with an old queen a young queen eats her way out of the sealed cell in which she was imprisoned. Once free she immediately rips open the cells in which other queens are developing. This prevents any rivals from maturing. Sometimes the workers destroy all other queens but one—held in reserve should anything happen to the first queen to emerge. If all goes well with the new queen, the one in reserve is eventually killed. There are times when a recently emerged queen finds it necessary to give some of her potential rivals a thrust with her sting—not barbed like those of the workers but long and pointed.

After a few days in the hive a young queen takes off on what is to be her nuptial flight. This first venture outside the hive usually occurs on a sunny day and one that is also warm and windless. As the queen is an excellent flyer, only the strongest of the pursuing drones is able to reach her. A mating is then consummated while both are airborne. Shortly after a mating is effected the drone becomes a dying creature, and by the time it falls to earth it is dead.

Once the nuptial flight is over the queen returns directly to the hive where she begins a life devoted solely to egg production. This function is interrupted at about the end of a year when her time comes to swarm. Now she takes to the air for the second and probably the last time in her life. The nuptial and swarming flights and the time spent in clustering while scouts look for a new home are the only relief she ever has from her true destiny as a queen. For as soon as she is settled in a new, man-made hive or a natural one, she commences to lay eggs once more, and at a rate of 1,500 a day during the three, four, or five years of her life.

The workers that remained in the old colony dominated by a new, young queen go about their business which includes the production of wax from glands on the underside of the body. A worker scrapes off the wax with its hind legs, transfers the sticky substance to its mouth where it is masticated and mixed with a special fluid. This is used to make the six-sided cells of the comb, with those for holding honey at the top and sides of the hive and those for broods at the lower and central parts. Any rough spots or cracks in the comb are covered or filled in with propolis, the bee-glue. The comb devised by the bee is highly functional, for the six-sided cells waste no space.

The eggs are placed in cells which differ slightly; the cell from which the queen emerges sixteen days after the egg is laid is similar in shape and appearance to a peanut shell; the egg-cell that houses a drone for twenty-four days is similar to, but larger than, those used for the storing of honey; and those for the eggs from which the worker bees develop are the same size and shape as the honey cells. The worker, smallest member of the colony, comes out of its cell at the end of twenty-one days. The life span of a worker that emerges early in the summer is only a matter of four or five weeks from the time it starts to fly. Those emerging late in the season overwinter in the hive, and the age to which these bees may live can be as much as eight months. The rate at which any of these bees develops within the egg is governed by variations in temperature.

One that is high speeds the development, while one that is low slows it down.

The drones born late in summer die with the season, whereas the queen and her workers overwinter within the hive. The workers surround the queen in a dense spherical mass; those nearest the queen are the least crowded, but those on the perimeter of this bee ball are jampacked together and act as an insulation. As the weather outside the hive becomes colder and colder, the bees at the center of the mass fan their wings. This activity generates heat. From time to time the bees inside relieve those on the outside by exchanging places with them.

The consumption of honey during the bees' least active period is thirty to forty pounds. The amount consumed depends upon the size of the colony, the temperatures from day to day outside, and the condition of the hive itself. A large colony in a poorly insulated hive eats a great deal of honey, for the workers constantly fan their wings to keep temperatures at a livable level. It is a matter of record that bee activity within the hive produced temperatures of 30° to 35° C. when the thermometer read 0° C. outside.

As such activity leaves a much weakened colony by spring, those responsible for the welfare of the six million colonies of bees in the United States see to it that in winter all hives are well insulated. This saves money, cuts down on the activity of the bees (which makes their aging much less rapid), and ensures strong, healthy colonies in the spring when agriculturists and orchardists will start renting bees to ensure pollination of their particular crops.

10 FLEAS

Dust you must if you would rid your dog or cat of the jumping insect known as the flea. In March 1958, an entomologist at the University of California, I. Barry Tarshis, stated that he had used new types of silica aerogel dust on forty dogs and eight cats The two dusts, then designated SG 67 and SG 77, were a complete success, for the fleas came out of the animals' hair and fur, fell off their hosts, and died within an hour. Today these flea-killers are on the market.

The usual fleas that harass cats, dogs, and man belong to the family *Pulicidae*. All members of this order, *Siphonaptera*, are wingless, narrow-bodied creatures distinguished by short antennae and long legs—legs that are muscled for jumping and which end in tiny clawed feet. The mouth parts of this parasite are equipped for piercing, injecting, and sucking.

The narrow body, actually somewhat flattened laterally, lets the flea move through the hair or fur of its host with ease. The long, powerful legs permit the animal to hop, skip, and jump for varying heights and distances. Most fleas can jump no higher than 6 inches, though 8-inch leaps have been recorded. As for standing broad jumps, the longest known distance covered by a few fleas is 13 inches. A peculiarity of a jumping flea is that the insect always lands looking in the direction from which it took off, and with its rear legs the first to touch the "ground." The large claws on the tiny feet assure a good grip when the animal finally settles down on its host. First it pierces the skin of a victim, then draws out the blood —the only food for adult fleas.

Usually the adult dog or cat flea is the one that man finds most bothersome. The human flea (*Pulex irritans*) is more likely to be found on such other animals as hogs, rats, and skunks. Man, however, was a preferred host in the Pacific Theater during World War II, as *The History of Entomology, World War II* relates:

On Okinawa our troops encountered *Pulex irritans*, the human flea, a species that has adjusted through the ages to a way of living in association with man not unlike the manner in which our common cat and

Human Flea, *Pulex irritans*

dog fleas live with our pets. The repellents and the DDT louse powder served a useful purpose in reducing the annoyance caused by this pest, but it was apparent that these materials were not a satisfactory solution to the problem.

In this country the species that causes the most discomfort is the dog flea (*Ctenocephalides canis*), with the cat flea (*C. felis*) a close second.

The dog flea is a cosmopolite that makes life exceedingly uncomfortable for various animals all over the world and throughout a great part of the United States. An area exempt from this flea and its infestations is the Rocky Mountain region and some intermountain states.

The egg from which a dog flea hatches is tiny, smooth, and white or yellowish white. A female expels an egg while she is on the host, and the miniature pellet falls into any convenient crack or crevice or wherever else there may be little accumulations of dust. The larva that hatches is a tiny white or yellowish creature that feeds on organic material in its vicinity. The larval interval of a flea's life is divided into three stages, the last of which sees the creature mature. Now it is ready to pupate and for this quiescent interval the flea spins a little cocoon. Pupation is over quickly, for in all it takes only thirty days for the flea to reach adulthood after hatching. On occasion the flea reaches adulthood in a somewhat shorter time or one that is a little longer—such variations are governed by temperatures.

The dog flea is one of some nine hundred species, including the oriental rat flea (*Xenopsylla cheopis*)—a carrier of plague and typhus. The germs of these diseases occur in the blood of infected rats. A flea feeding on the blood of such an animal introduces the infection into its own body. If such a flea makes a change in hosts, moving from rat to man, then there is danger that the individual may become infected. A flea is apt to disgorge partly digested blood or drop its feces near the bite. Either of these may get into the blood if the bitten individual scratches to relieve the itching. And there are times when the infected blood of the flea is forced into the wound by the feeding creature itself.

Today such animals as ground squirrels, meadow mice, and field voles in many parts of the West are infected with plague organisms. Infected mammals have been found in plant and animal communities as far east as South Dakota, Kansas, and Oklahoma.

The flea has been troubling all sorts of animals for a long, long time. Presumably there were fleas some 47 million years ago during the Oligocene period—a period in which a "blue earth" produced amber. Bits of vegetation and any number of insects were imprisoned when this yellowish or brownish mineral was in the making. One of these insects is the only known fossil flea, *Palaeopsylla klebsiana*.

11 OTHER ORDERS

The insects decribed here are a heterogenous collection such as any beginning entomologist might make. They include a familiar household pest; one that is unique in the way it finally achieves adulthood; and another well known to those who enjoy fresh-water sports fishing.

In this collection is the European earwig, truly representative of all the species in the order to which it belongs; the bristletail, one of our most primitive insects that develops directly from young to adult without the slightest sign of metamorphosis; and the green lacewing, belonging to an order in which the members differ so greatly in form as if to seem unrelated, and which are, for the most part, not too well known. Then there are the mayflies, the stoneflies, and the caddisflies, all creatures of fresh-water environments but in no way related to the true, or two-winged, flies.

But each species in this chapter, like the others in *Familiar Insects of America*, is a part of the world we live in. Any of these insects is worth study, either because you wish to add to your own general knowledge of this phase of natural history or because you would like to contribute something specific in the way of a new fact to the field of entomology.

The members of this order are among the most primitive of all insects. And though there are some 2,500 species of these small, wingless creatures throughout the world, not a great deal is known about their life histories. They are distinguished by long, segmented antennae, and three long, tail-like appendages that resemble bristles, the reason for their common name.

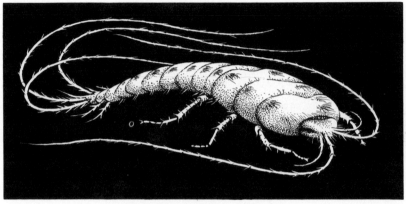

Silverfish, *Lepisma saccharina*

Two of the bristletails are the silverfish (*Lepisma saccharina*) and the firebrat (*Thermobia domestica*). These insects are familiar to almost any householder throughout the world and are well-known and feared by those who have any concern for collections of books. The silverfish thrives when the temperature is 80° F., but is frequently found in cooler places such as the basements of recently constructed buildings. The firebrat, as might be guessed, is an insect of hot places, and a temperature of 98° F. is one in which the insect seems to exult. Both are night feeders, and by day take refuge behind baseboards, window and door frames, in bookcases and the cracks in closets.

The silverfish and the firebrat have the simplest development; they undergo no radical changes, but merely increase in size the form they had at hatching, and develop reproductive organs. Maturing for these two is slow, and may take three to twenty-four months from the day of hatching. Growth is governed by temperature and humidity—factors that also influence the length of time it takes the eggs to hatch.

A female silverfish lays eggs at any time during the year; she usually deposits them in protected spots. There are occasions, however, when eggs are laid right out in the open—perhaps by a female little concerned with perpetuating the race or one whose egg-laying time came before she was able to reach privacy and seclusion.

Only a few eggs are laid at a time, but seemingly to compensate for the small number in each clutch, egg-laying may be extended for several weeks. The eggs are whitish, oval, and not more than one thirty-second of an inch in length, and the time it takes for hatching may be two weeks or a full eight weeks.

The firebrat lays several clutches of fifty eggs each. At first the soft eggs of this insect are opaque white, but take on a yellowish tinge before they hatch—a matter of two weeks.

The adult silverfish is slender, scaled, and has a lengthwise body measurement of an inch. The scales on the body are all a pearly gray. Though the firebrat is much like the silverfish in body form and general appearance, some of its scales are brown. This gives the creature of hot places a mottled appearance.

Each insect has a pseudonym. The one for the silverfish is "slicker," perhaps because it can get out of sight so quickly. That of the firebrat is "asbestos bug," a nickname that was bestowed on it because the insect feeds on, among other things, the sizing in the asbestos insulation with which steam pipes are wrapped.

These household pests and eaters of paste and glue in bookbindings can be controlled by a dust in which there is 10 per cent DDT or a spray with a petroleum base containing 5 per cent DDT. Control is not lasting—a few weeks at best—whereas the staying power of these two primitive insect forms seems to be enduring. Bristletails are the third oldest insect order on geological record. Fossil remains have established this fact, for evidence has been found from the Jurassic Age—which began approximately one hundred and fifty million years ago, and was a time when the reptiles were in the ascendancy.

STONEFLIES
Order *Plecoptera*

Insects of fresh-water communities throughout North America are devoured in quantities by trout, large-mouth black bass, and other sport fishes. The bass or trout on which you dine commonly dines on the stonefly—represented on a world-wide basis by some 1,500 species and in North America by two hundred or so varieties.

The stonefly, an insect with transparent wings, is also known by such regional names as "rock fly," "shad fly," and "trout fly." But no matter the name and no matter the place, people will know what insect you mean if you say stonefly, as this name is used for *no* other insect.

Occasionally you will find an adult stonefly airborne above a stretch of stream where the water flows fast. More frequently you are apt to find this large-headed insect crawling over water-washed rocks. For it is one of the most inept flyers among our various winged insects, though adults do fly some distance from the water to mate. This union marks the end of life for a male, who dies shortly thereafter. The female returns to water on whose surface she deposits 5,000 to 6,000 minuscule eggs, carried by some species in a tiny sac. As soon as the last of her eggs are expelled the female dies.

The stonefly that hatches from one of the eggs sized like a pin point is a tiny creature with an unusually large head, an extremely flat body, and two long filaments attached to the rear of the abdomen. At the bases of the three pairs of legs and on the last segment of the abdomen are a number of hairlike processes—little outgrowths that serve as gills so the nymph can get oxygen from the water.

Some nymphs feed on minute animals in their environment, others are vegetarians and nibble fresh-water aquatics. In turn hundreds and hundreds of nymphs hatched from the thousands and thousands of eggs are food for fishes that in the early stages of their development eat only fresh-water insects. The nymph that survives the chain of life in its own community undergoes several molts before it is ready to leave the water. Now a mature nymph and a survivor of the dynamics of food utilization, it crawls out of the water, then climbs up onto the stalk of some plant or up the face of a stream-side rock. It clings to either support and remains so until the skin splits down the back. This releases an adult stonefly—easily recognized because it has such a large head, four large wings of about equal size, long antennae, and two long tail-like streamers attached to the rear end of its pale brown body. The hind wings are broad and constructed like a fan. This permits a resting insect to fold the wings flat over its back.

Various species of stoneflies emerge from the mature nymphal state at different seasons. The winter stonefly (*Taeniopteryx nivalis*) may emerge on any day between New Year's and the first day of May. And there are years in which this species is so abundant that the snow has a mobile coating of black as the insects crawl back and forth across the surface.

Another source of food for fishes is unique because it is the only one of its kind to molt after acquiring fully developed wings. This is the mayfly of the order *Ephemeroptera*, an insect with a delicate body and one that usually has four wings (though some exceptions have only two), with the front pair much larger than those to the rear. The mayfly is found along streams or in the vicinity of ponds and lakes in whose waters the nymphs develop.

Before a mayfly becomes an imago, assumes its perfect adult form, it reaches a stage known as the "subimago." At this point in its life the insect settles itself in an upright position on some sort of perch with the wings also held in an upright position. Then as a prelude to the last stage of its life, the insect brings the wings into a horizontal position, fluttering them momentarily. Apparently this action must help—perhaps even causes—the skin on the back between the wings to split, thus enabling the insect to pull out the thorax and the head. With the end of the abdomen still in the old skin, the mayfly suddenly tilts so far backward that it hangs head down. It remains so for a matter of minutes, then works itself back into a heads-up position, finally pulling itself out of the last skin to be shed.

The now fully developed adult does not take off at once; it waits beside the former specter of itself until dusk gives way to dark. Then the adult takes leave of its former shape to fly off into the night, wings shimmering gold as it passes through a shaft of moonlight or comes into one of artificial light.

The mayfly will be a thing of beauty for a short time only. The life span of this insect in its adult form is often but a few hours and hardly ever more than three days. The short shimmering life of the adult mayfly is the reason for the name of its order, *Ephemeroptera*—derived from the Greek *ephemeros*, meaning "day."

EARWIGS
Order *Dermaptera*

In November of 1950 the Washington (D. C.) *Star* carried a wire-service item from Copenhagen that stated, "An insect called the earwig caused the loss of three Danish motorships valued at 350,000 kroner ($50,000) last night."

The loss was due to an earwig that got into the acetylene burner of a lighthouse in Greensund Belt. The insect stoppered the feed line and before anyone discovered why no fuel was flowing to the burner the flame had been extinguished for seveny-five minutes. The blacking out of the lighthouse beacon caused four skippers to run their vessels aground. Though three of the motorships sank, no lives were lost.

Probably the ship-sinking earwig was the European species (*Forficula auricularia*)—a reddish-brown creature nearly three-quarters of an inch in length, and distinguished by tail-like appendages shaped somewhat like forceps. Of all the thousand or so earwigs, the European is the most cosmopolitan, for it has traveled in potted plants to almost every temperate and tropical region. The insect was unknown, or at least unidentified as such, in the United States until 1909. In that year it was found in the vicinity of Portland, Oregon, and two years later another colony was discovered at Newport, Rhode Island. In 1953 large colonies were flourishing in and around Westport and Green's Farms—two communities of

New York's exurbia. One species (*Anisolabis maritima*) belongs to plant and animal communities in the vicinity of the high-water mark on the beaches of the United States.

The name of this insect is thought to derive from "earwing," for in those species that are winged, the rear pair is shaped somewhat like the outline of the human ear. This pair of wings is folded in an elaborate manner, both lengthwise and crosswise, under the short forewings. The insect does not as sometimes supposed enter the human ear, then burrow its way through the inner ear and into the

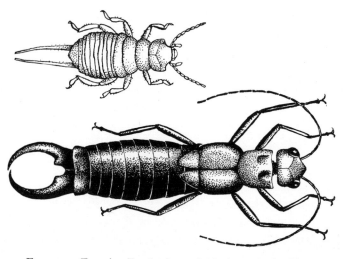

European Earwig, *Forficula auricularia;* nymph above, adult below

brain. If an earwig gets into anyone's ear the insect is probably seeking a hiding place.

The earwig overwinters as an adult or in the egg state, the eggs being laid in the fall. Some female earwigs act like broody hens, with their smooth white eggs that are laid in protected spots or in the ground. A female watches over the eggs and stays with them until the young have had the first of four or five molts. After the last molt the adult may be winged or wingless. Those with wings fly but little, and males can be distinguished from females because the forceps structure is larger and more curved.

By day the earwig hides in almost any place that affords protection: crevices of buildings, cracks in the ground, among fallen leaves and other litter. It is apt to be numerous in spots wherever garbage is dumped or in partially filled bogs or other damp places.

By night the insect comes out to feed on fruits and vegetables, on other insects and such slow-moving animals as the snail, and on decaying vegetation. A bulletin of the U. S. Department of Agriculture describes the insect as a hazard to health because "it feeds on filth."

A few of the world's thousand or so species are considered somewhat beneficial, for they feed on other insects classed as pests. Of this number there are about twenty native or introduced species in the United States. And gardeners should be heartened that among the twenty only the European earwig is apt to be troublesome to flowers and vegetables.

LACEWINGS
Order *Neuroptera*

One family in this order goes by the name green lacewings. These insects, the *Chrysopidae*, are small delicately formed creatures with soft bodies, wings that look as if they were made of net, and extremely long backward-curving antennae. The usual allover body color is a delicate green, though some go contrary to the general rule and flout color conformity by having touches of red, yellow, or black.

The green lacewings are also known as "golden eyes" and "stink flies." The insect comes by both names naturally: the color of its eyes is like that of freshly minted gold; and the insect can, when alarmed, emit a fluid that in the language of Audubon is foulsmelling enough "to offend the olfactories."

The green lacewing, the golden eye or the stink fly hatches from a tiny egg the adult female deposits on the tip of a little stalk, thin as a thread but stiffened and attached to a leaf. Sometimes the stalk serves as food after the infant lacewing hatches. Upon emergence from the egg the larva remains at the tip of the stalk, swaying back and forth. This swishing through the air helps to harden the soft body of the creature which as yet shows no sign of wings. When it is sufficiently armored to face its world, the larva is ready to begin hunting aphids and other small destructive insects, which it devours in enormous quantities.

The lacewing is an insect that undergoes a complete metamorphosis, passing its quiescent interval in a whitish little cocoon that it spins for itself. It emerges from the cocoon as an imago, the perfect adult form when it measures 6 inches in length, has brilliant golden eyes, and great shimmering wings. The advent of this creature in its final form is assurance there will be more to help keep in check the aphids—minute sucking insects that damage arborvitae, chrysanthemums, and melon plants—to name three on a list of more than forty damaged by aphids.

CADDISFLIES
Order *Trichoptera*

During the 1950's a creel census showed that about 10 per cent of our licensed fishermen catch nearly 90 per cent of the nation's trout. The experts pull native and introduced species and the resultant hybrids out of streams in which riffles kick up white water or from lakes and tarns in which the water is glacier cold, gin clear, and full of fighting fish.

In the East some of these anglers cast for brown trout in the Beaverkill, a broad, winding, gravel-bottomed stream in the Catskill Mountains of New York. Here as a boy I still-fished from a large flat rock while my father whipped the stream with a long, old-fashioned bamboo fly rod. In the West a certain number of these expert trout fishermen try for native species in countless mountain-born streams including Bear Creek, tiny, fast-flowing tributary of Montana's Blackfoot River, in which I caught my first rainbow trout.

Among the lures of the experts there must be some that simulate the caddisfly, an insect that comes off the water in fantastic numbers as winged adults. Throughout the United States, in southern

Caddisfly, *Ptilostomis semifasciata*, adult above, its larva second
from bottom; other drawings show larvae of various other species
with characteristic cases

Canada, and in northern Mexico there are more than two hundred species of caddisflies, many of which are prominent in the diet of trout and young salmon. Among the thirteen families into which the two hundred species are separated, only two live in salt water and only half a dozen or so are found on land. The habitat of the land caddisfly is in various mosses, bright-green and saturated with moisture, that cover the ground around the bases of trees.

The caddisfly belongs to the insect order *Trichoptera*, and is related to certain moth families and also related, though less closely, to the scorpionflies—one of the families of a small order of insects known as the *Mecoptera*. The name of the order *Trichoptera* means "hairy-winged," and as an adult the caddisfly brings to mind a small moth because the wings are hairy and speckled. Some are so small as to be practically immeasurable, while others have a wingspread of as much as 2½ inches.

Some adults are strong enough flyers to cover several miles in a night if attracted by distant lights. In addition to the night-flying species there are a number that are active during the day. Perhaps you have seen swarms of them "dancing" above the surface of the water from which they but recently emerged. Still others are found in the vicinity of rocks covered with lichens. If such a caddisfly is disturbed, it runs swiftly over the lichens, hurls itself into the air, and makes such a fast getaway that you are unable to follow it with the eye.

Adult caddisflies—sometimes spelled "caddice-fly"—mate in flight above the water. As a rule the male dies as soon as the mating is consummated, and the female lives only long enough to lay several thousand eggs. She deposits them on submerged parts of water plants and water-washed rocks. Each mass is usually covered by a gluelike substance that is either green or bluish green. The egg masses of some species do not have any particular form, but one species deposits them in a circlet that hangs from plants or is attached to the upper sides of the water plantain or water-lily. A few species deposit eggs in a long, unbroken string, but an exception to this rule is *Triaenodes bicolor*, a caddis that lays its eggs in a spiral.

Sometimes an egg hatches within a few days, but at the most it is never longer than two weeks. The newly hatched larva immediately crawls out of the egg mass. If it is under water the larva is right where it wants to be, but if it hatched on the leaf of an aquatic plant, it has to tumble off and into the water.

Among caddisflies some are known as case-makers because the larvae fashion a protective covering. The young insect starts the case by plastering its underside with grains of sand, bits of stream vegetation, and other debris of its watery habitat. The accumulation is held in place by a silken thread excreted from a gland at the edge of the labium, the lower lip. The thread has an adhesive property that holds the bits of this and that together, and as the insect enlarges the case to meet the demands of its increasing size, it uses the sticky silken thread to hold together the necessary additions.

The design of the case varies with the species; one larva puts together a spiral-shaped case, another builds a shield-shaped affair. The case of *Triaenodes bicolor* is elongated, and is carried wherever the insect goes. One of its three pairs of legs is shot out through little openings. Slender and fringed, the legs serve as oars to row the creature from one place to another. And there is at least one species of case-making larva that uses bits of shells from freshwater clams for its protective covering.

A different group of caddis larvae are known as net-spinners. With silk secreted from the gland on the labium, they "weave" nets, webs, or seines, and one of them works so fast that within a few hours it has built itself a funnel-shaped affair. This net funnel or those of any other design serve two purposes; they act as a protective covering and also as a trap to catch food that floats downstream. As a net-spinning larva grows, it makes adjustments in its covering to meet the increased size or often builds an entirely new one.

The larval food of the caddisfly may be either plant or animal. A case-making species is apt to be a vegetarian, and may eat algae, various green plants, and also bits of decayed vegetable matter. Many that make nets, seines, or webs are carnivorous, and feed on all manner of small animals that are caught in these traps—other small insects, crustaceans, and recently hatched fish. If the larvae of the seine-making species get into the rearing troughs of a salmon or trout hatchery, they are a minor menace to the fingerling fish, but in natural waters they are in turn food for many other animals.

The gravelly stream bottoms beneath fast-flowing waters are ideal environment for insects whose oxygen requirements are high. Areas in which riffles occur usually have many more insects than pools or the quiet stretches of streams. In addition to caddis larvae, you will find the early stages of such insects as mayflies, stoneflies, various beetles, and some true flies.

The caddisfly is in the diet of the small-mouthed bass, and the insect makes up a large part of the diet of the trout—a fish that eats caddis in all life stages. If the species is a case-maker, the trout tries to blow or suck the larva out of its case. If this is not possible, the trout swallows the larval caddis, case and all.

One species (*Anabolia nervosa*) "out-smarts" a hungry trout, for this case-maker attaches its house to a "large" twig. The twig is an obstacle that makes it impossible for a trout to gobble down *A. nervosa*—apparently endowed by Nature with the know-how of self-preservation.

Fishes are not the only animals that eat these "flies." The bat takes a number of the larger species, and among birds the mallard duck, the coot, some grebes, and the sandpiper and the snipe feed on caddisflies. And in Great Britain the caddis is in the diet of eels.

Once the larva is fully grown it undergoes certain modifications to get ready for pupation. Now its legs are folded into a different position than was habitual during the larval stage. As a rule the larva about to undergo pupation anchors itself to a stick, stone, or weed by throwing out a few strands of gluelike silk. Some larvae encase themselves in a cocoon—tough, leathery, brown—which the insect manufactures by secreting a fluid that hardens. Now comes the interval when no outward change is apparent, but inside changes are taking place that transform the insect into a winged creature.

The day arrives when certain pupae are ready to swim or crawl to the surface. They are able to do so because the antennae, wings, and legs are free—not bound to the body in any way. The swimmers use the middle pair of legs to row to the surface, while the crawlers use clawed tarsi to pull themselves up plant stems or onto rocks and debris along the banks of streams. As soon as any species of caddis reaches the water's surface, the skin splits open. This releases the winged adult—a mothlike creature that frequently takes to the air in midstream by using the cast-off skin, somewhat as an airplane takes off from a carrier.

Because trout feed on all life stages of the caddisfly, the lures that simulate the insect are of two types. For wet-fly fishing the lure is apt to be similar to a caddis pupa at the swimming stage, immediately preceding the time it is about to break water. The technique with this type of lure, according to various masters, is to make the bogus insect behave like a swimming pupa—a nice trick if you can do it! If the time, the place, and the weather dictate dry-fly fishing, the lure is similar in appearance to the mothlike adult—a simulated lure that is not so popular, perhaps, as those tied to resemble mayflies.

In England the names of some dry flies have become the common names of various species of caddis. A few such are Grouse Wing, Red Sedge, Welshman's Button, and Black Silverthorns. In North America, anglers use such dry flies as Grannom, Bucktail Caddis, and Queen of the Waters—names that make the eyes of the dry-fly fisherman sparkle or take on a faraway look—depending upon his nature.

In Conclusion

These are some of the 82,000 or more insects of North America —a land of such varied life zones that there are extreme differences in plant and animal communities. The extremes permit the amateur or professional naturalist the greatest scope imaginable for studying the ecology of one or more areas. He can see the interrelationships of the insects and other animals and the plants in his own neighborhood or he can study the ecology of some far-distant area in order to learn how that particular "other half" lives. And in the study of near or far places the observer with an alert eye and the patience of a horticulturist waiting for a century plant to bloom is almost certain to discover a new aspect of the land he lives in and on which he depends for survival.

APPENDIX

GLOSSARY

Abdomen: major body division behind head and thorax.

Acquired characteristic: trait acquired by individual (animal or plant) in response to an environment.

Antennae: slender, flexible appendages on head; feelers.

Biota: flora and fauna of region; plant and animal community.

Brood: the young; usually the larvae.

Castes: various classes of individuals of social insects; each class differs from the others in appearance and each has its own particular function in life of the colony.

Cephalothorax: head and thorax taken together.

Chrysalis: pupa of an insect, especially that of butterfly.

Cocoon: silky covering spun by mature moth larva to protect pupa.

Colony: group of same species living together.

Community: group of organisms related by environmental requirements; the plant and animal community of any given area.

Complete metamorphosis: successive life stages in which radical changes in form and structure take place.

Compound eye: eye of many separate optical units or facets; one on each side of head.

Diapause: temporary stoppage of activity or growth at immature stage; special type of hibernation for insects.

Dimorphism: existing in two forms; usually peculiar to butterflies; both forms hatch from same lot, or clutch, of eggs.

Dorsal: toward the back; upper surface.

Ecology: science dealing with mutual relations between living organisms and their environment.

Elytra: beetle's hard front wings; the wing covers.

Embryo: inactive stage when organism is first developing.

Endoskeleton: internal supporting structure; skeleton on inside.

Entomology: science of insect life.

Exoskeleton: external supporting structure; skeleton on outside (as with insects).

Facet: subdivision of compound eye.

Gene: factor determining heredity; part of chromosome (the definite number of cells of given species).

Genetics: science of heredity.

Halteres: short, stalked knobs on sides of a fly used for balancing when in flight.

Honeydew: sweet liquid exuded by aphids, scale insects, and other *Homoptera* (same-winged insects); ant food.

Host: plant or animal at whose expense a parasite obtains food, shelter, or other requirements.

Incomplete metamorphosis: growth by which miniature of parent matures by series of molts and develops wings while so doing, if it is to be a winged insect.

Instar: intervals between molts; *see,* Stadium.

Labium: lower lip of insect.

Mandible: jaw.

Metamorphosis: changes in form and structure during insect development; *see,* Complete and Incomplete Metamorphosis.

Molt: shedding skin in process of growth.

Morphology: study of structure.

Nectar: concentrated sugar solution exuded by petals of flowers.

Nest: structure or excavation made by colony of social insects—ants, bees, wasps, termites.

Nymph: immature stage of insect with incomplete metamorphosis; that is, stage in life of insect marked by three periods: egg, nymph, adult.

Ocellus: simple eye; *Ocelli,* simple eyes, usually three, on top of head between compound eyes.

Organ: cell or tissue group functioning as unit.

Organism: single plant or animal behaving as unit.

Ovipositor: specialized insect organ for depositing eggs.

Palps: little "fingers" on jaws of insects and other creatures.

Parthenogenesis: capable of reproduction from unfertilized eggs

Physiology: study of function.

Posterior: toward the rear; the hinder end.

Predator: animal that lives by preying on other animals.

Prepupa: mature larva, quiescent, nonfeeding, of some insects.

Primary reproductives: sexually functional termites with wings.

Primordia: earliest formed organ.

Prolegs: abdominal legs of caterpillar (not true legs such as those attached to thorax), lost when insect becomes fully adult.

Propolis: resins collected by honey bee; the bee-glue used to seal and weatherproof dwellings and structures.

Pupa: form assumed after larval stage and preceding start of adult stage.

Pupation: act of becoming a pupa.

Queen: sexually functional female.

Secondary reproductives: sexually functional termites in which wing-pads are short or lacking.

Scientific name: name given species of animal or plant; it consists of generic name (always capitalized) and specific name (never capitalized); the form is Latin. Designation of species by two names is known as the binomial system of classification; introduced by Carolus Linnaeus in the 1750's.

Simple eye: one consisting of single optical unit.

Social: living in family groups.

Soldier: ants, the workers; termites, caste of large individuals.

Species: group of individuals sufficiently alike to have had similar parents.

Spinnerets: small pockets at end of insect's body which hold liquid used for its web.

Spiracle: opening into trachea.

Stadium: time interval between molts; *see* Instar.

Subspecies: subdivision of species; rank below species and usually lowest category in classification.

Swarm: a single queen (though sometimes several) and workers that leave old colony to start new one; mass migration of insects.

Tarsus: terminal division of insect leg.

Taxonomy: science of plant and animal classification.

Thorax: major division of animal body immediately behind head.

Trachea: air tube.

Tympanic membrane: vibrating membrane involved in hearing.

Wingpad: undeveloped wings of active pupa.

Worker: sexually undeveloped adult; "work horse" of colony-living insects.

Suggested Reading and References

American Social Insects, by Charles D. Michener and Mary H. Michener. 267 pp., illus., index. D. Van Nostrand Company, Inc., New York. 1951.

Animals Forms And Patterns, A Study of the Appearance of Animals, by Adolf Portmann; trans. by Hella Czech. 246 pp., illus., index. Faber & Faber, Ltd., London. 1952.

Animals Without Backbones, by Ralph M. Buchsbaum. 405 pp., illus., index. (Revised Edition.) University of Chicago Press, Chicago. 1948.

Ants, The, by Wilhelm Goetsch; trans. by Ralph Manheim. 169 pp., illus., reading list. University of Michigan Press, Ann Arbor. 1957.

Applied Entomology, by H. T. Fernald and Harold H. Shepard. 285 pp., illus., index. (Fifth Edition.) McGraw-Hill Book Company, Inc., New York. 1955.

Arthropod Anatomy, by R. E. Snodgrass, 363 pp., illus., index. Comstock Publishing Associates, Cornell University Press, Ithaca, N. Y. 1952.

Audubon's Butterflies, Moths, and Other Studies, compiled and edited by Alice Ford. 120 pp., illus., index. The Studio Publications, Inc., in association with Thomas Y. Crowell Company, New York. 1952.

Bumble Bees and Their Ways, by Otto Emil Plath. 201 pp., illus., index. The Macmillan Company, New York. 1934.

Butterfly Haunts, by L. Hugh Newman, with a Foreward by Brian Vesey-Fitzgerald. Unpaged, photographs and descriptive notes. Classified List of British Butterflies. Chapman & Hall, London, 1948.

Caddis, by Norman E. Hickin. 50 pp., illus. Metheun & Co., Ltd., London, 1952.

City of the Bees, by Frank S. Stuart. 243 pp. McGraw-Hill Book Company, Inc., New York. 1947–1949.

Collecting, Preserving, and Studying Insects, by Harold Oldroyd. 327 pp., illus., The Macmillan Company, New York. 1958.

Edge of the Sea, The, by Rachel Carson. 276 pp., illus., index. Appendix: Classification of Seashore Animals. Houghton Mifflin Company, Boston. 1955.

Fabulous Insects, The, edited, with an Introduction, by Charles Neider. 278 pp., including sources. Harper & Brothers, New York. 1954.

Field Guide to the Butterflies, A., by Alexander B. Klots. 349 pp., illus., index. Houghton Mifflin Company, Boston. 1951.

Garden Friends and Foes, by Richard Headstrom. 219 pp., including appendix, illus. Ives Washburn, Inc., New York. 1954.

Garden Enemies, by Cynthia Westcott (The Plant Doctor). 261 pp., illus., index. D. Van Nostrand Company, Inc., New York. 1953.

Gardeners Bug Book, The, by Cynthia Westcott. 590 pp., illus., index. Edited by F. F. Rockwell. The American Garden Guild, Inc. and Doubleday & Company, Inc., New York. 1946.

General Entomology, by S. W. Frost. 524 pp., illus., index. McGraw-Hill Book Company, Inc., New York. 1942.

Genetics and the Origin of Species, by Theodosius Dobzhansky. 364 pp., illus., index. Third Edition Revised. Columbia University Press, New York. 1951.

Grasshoppers of the Mexicanus Group, Genus *Melanoplus (Orthoptera: Acrididae)* by Ashley B. Gurney and A. R. Brooks. No. 3416—From The Proceedings of the United States National Museum, Vol. 110, pp. 1–93; 18 figs., 5 plates. Smithsonian Institution, U. S. Government Printing Office, Washington, D. C. 1959.

Handbook of Insect Enemies of Flowers and Shrubs, by C. A. Weigel and L. G. Baumhofer. 115 pp., illus., index. Miscellaneous Publication No. 626, U. S. Department of Agriculture, U. S. Government Printing Office, Washington D. C. 1948.

History of Entomology in World War II, by Emory C. Cushing, Colonel, U. S. Army, Retired. 117 pp., illus., index. Publication 4294, Smithsonian Institution, Washington, D. C. 1957.

Hive of Bees, A, by John Crompton. 180 pp., illus., index. Doubleday & Co., Inc., New York, 1958.

How Animals Develop, by C. H. Waddington. 128 pp., illus., index. George Allen & Unwin Ltd., London. 1935.

How to Know the Immature Insects, by Hung-fu Chu. 234 pp., illus. index. Wm. C. Brown Co., Dubuque, Iowa. 1958.

Insect Book, The, by Leland O. Howard. 429 pp., index, illus. Doubleday & Company, Inc., New York. 1923.

Insect Guide, The, by Ralph B. Swain, illus. by Su Zan N. Swain. 261 pp., illus., index, "Orders and Major Families of North American Insects." Doubleday & Company, Inc., New York. 1952.

Insect Migration, by C. B. Williams. 235 pp., illus., index. The Macmillan Company, New York. 1958.

Insect World of J. Henri Fabre, The, with an introduction and interpretive comments by Edwin Way Teale. 333 pp., index. Dodd, Mead & Company, Inc., New York. 1949.

Insects, A Guide To Familiar American Insects, by Herbert S. Zim and Clarence Cottam. Golden Nature Guide. 160 pp., illus., index, list scientific names. Sponsored by The Wildlife Management Institute. Simon and Schuster, New York. 1951, 1956.

Insects, The Yearbook of Agriculture, 1952, Editor, Alfred Stefferud. 780 pp., illus., index, with 72 additional color plates and life histories. U. S. Department of Agriculture, U. S. Government Printing Office, Washington, D. C. 1952.

Insects and Diseases of Vegetables in the Home Garden, by L. B. Reed. Home and Garden Bulletin No. 46. 48 pp., illus., index. U. S. Department of Agriculture, U. S. Government Printing Office, Washington, D. C. 1956.

Life of the Bee, The, by Maurice Maeterlinck. Various editions (two current) since its translation into English in 1902.

Manual for the Study of Insects, by John Henry Comstock and Anna Botsford Comstock and Glenn W. Herrick. 401 pp., illus., index. 22nd edition, revised. Comstock Publishing Company, Inc., Ithaca, N. Y. 1938.

Nature of Natural History, The, by Marston Bates. 309 pp., index. Charles Scribner's Sons, New York. 1950.

Moth Book, The, A Popular Guide to a Knowledge of the Moths of North America, by W. J. Holland. 479 pp., illus., index. Doubleday & Company, Inc., New York. 1922. (See also Holland's *The Butterfly Book*.)

North American Deserts, The, by Edmund C. Jaeger, with a chapter by Peveril Meigs. 308 pp., illus., index. Stanford University Press, Stanford, Calif. 1957.

Of Ants and Men, by C. P. Haskins. 244 pp., illus., index. Prentice-Hall, Inc., Englewood Cliffs, N. J. 1939.

Parasitic Animals, by Geoffrey LaPage. 351 pp., illus., index. Cambridge at the University Press. 1951.

Praying Mantids of the United States: Native and Introduced, by Ashley B. Gurney, Publication 4037, from the Smithsonian Report for 1950, Pages 339–362, with 9 plates. Smithsonian Institution. U. S. Government Printing Office, Washington, D. C. 1951.

Textbook of Entomology, A, by Herbert H. Ross. 519 pp., illus., index. (2nd Edition.) John Wiley & Sons, New York. 1956.

Ways of the Ant, by John Crompton, 242 pp., illus., index. Houghton Mifflin Company, Boston. 1954.

Web of Life, The, by John H. Storer, with an introduction by Fairfield Osborn. 144 pp., including bibliography. The Devin-Adair Company, New York. 1954.

Woodland Ecology, by E. G. Neal. 117 pp., illus., index. Harvard University Press, Cambridge, Mass. 1959.

Wonderful World of Insects, by Albro T. Gaul. 290 pp., illus., index. Rinehart & Company, Inc., New York. 1953.

World of Butterflies and Moths, The, by Alexander B. Klots. 207 pp., illus., index. McGraw-Hill Book Company, New York. 1958.

Zoology, by A. M. Winchester. 437 pp., illus., index. D. Van Nostrand Company, Inc., New York. 1947.

Zoology, General, by Gordon Alexander. 290 pp., illus., index. A summary of biological principles with a survey of the animal kingdom. Includes final examination and answers. Keyed to standard textbooks. College Outline Series No. 32. Barnes & Noble, Inc., New York. Tenth printing, 1956.

FOR YOUNGER READERS:

Butterflies and Moths, A Study of the Largest and Most Beautiful of the Insects, by Richard A. Martin. 56 pp., illus., index, with a table of butterflies and moths illustrated, their family, common, and scientific names and foods eaten by each species. Simon and Schuster, Inc., New York. 1958.

4-H Insect Club Manual, Agriculture Handbook No. 65, by M. P. Jones. 64 pp., illus. U. S. Department of Agriculture, U. S. Government Printing Office, Washington, D. C. 1951.

Grassroots Jungles, by Edwin Way Teale. 240 pp., illus., index. (Revised Edition.) Dodd, Mead & Co., New York. 1944.

Insect World, The, by Hilda Harpster. 211 pp., illus., index. The Viking Press, New York. 1956.

Insects and Their World, by Carroll Lane Fenton and Dorothy Constance Pallas. 96 pp., illus. The John Day Company, New York. 1956.

Introducing the Insect, by F. A. Urquhart. 287 pp., illus., index. Henry Holt and Company, Inc., New York. 1949.

Junior Book of Insects, The, by Edwin Way Teale. 249 pp., illus., index. E. P. Dutton & Company, New York. 1953.

INDEX